The Legacy of Marxism

The Legacy of Marxism

Contemporary Challenges, Conflicts and Developments

**EDITED BY
MATTHEW JOHNSON**

Continuum International Publishing Group

The Tower Building	80 Maiden Lane
11 York Road	Suite 704
London	New York
SE1 7NX	NY 10038

www.continuumbooks.com

ISBN: 978-1-4411-4302-0 (hardcover)
978-1-4411-0349-9 (paperback)

Library of Congress Cataloging-in-Publication Data
A catalog record for this book is available from the Library of Congress.

Typeset by Deanta Global Publishing Services, Chennai, India
Printed in the United States of America

CONTENTS

ACKNOWLEDGEMENTS

This collection was the result of a project developed by the journal *Global Discourse* (global-discourse.com). As editors, Mark Edward and I sought to examine the contemporary relevance of Marxism by holding a conference entitled 'Examining the Relevance of Marx and Marxism to Contemporary Global Society' at Newcastle University on January 29th and 30th, leading to two special issues of *Global Discourse*. Some of the papers in this collection are drawn from the conference and the special issues and it is important that I acknowledge the contribution of those who helped in the organization of both: Russell Foster for dealing with emails and administrative tasks prior to the event as well as contributing greatly over the weekend of the conference; Gerard Thomas for assisting with the organization of the evening meal and refreshments; Megan O'Branski for her help during the conference and for her work as an editorial assistant; Esteban Castro for his enthusiasm and for chairing a panel; Paul Reynolds for his advice on the nature and format of the conference; William Maloney for supporting the event and Norman Geras and Stuart Sim for their keynote speeches; Steven Robinson for assisting in the processing of submissions; the referees for their comprehensive and constructive reviews; Mark Cowling for his advice and the publishers who provided review copies of the books in the symposia.

In relation specifically to this collection, I would like to thank Norman Geras for his advice and comments; Kay for her proof-reading; Selina for her enthusiasm, encouragement, cooking and financial support; Ell for improving my self-image by being more sarcastic and morbidly depressed than me and Mark Edward for his magnanimity. In particular, I must recognize David Walker's ceaseless, though reluctant, contribution to my career. As well as embellishing my cricketing abilities by serving up duff long-hops and half-volleys during three-man matches in Saltwell Park, David has also tolerated persistent requests for assistance with publications, providing a generous endorsement of this book. I thank him for his ten years of grudging toleration.

Matthew Johnson
Newcastle upon Tyne
25 November 2011

CONTRIBUTORS

Norman Geras

Norman Geras is Professor Emeritus in Politics at the University of Manchester, where he was a member of the Department of Government from his appointment in 1967 until he retired in 2003. Between 1997 and 2001 he was Head of the Department. He was a member of the editorial committee of *New Left Review* from 1976 to 1992 and a member of the editorial committee of *Socialist Register* from 1995 to 2003.

Among Norman Geras's books are *The Legacy of Rosa Luxemburg* (1976), *Marx and Human Nature: Refutation of a Legend* (1983), *Solidarity in the Conversation of Humankind: The Ungroundable Liberalism of Richard Rorty* (1995), *The Contract of Mutual Indifference: Political Philosophy after the Holocaust* (1998) and *Crimes against humanity: birth of a concept* (2011). He has also had essays and papers published in academic and professional journals, including *New Left Review, Review of International Studies, Journal of Applied Philosophy, Res Publica, Journal of the British Society for Phenomenology, The European Legacy, Dissent, Imprints* and *Critical Horizons*. Since 2003 he has been blogging at *normblog* (http://normblog.typepad.com/normblog/). He was the principal author of *The Euston Manifesto* (2006). Norman Geras is also the author of two cricket books: *Ashes '97: Two Views from the Boundary* (with Ian Holliday); and *Men of Waugh: Ashes 2001*.

Joseph V. Femia

A political theorist, Joseph V. Femia is the author of several books: *Gramsci's Political Thought* (Oxford University Press, 1981), *Marxism and Democracy* (Oxford University Press, 1993), *The Machiavellian Legacy* (Macmillan, 1998), *Against the Masses: Anti-Democratic Thought since the French Revolution* (Oxford University Press, 2001), *Machiavelli Revisited* (University of Wales Press, 2004) and *Pareto and Political Theory* (Routledge, 2006). He has also edited volumes entitled *Vilfredo Pareto for the International Library of Essays on the History of Social and Political Thought* (Ashgate 2009) and, with G.Slomp and A. Korosenyi, *Political Leadership in Liberal and Democratic Theory* (Imprint Academic 2009). He has also published articles in a wide range of academic journals, including *Political Studies, British Journal of Political Science, History of Political Thought,* and *Political Theory*. He has served on various editorial boards, and is co-founder and co-convenor of 'Workshops in Political Theory', the main international conference for political theorists, held annually in Manchester. He has held visiting appointments at the European University Institute in Florence (1989–90), Yale University (1981–82) and Princeton University (1997). Before coming to Liverpool, he taught at the Universities of Oxford and Manchester. Professor Femia is Subject Leader for Politics and Chair of the School's Research Ethics Committee. He teaches three undergraduate modules (POLI 201: History of Political Thought, POLI 202: Twentieth Century Political Thought and POLI 315: Marxism and Democracy) and contributes to the M.A. module on International Relations Theory (POLI 132).

Alan Johnson

Alan Johnson has been working at Edge Hill University in the Social Sciences Department since 1991. He was made a Reader in 2001 and a Professor in 2007. His research has mostly been about the intellectual history of the Left and social movements. He has been active on the left and in social movements since 1979 when he worked as a volunteer in the Days of Hope bookshop in Newcastle; he was an editorial board member at *Socialist Organiser* in the 1980s, at *Historical Materialism* (1990–2003) and *New Politics* (1999–2003). He has been involved in supporting the Iraqi trade unions since 2003, co-authoring *Hadi Never Died: Hadi Saleh and the Iraqi Trade Unions* (2006, TUC) with Abdullah Muhsin. In 2005, he founded the online quarterly journal *Democratiya* and edited 16 issues (now archived at the British Library and at the Dissent website) until merging *Democratiya* with the US journal *Dissent* in 2009. He blogs at *Comment is Free* and now at the new translatlantic blog created by the merger of *Democratiya* and *Dissent*, Arguing the World. He co-authored The Euston Manifesto and has been involved with the 'Progress' think tank, especially its Progressive Internationalism policy group.

In 2008–10 he was engaged in consultancy work for the Research, Information and Communications Unit (RICU), which is based in the Office of Security and Counter-Terrorism (OSCT), using social movement theory and in-depth interviewing to examine the dynamics of 'radicalisation' and 'deradicalisation' and effective communications to encourage desistence and disengagement.

Paul Bowman

Paul Bowman, Cardiff University, is the author of *Post-Marxism versus Cultural Studies* (Edinburgh UP), *Deconstructing Popular Culture* (Palgrave), *Theorizing Bruce Lee* (Rodopi), and editor of *Interrogating Cultural Studies* (Pluto), *The Truth of Žižek* (Continuum), *Reading Rancière* (Continuum) and *The Rey Chow Reader* (Columbia UP). He has edited special themed issues of the journals *Postcolonial Studies*, *Social Semiotics*, *Educational Philosophy and Theory* and many issues of *Parallax*. He has recently completed a book called *Beyond Bruce Lee*, is preparing a collection on Rancière and Film and is working on a study of Rey Chow. He is on the editorial board of *Culture Machine*, *The Poster* and *Ctrl-Z: New-Media-Philosophy*.

Ronaldo Munck

Professor Munck has authored or edited more than 20 books on various topics related to globalization, international development and social movements as well as over 100 academic journal articles. His books have been translated into French, Spanish, Portuguese, Italian, Arabic, Korean, Turkish Chinese and Japanese. He serves on the editorial boards of a number of international journals including Globalizations, Global Social Policy, Global Labour, Labour History and Latin American Perspectives. He represents DCU on the board of the Centre for Cross Border Studies, on NorDubCo, the Ballymun and Whitehall Partnership, the Creative Dublin Alliance and on the Financial Development and General Strategic Policy Committee of Dublin City Council. He is the Irish representative of the Council of the Development Studies Association of UK and Ireland. He has acted as External Examiner at Cambridge University, the London School of Economics, University of Warwick, Queen's University Belfast, National University of Ireland Maynooth, the Open University, University of Sussex, University of Lancaster, University of Florence, Leiden University, Institute of Social Studies: The Hague. Recent keynote speeches include the International Society for Third Sector Research in Bangkok, the Migration and Informal Labour Conference in Istanbul, the International Transport Workers Federation in Oslo, the Critical Development Forum in Zacatecas, Mexico, the Latino(a) Migration Futures at Omaha, US and the International Development Studies Association in Montreal, Canada. Currently Professor Munck is coordinator of the Irish Aid funded inter-university project the Irish African Partnership for Research Capacity Building (www.irishafricanpartership. ie), editor of Translocations, an inter-university online journal on migration and social transformation in Ireland (www.translocations.ie) and is Visiting Professor of Labour and Migration Studies at the University of Linkøping in Sweden.

Matthew Johnson

Matthew Johnson is a British Academy Postdoctoral Fellow at the University of York. His research interests lie in the assessment of cultural practices, with a monograph entitled *A Theory of Cultural Evaluation* to be published by Palgrave in early 2012. He has particular interest in invasive rites, such as male and female genital mutilation, and in the potential contribution of Marxism to the examination of cross-cultural encounters. He has published articles in *Ethnicities*, *Social Indicators Research*, *Educational Theory* and *Critical Review of International Social and Political Philosophy* and taught at the University of Queensland and the University of Iceland. He is the founding editor of the interdisciplinary journal *Global Discourse* (www.global-discourse.com) and co-editor of *Studies in Marxism* and has refereed articles for *Ethnicities*.

Lawrence Wilde

Lawrence Wilde is Professor of Political Theory at Nottingham Trent University in England. He is the co-author (with Ian Fraser) of *The Marx Dictionary* (London: Continuum) and sole author of *Erich Fromm and the Quest for Solidarity* (New York: Palgrave, 2004), *Ethical Marxism and its Radical Critics* (Basingstoke: Macmillan, 1998), *Modern European Socialism* (Aldershot: Dartford, 1994) and *Marx and Contradiction* (Aldershot: Avebury, 1989). He is editor of *Marxism's Ethical Thinkers* (Basingstoke: Palgrave, 2001) and co-editor (with Mark Cowling) of *Approaches to Marx* (Milton Keynes: Open University Press, 1989). His current research focuses on the concept of solidarity and employs a radical humanist perspective, as outlined in 'A Radical Humanist Approach to the Concept of Solidarity' in *Political Studies* 52 (1) 2004 and 'The Ethical Challenge of Touraine's "Living Together"' in the *Journal of Global Ethics* 3 (1), 2007. He is currently working on a book, *Global Solidarity*, for Edinburgh University Press.

Mark Cowling

Dr Mark Cowling is Professor of Criminology and Marxism at Teesside University. He is the convener of the Political Studies Association Marxism Specialist Group, and, as a consequence, has been the editor or joint editor of four edited volumes on aspects of Marxism. He is also the editor of *Studies in Marxism* and the author of *Marxism and Criminological Theory: A Critique and a Toolkit* (Houndmills: Palgrave, 2008) and *Date Rape and Consent* (Aldershot: Ashgate, 1998).

Andrew (Chengyi) Peng

Andrew (Chengyi) Peng obtained his PhD degree in the Department of Public and Social Administration at City University of Hong Kong in 2011 and is currently a researcher at the Chinese Academy of Social Sciences in Beijing. Previously he was the first one to be supported by China's 'Project of Hope' to study abroad and attained his BA and MA degrees in political science at St. Thomas University and University of British Columbia in Canada respectively. His research interests include comparative political philosophy, classical political thought, constitutionalisms and political thoughts in contemporary China. His dissertation *The New 'Romance of Three Kingdoms': The Competition of Three Constitutional Blueprints for Twenty-first Century*

China seeks to crystalize and compare the three constitutional discourses advocated for the future of China.

Terrell Carver

Terrell Carver is Professor of Political Theory at the University of Bristol. He has published extensively on Marx, Engels and Marxism, including theoretical and biographical studies, textual editions and translations. His work has been translated into Chinese, Japanese, Korean, French, German and Farsi. Recently he has given papers and keynote speeches at a number of universities in China, including Tsinghua, Peking, Renmin, Beijing Normal, Fudan and Nanjing.

Oliver Harrison

Oliver obtained his BA Politics from Nottingham Trent University in 2003, his MA in Social and Political Thought at the University of Warwick in 2004 and his PhD in Politics from the University of Nottingham in 2011. His PhD research used Marx's theory of revolutionary subjectivity as a benchmark for assessing the post-Marxist nature of the work of Ernesto Laclau, Antonio Negri and Alain Badiou. Oliver is interested in theories of collective subjectivity, sociological theories of revolution and modern ecological thought. He teaches various modules in Political Theory at Nottingham Trent University, and while aiming to secure a book contract for his PhD thesis, is also developing the future MA in Politics at NTU.

Stuart Sim

Stuart Sim retired as Professor of Critical Theory in the English Dept., University of Sunderland, 2008. He is currently Visiting Professor in the English Dept., Northumbria University. He has published widely on the subject of critical theory, particularly postmodernism and poststructuralism. Among his recent books are *The Carbon Footprint Wars: What Might Happen If We Retreat from Globalization?* (EUP, 2009), *The End of Modernity: What the Financial & Environmental Crisis Is Really Telling Us* (EUP, 2010) and the edited collection *The Lyotard Dictionary* (EUP, 2011). Forthcoming in June is his edited collection *The Routledge Companion to Postmodernism* (3rd edition).

Introduction

Matthew Johnson

Marx's nineteenth-century thought provided the intellectual inspiration for a range of twentieth-century political movements and academic approaches, each with distinctive features and each, unfortunately, complicated by failings and contradictions. With the fall of the Soviet Union and its satellite states, and the emergence of an economically reformed China, the events of the final years of the twentieth century seemed to have granted credence to Francis Fukuyama's *End of History* thesis. At the same time, the academic left gravitated towards approaches which eschew 'authoritarian', 'essentialist' and 'ethnocentric' elements of orthodox Marxism. As a result, Marxism has seemed to be in danger of slipping from a method and subject of social scientific inquiry, to an object of historical intrigue or even indifference. Yet, given the nature and gravity of the events and issues of this new century, Marxism as both a political movement and an academic approach should be as relevant as ever.

In order to consider its relevance, we have to consider, first, the various ways in which Marxism since the time of Marx has been fractured and splintered and developed and evolved in various directions. There are several trajectories which are considered in this book. The first trajectory is the revisionism of Eduard Bernstein – the father of evolutionary socialism. For Bernstein, Marx's empirical claims regarding the laws of historical development were confounded by the experiences of capitalism. The chances of achieving real socialist ends lay most prominently in the recognition of proletarian demands within the existing liberal democratic framework, with the attainment of rights a core goal of political praxis. The second trajectory is the autocratic vanguardism of Lenin, which, combined with his understanding of imperialism as the highest form of capitalism, laid the foundation for revolutionary action in the developing world. Lenin's Bolshevism served to shift the attention of Marxism from the developed West to impoverished, developing regions of the world. This movement was strengthened by the emergence of Mao Zedong's Sinicized Marxism, with its focus on agrarian relations of production and the revolutionary potential of peasants.

The association between socialism, the developing world and anti-imperialism was firmly entrenched by the thought and praxis of guerrilla figures, such as Che Guevara, Fidel Castro and Ho Chi Minh. From the protest movements of the 1960s onwards, various positions have emerged which have sought to incorporate external intellectual resources in order to revitalize the radical left. Some, such as Slavoj Žižek, have retained their Marxist identities, while rehabilitating Hegel and adopting elements of such figures as the psycho-analyst Jaque Lacan. The third trajectory, post-Marxism, differs both in content and identity. Post-Marxists have drawn intellectual inspiration from Marxism's rejection of capital and retained elements of the thought of self-professed Marxists, such as Antonio Gramsci and Mao, while increasingly moved towards postmodern positions on essentialism, materialism, voluntarism, pluralism and democracy, as exemplified by Ernesto Laclau's and Chantal Mouffe's seminal *Hegemony and Socialist Strategy*.

The revisions made by and within each of these trajectories have been in response to perceived deficits or oversights in classical and, subsequently, orthodox Marxism. These revisions have themselves, though, led to significant paradigmatic quandaries. Whether attempting to conserve, transcend or reject elements of Marx, those influenced by his work have to deal with the legacy of Marxism in light of several contemporary events.

Contemporary conflicts, challenges and developments

The beginning of the twentieth century saw significant confidence in neoliberalism, the Washington Consensus and the possibility of a truly integrated global economy. Some talked readily of the need for global governance as what were intended originally as trading blocs, such as the European Union, expanded and took increasingly political forms. While international economic institutions such as the WTO and IMF focused much of their attention on facilitating liberalization and privatization in developing countries, the most significant economic success stories appeared to emanate from states, such as China and India, which maintained substantive commitments to protectionism and public ownership. Those countries which appeared to have benefited from elements of neoliberal engagement with the global economy, such as Iceland and Ireland, found themselves at the heart of the late-2000s global financial crisis, having previously maintained that the rapid increases in real estate prices, which had brought dramatic growth, were both genuine and sustainable. Now, with those claims seriously undermined, the Washington Consensus has come to appear anything but consensual and neoliberalism as a project has been damaged, though certainly not defeated.

At a time when confidence in neoliberalism was perhaps at its height, the United States suffered the attacks on 11th September 2001. This marked the most dramatic incident in the campaign of Jihadist groups against Western targets and Western people as well as those in other parts of the world deemed to exist in contradiction to their theology or aims. The resulting campaigns waged by US-led coalitions against regimes in Afghanistan and Iraq marked the most brutal incidents in a decade of conflict in the Islamic world. Even now, with the stiflingly slow development of a broadly democratic system in Iraq and the death of Osama bin Laden in Pakistan, these conflicts seem certain to continue, with their wider effects throughout the region and among migrant groups in Western countries unquantifiable. Alongside these conflicts, Western states continue to offer varying degrees of support to Israel, particularly in its confrontations with Hamas and Hezbollah, and have recently become involved militarily in the civil war in Libya.

One extremely significant development, in the context of 'The War on Terror' has been the invocation by liberal states of security imperatives to justify constraints on civil liberties. Autocratic or authoritarian societies, such as China and those currently being attacked or overthrown in the Middle East and North Africa, have often been criticized, by liberals in particular, for these actions on the basis that constraints served simply to ensure the stability and security of the regime against populaces whose interests were regarded as naturally antagonistic. However, the first decade of this century has seen steady encroachments on individual entitlements, among other things, to privacy, freedom of speech and freedom of movement. The actions taken by successive governments throughout the liberal world have, at times, appeared anything but liberal.

Now, with the most significant international proponents of the unconstrained market mired in conflict and debt, it would seem that the opportunity for Marxist contributions to debates regarding the future of the world is significant. However, such responses to the events and processes outlined above have been markedly negative and reactive. That is, the most visible popular opposition to neoliberalism, the finance crisis, the conflicts in the Middle East and encroachments on civil liberties has been encapsulated in a series of 'anti-s': anti-capitalism, anti-globalization, anti-war and anti-imperialism.

This contemporary trend, which some have seen as a continuation of the spirit of revolt from 1968, emerged most clearly in the final year of the previous century. Since 1999, self-professed anti-globalization and anti-capitalist campaigners have led public protests against global capitalism and the organizations and institutions, such as the WTO, IMF and G7, deemed responsible for propagating the expansion of neoliberalism. This has resulted in direct action in, among other places, Seattle, Washington, Genoa, London and Athens. Such protests have garnered significant attention in the media and have served to associate leftist politics with opposition. At the same time, anti-war and anti-imperialist groups have opposed US-led actions in Afghanistan, Iraq and elsewhere, Israeli actions against Hamas and Hezbollah and, now, NATO bombing in Libya.

While there are various reasons to support or oppose these positions (to be clear, the contributors to this volume are likely to adopt a range of different positions on each of these issues), 'Marxism' has found itself almost exclusively associated with or subsumed within movements of opposition and reaction. Although this may afford Marxists a means of involving themselves in broader movements, it also serves to lower the profile of Marxism and hinder the articulation of certain Marxist or even post-Marxist alternatives. It is important that these alternatives, however diffuse and contradictory, be developed and articulated and that the different forms of the Marxist left become defined by what they seek constructively to offer, rather than by what they oppose. Only by engaging openly and fully in ultimately normative questions of the nature, form and desirability of revolutions, the shape and scope of democracy, the actions of opponents of capitalist societies, the content and possibility of distributive justice, the place of civil liberties in socialist societies, the shape of constitutions and the relative weight afforded consequentialism and deontology, and the possibility of legitimate diversity in political form, will leftist approaches be able to escape pragmatic anonymity.

The project of post-Marxism was intended as a response to these questions in order to create a scheme capable of making real political progress, with essentialist understandings of human nature and justifications for authoritarian politics rejected in favour of inclusive, pluralist radical democracy. Yet, while these ideas have gained currency within, and often beyond, the radical left, there remain pressing concerns about the viability of post-Marxism as a project. Does it have the organizational capacity and can it exert the emotive appeal to attract and sustain support for the radical democratic alternatives it proposes?

This book is an attempt to outline the challenges faced by those influenced by Marx and to put forward a range of ways in which the left, in its various, diverse ideological forms, can make real, substantive and positive contributions to contemporary debates and concerns.

Structure of the book

While the contributors to this collection may disagree, in some cases fundamentally, on the nature of, and responses to, contemporary challenges, conflicts and developments (and, perhaps, to the phrasing of this introduction), there exists a recurring theme of reflection: on paths chosen, on strategies adopted and on paradigmatic shifts. This serves, not simply to provide an account of where particular branches of the Marxist left stand in relation to current issues, but to identify lessons from the past which can enable those influenced by Marx to achieve relevance in the future. There are no impenetrable boundaries between sections of the collection precisely because the issues with which the chapters engage are broad and dealt with in different ways by different paradigms. The chapters within the volume are eclectic, representing the diversity and fragmentation within the field, but build upon one another. They move from definitional work on the meaning of Marxism to critical concern regarding forms of revolutionary praxis and dismissive approaches to developing societies, to substantive engagement with the global justice debate, to consideration of principles and processes of justice and the scope for pluralism within Marxist constitutions, to the nature of revolutionary subjectivity in post-Marxism and, finally, to evaluation of post-Marxism, its effect on Marxism and its potential actively to foster political change, returning to and expanding upon the core concerns of Norman Geras in Chapter 1. If there is a thematic structure to the collection, it is that the early chapters deal with Marxism and its relationship with liberalism, the middle chapters focus on the practical application of Marxism and the influence of local conditions, while the final chapters examine post-Marxism.

Norman Geras has been at the forefront of Marx scholarship for several decades. In recent years he has contributed to public discourse on current affairs through his widely read normblog.typepad.com. Well known for his iconoclasm, Geras sets about examining what it means to be a Marxist, putting forward three core definitions: personal, intellectual and socio-political. Through analysis of these definitions, Geras argues that attempts to circumscribe Marxism by those on the Marxist left should be rejected. Citing apologetic or ambivalent responses to apparently regressive or anti-democratic movements and regimes, he claims that the Marxist left has served to stifle possibilities for diversity, plurality and debate within the left over such issues as international intervention or the participation by Israeli academics in public discourse. Rather, Geras claims that a range of Marxist-influenced approaches can, and should, be developed, in particular, those which seek reconciliation with that other, much maligned, Enlightenment approach – liberalism. In order to rejuvenate itself and to play an important role in socio-political life, Geras believes that the left needs to supplement contextual understanding of the functioning of societies and critical assessment of inequalities with acknowledgement of the comparative successes of democratic societies despite their flaws.

In Chapter 2, Joseph Femia explores the scientific credentials of Marxism. For Femia, those who examine this aspect of Marx (and Marxism) usually adopt one of two contrasting positions. Marx is either depicted as a great scientist, on a par with Copernicus, whose findings are 'objective truth' (as in the case of Plekhanov), or he and his followers are derided as scientific imposters, whose elastic terminology allows them to explain away any contrary evidence (as in the case of Popper). In Femia's opinion, Vilfredo Pareto, the pioneering Italian sociologist, provided a more measured evaluation. To Pareto, Marx made two impressive scientific discoveries: that the struggle between social groups is a key element in social life and that moral and political ideas are historically and culturally variable rather than universal and timeless. However, according to Pareto, Marxist 'science' had been subverted by the 'essentialism' Marx inherited from Hegel (resulting in metaphysical concepts such as 'surplus value' and the 'dialectic'), and by the intense moralism he inherited from the utopian socialists (accounting for the obvious value preferences that coloured his description of capitalism). Femia, for the most part, endorses Pareto's analysis, but also notes that his attack on Marx's use of abstraction might be considered somewhat unfair, given that Pareto himself insisted – when he was not discussing Marx – that abstraction was essential to the scientific enterprise. The value of Pareto's account, for Femia, lies in his assertion that Marx sought, 'with limited success, to unify two contrary human impulses: the one that drives us to extend our knowledge of the external world and the one that impels us to seek the existential comfort of metaphysical postulates'.

Alan Johnson, in Chapter 3, builds upon Geras' chapter in his examination of Slavoj Žižek's theory of revolution. Žižek has gained attention in recent years as one of the key intellectual figures on the radical left, stimulating interest in Marx and critical theory in general through his melding of Marxian, Hegelian and Lacanian thought. For Johnson, however, this contribution is far from an unalloyed good. Drawing on his personal engagement with Žižek, Johnson highlights a number of troubling trends towards violent, totalitarian and 'psychotic' politics. For Johnson, there is good reason to treat cautiously Žižek's faith in *a priori* Hegelian dialectical models of development and Blanquist forms of praxis which lead him to inflict revolution in order to make reality conform to transhistorical laws. Johnson argues that Žižek's understanding of revolution as a self-less, voluntaristic Badiouan 'Event' is derived from a misconceived application of the Lacanian 'Act'. Johnson draws on the anti-totalitarian resources of Charles Lefort to suggest that Žižek's thought amounts to an all-pervasive and narcissistic desire for abstraction from society, a spiritualized aesthetic of death and a totalitarian communitarianism. Johnson then demonstrates the fundamental dislocation of this approach from the validation of autonomy, self-realization and maturation in Marx's account of revolution before concluding that Žižek's theory of revolution, by repeating a number of twentieth-century tragedies, serves simply to undermine two aims which should be central to the left: the extension of the democratic revolution and the 'complete reconceptualization of the political in the light of the totalitarian experience'.

In affirming and expanding upon Alan Johnson's contribution, Paul Bowman, in Chapter 4, reflects on the objects and nature of Žižek's polemics and their reception in left-leaning circles. Bowman's focus lies on the difficulty of reading and disentangling Žižek's eclectic, erratic and inconsistent works and his tendency to reject critiques, such as those of Johnson, as 'misreadings'. For Bowman, Žižek contradicts his occasional self-professed objectivism by rejecting as inaccurate attempts to present a 'true' position on his work. This may, unintentionally, suggests Bowman, be seen as a virtue, with Žižek demonstrating commitment to provocation and critique, rather than consistency. However, more often than not, it is used simply to side-step accusations of the sort levelled by Johnson, without dealing adequately with the troubling trends which litter his work. For Bowman, Žižek's use of cultural studies as a term of derision is grounded in the sort of caricaturing found among the reactionary right. Tracing a demonstrative encounter from one of his own edited collections, Bowman argues that, while Žižek's polemical style maps swiftly significant debates, disputes and controversies, it does so by '*not* reading, *not* engaging, *not* reflecting and *not* seeking or digging to find out whether things are actually as Žižek says they are'. This, claims Bowman, leads Žižek's work to read like a series of jokes directed at the subjects of concern – women, homosexuals, ethnic minorities, etc. – for many in cultural studies and the broader left. Bowman suggests that, while it is possible for the intellectual left to laugh at its own contradictions, Johnson's work, among others, shows Žižek to be, in some measure, worryingly ill-disposed towards these groups and the movements which see their status as being of fundamental concern to modern, leftist, democratic politics. For Bowman, it is this dislike for minorities and democratic politics which is significantly consistent throughout Žižek's work, revealing a man transfixed and possibly threatened by the multicultural transformation of the world and the dissolution of the traditional monopoly by white men of academic power.

In Chapter 5, Ronaldo Munck examines the legacy of Marxism's engagement with development. He traces the shift from the 'ambiguity' of classical Marxism with regard to Ireland and Russia, through the realization of Marxism–Leninism as a development ideology, the subsequent emergence, in the 1960s and 1970s, of Marxism as a primarily Third World ideology of nationalist anti-imperialism, and the later flourishing of capitalism in China and India, to the anti-globalization movements of the 1990s. Munck claims that, today, Marxism is not a key player in development debates, not least because of the ideological victory of the neoliberal approach which dominates even the critical voices of those such as Joe Stiglitz. To regain relevance, Munck argues that Marxism must engage substantively in dialogue with postcolonial and post-development thought in order to 'regain some of the dialectical subtlety of the founders of Marxism and develop guides to action rather than proclamatory critiques'.

In Chapter 6, I seek to link elements of the concerns of Geras, Johnson and Munck in assessing the alliances formed in recent years between Marxists and regressive socio-political forces. In an era in which the left has become increasingly associated with anti-movements, I suggest that one of the most disturbing and counter-productive developments has been the desire of certain self-professed Marxists, such as the Socialist Workers Party (SWP), to channel opposition to capitalism, imperialism and war, into support for 'native', 'anti-imperialist' and, often, Islamist forces, particularly in Palestine, Lebanon, Iraq and Afghanistan. I argue that this is anything but Marxian. I consider, first, Marx's stagist defence of capitalist expansionism before examining his opposition to imperialism in his late writings on Russia. I suggest that, cutting through these apparently contradictory positions on imperialism, there is belief that actions be evaluated according to the extent to which they increase the potential for needs to be satisfied and capabilities promoted. I claim that, even if Western imperialism is judged to have been a poor means of achieving this good, there is still no reason to support Islamist groups in Iraq and Afghanistan. Putting forward a series of reasons for the attraction of certain Marxists to these groups, I argue that what is required is a Marxism which looks beyond its 'anti-' focus and comes to engage more fully in promoting a positive account of progress grounded in the sort of interests identified by Marx as being universal to the species.

One means of regenerating the positive focus of the left is examined by Lawrence Wilde in Chapter 7. Noting the absence of Marx from contemporary debates on global justice, Wilde argues that there is both scope and need for Marxist engagement in moral discourse. He claims that Marx's own reluctance to advance moral positions was due to a tactical desire to avoid a utopian socialism ignorant of existing conditions and parameters of action. Beneath this, for Wilde, lies a universal *eudaemonistic* ethics which was explicit in Marx's early writings and implicit in his mature political economy. With faith in proletarian movements undermined by the experiences of the twentieth century, Wilde argues that it is essential that Marxists engage morally in the global justice debate as part of the global class struggle against, in particular, neoliberalism. To this end, he demonstrates the way in which Marx's essentialist *eudaemonistic* ethics can assist in actualizing the apparent aims of one key paradigm of global justice – Martha Nussbaum's capabilities approach. Wilde argues that the value of the approach is constrained by Nussbaum's political liberalism and its commitment to private property, which fails adequately to acknowledge the importance to human flourishing of fundamental, structural change to existing, inegalitarian socio-economic systems. For Wilde, in order effectively to realize Nussbaum's ten principles for global justice, we need to transcend liberalism by acknowledging the need for both political and socio-economic equality and rejecting historical commitments to charity in favour of attempts to address the structural causes of inequalities.

In Chapter 8, Mark Cowling examines Marxist contributions to criminological thought, noting in particular the consequences of developing a society to promote the sort of ends outlined by Wilde in Chapter 7 on accounts of crime. He begins by rejecting the association made by Marx and Engels of crime with the lumpenproletariat, highlighting links between that account and the neoliberal account of welfare dependency, before arguing that any use of alienation theory is too vague to be of comprehensive value. He then examines the possibility that crime may be part of the reproduction conditions of capital, highlighting stark differences between capitalist criminal justice systems to argue that it is merely a contingent, rather than necessary, condition. Cowling then argues that law has some substance independent of ruling class interests and can be used under limited circumstances to defend workers, before turning his attention to Rawls' notion that criminal acts disturb just patterns of distribution. Examining disparities in the way in which middle class and street crime are prosecuted, Cowling suggests that there is significant scope for Marxists to link together distributive and criminal justice. Finally, Cowling comes to consider whether crime will disappear in a communist society. He claims that it will not. Indeed, even if a communist society is otherwise attractive, there is reason to believe that activities which are currently legal will be criminalized. With the eradication of private property, a communist society will have to decide, for example, from a range of incompatible activities such as farming, house building, rambling and quad biking, for which ends the countryside can be used. Those whose ends are rejected may wish to subvert the society and state (in whatever form it remains). Likewise, while subjective constraints on sexual behaviour would presumably be rejected, there might still be crime motivated by immanent feelings of jealousy or passion. There might also be continuing debates regarding ages of consent and extreme forms of degradation.

In Chapter 9, Chengyi Peng examines the development and implications of Sinicized Marxist Constitutionalism (SMC) in light of over three decades of party-led reform. Peng begins by outlining reasons for the development of SMC, citing codification of law since the Cultural Revolution, the dissemination of liberal constitutional ideals from the West and response to these ideals by 'New Confucians' and the growth of interest in the 'Chinese Model' within academia. Peng then presents five approaches to understanding the contents of SMC: a homogenizing Western Liberal Constitutionalism; an empirical transitionalism towards liberalism; Marxist Party State with rule of law; Marxist Party State pillared with orthodox ideology and, finally, Marxist party-state supported by a new organic eclectic ideology. Peng argues that it is this final approach, which assumes the existence of an organic unity of 'the leadership of the Party, the position of the people as masters of the country, and the rule of law', all guided by a set of eclectic ideological imperatives, which is most plausible. The institutions are seen to seek to reconcile and achieve harmony between apparently competing consequentialist and deontological imperatives, with the materialism of Marxist approaches contrasted with rights-based tenets in liberal approaches. For Peng, it is the distinctive way in which this is being resolved which lies at the heart of Sinicized Marxist constitutionalism, with significant academic interest now focused on its accompanying form of jurisprudence. This has the potential, suggests Peng, to challenge the hegemony of WLC and homogeneity of constitutional ideals.

Terrell Carver examines this possibility in Chapter 10. Responding to the core claims and tenets of Peng's thesis, Carver outlines internal contradictions and tensions in 'Western' constitutionalism. Tracing the bloody, unpredictable and often contingent development of Western constitutions, Carver argues that the notion of the United States as an ideal embodiment of constitutionalism is flawed and serves simply to neglect the heterogeneity of constitutional forms. Comparing the systems of the United States, United Kingdom and elsewhere to the constitutional tenets of Locke, Carver demonstrates that the definition of, and relationship between, apparently indispensible components of constitutionalism, such as democracy, separation of powers, rule of law and party politics, are anything but fixed, uncontested and inevitable. For Carver, there needs to be serious recognition of legitimate local influences on constitutional forms, including, potentially, in China, and protest at illegitimate ones such as the global war on terror. Carver then brings the discussion to the relationship between Marx and Marxism and constitutionalism, highlighting Marx's own partially instrumental, liberal democratic sympathies and desire to achieve a transcendence, rather than rejection, of liberalism by removing traditional obstacles to the development of forces of production and, ultimately, human flourishing. Placing these concerns in the present, Carver asks whether liberal democracy is any more capable than one-party governance of achieving instrumental goods associated with the development of the forces of production or whether a system such as that in China is a mere 'pragmatic and moral perversion' of capitalism. Explaining that Marxism is a perfectionist, outcome based, rather than a procedural, deontological, paradigm, Carver argues that discussions in China about the place and extent of individual rights are understandable. Indeed, for Carver, in an age of excess in the private sector and austerity in the public, this is one key issue which remains of great importance globally.

The focus of the book now moves towards examination of an approach which has sought to acknowledge diversity while claiming to develop a radical, revolutionary alternative to both Marxism and liberalism: post-Marxism. As Oliver Harrison explains in Chapter 11, however, the break from Marxism is far from conclusive in the thought of post-Marxists such as Ernesto Laclau and Alain Badiou. For Harrison, the fact that these thinkers employ the thought of self-professed Marxists, Antonio Gramsci and Mao Tse-Tung, to seek to break from Marx means that a Marxist heritage remains. Harrison traces closely this heritage by comparing and contrasting the specific accounts and conditions of revolutionary subjectivity in Marx, Laclau and Badiou. Through this extensive analysis, Harrison agrees with Laclau that, while, as for Marx, a crisis is a pre-condition of revolution, revolution is immanent in the existing conditions of society only insofar as it enables revolutionary subjectivity. Despite his post-Marxist disdain for meta-narratives, Badiou conserves elements of dogma in his insistence on universal, though not totalizing, truths. The overarching message drawn from the chapter is that breaking from Marxism while remaining on the critical left is easier said than done.

This conclusion is examined further in Stuart Sim's evaluation, in Chapter 12, of the historical development and current status of post-Marxism, particularly with regard to its relationship with and influence on

Marxism. For Sim, one of the key features of post-Marxism has been the adoption of postmodern tenets, particularly with regard to the rejection of authoritarianism and essentialism and affirmation of pluralism and diversity. He argues that, beyond this unifying feature, there are elements which define two broad post-Marxist traditions. The first was developed by Laclau and Mouffe as part of a project to revitalize the left, ridding it of the harmful legacies of Marxism, such as its extremely prescriptive understanding of revolutionary subjects, and enabling it to promote more clearly radical democracy through engagement with ethnic minorities, feminists and those concerned with the environment. The second was developed by Lyotard and Baudrillard as a form of anti-Marxism, favouring uncontrollable contingency, unpredictability, 'little narrative' and pragmatic *ad hoc* single-issue protest in place of the universalizing tenets of historical materialism, grand narratives and positive accounts of the ways in which to bring about radical social change.

CHAPTER ONE

What does it mean to be a Marxist?*

Norman Geras

I should like to begin by thanking the organizers of this conference for inviting me to take part. I am particularly glad of the opportunity to speak on this topic since it is one I have thought much about in recent times, feeling as I do that there are ways in which I continue to be a Marxist, but also that there is one way in which I don't. I'll get to that later. Let me also say at the outset, having brought up the subject of my own relationship to Marxism, that I shall be making further reference to it here. The issues I want to discuss are of quite general import; but I haven't found it possible to discuss them in a general way without at the same time touching on this individual, biographical dimension.

I shall distinguish three meanings of 'being a Marxist'. I don't say that these exhaust the field of possible meanings. They are merely three meanings of interest to me and around which I find it convenient to organize my thoughts. To signal the general shape of what I will go on to say, these three meanings may be labelled, for short, *personal, intellectual* and *sociopolitical* ways of being a Marxist. I deal with them in turn.

---

*Paper presented at the 'Examining the Relevance of Marx and Marxism to Contemporary Global Society' conference on 29th January 2011.

Personal

This first meaning is conceptually quite straightforward, but it is not uninteresting for all that. For someone to be a Marxist, in the first – personal – sense I want to distinguish, he or she must (a) subscribe to a significant selection of recognized Marxist beliefs and (b) describe him or herself as a Marxist. Let me elaborate on each of those two points.

(a) I put it the way I do – speaking of *a significant selection* of recognized Marxist beliefs – because I don't think there is any single essential, or obligatory, tenet of Marxist doctrine or theory without which a person must fail in their self-identification as a Marxist. In my experience this is not always agreed among Marxists themselves. I have come across people who regarded acceptance of the labour theory of value – or, more bizarrely, of the falling rate of profit – as a *sine qua non* of authentic Marxist identity. More famously perhaps, Lenin wrote in Chapter 2 of *The State and Revolution* that 'Only he is a Marxist who *extends* the recognition of the class struggle to the recognition of *the dictatorship of the proletariat*' (Lenin 1949: 33). But given the breadth as well as the historical age of Marxism, and the consequent intellectual diversification of it, such attempts to pin down a single compulsory requirement of Marxist belief strike me as absurd. As Stefan Collini (2011) wrote in *The Guardian* a week ago, 'A quite extraordinarily rich and sophisticated body of ideas developed, and continues to develop, under this label' – he is referring to Marxism – and as Marxism has not been a church (despite certain religion-like features displayed in some of its branches; despite the view of certain of its critics that it is a secular variant of religion), it is not up to anyone to decree that adherence to any single thesis is indispensable to being a Marxist.

Naturally, it would not be sensible to call someone a Marxist on the basis of his or her signing up to some isolated and inconsequential proposition(s) lifted from, say, *Capital* or the *Communist Manifesto*, and that is why I refer, in the first condition above, to adherence to some significant plurality of Marxist beliefs. I shall give an illustration of the point. When asked a few years ago whether I still thought of myself as a Marxist, I answered that I did, and gave three reasons why I did. They were: (i) that historical materialism is broadly true – or perhaps it would be more accurate to say here, where I'm not spelling out the whole answer with its qualifications, true enough; (ii) that Marxism involves an 'enduring commitment to the goal of an egalitarian, non-exploitative society'; and (iii) that I valued 'Marxism's focus upon what is sometimes called the problem of agency: the problem of finding a route, the active social forces, between existing historical tendencies and the achievement of a substantially egalitarian society'. I would still, today, give these reasons for my being a Marxist; and I offer them also as an example of how being a Marxist depends, in the first of the two conditions I have proposed, on affirming some significant conjunction of Marxist beliefs.

What about the second condition? This is (ii) that the person who affirms the relevant beliefs *describes* him or herself as a Marxist. I add it as a second requirement not only because, Marxism not being a church, nobody is in a position to insist for anyone else on their membership of it: Marxism is a broad intellectual tradition, and one is free to adhere to it or not, as one chooses. But there is an additional reason for this possibility of choice, one that has long been clear to me as a matter of simple experience and that I shall now try to exemplify in quasi-formal terms.

Imagine someone who sees himself as a Marxist, but not in the sense of slavishly adhering to every important element of what he takes to be Marxist thinking; in the sense, rather, of using his critical faculties to distinguish what is right from what is wrong in that tradition and upholding only those elements he sees as viable. Thus, he says that he is a Marxist *because* of p, q and r, all these being aspects of Marxist thought which he takes to be true and/or valuable, and *despite x, y* and z, also aspects of Marxist thought but which he thinks are wrong and to be rejected. Now, here is a second person and she, it just so happens, reverses the weighting put on the very same pair of sets of components of Marxist thought. She says that she is not a Marxist, this *because* of x, y and z, which she, like the other guy, thinks are wrong, and *despite p, q* and r, which she too finds true and/or valuable, but not true or valuable enough to outweigh the wrongness and disvalue of x, y and z. These are two people, in other words, who agree that Marxism is good in the very same ways and no good in the very same ways; yet the two of them divide over whether to call themselves Marxists.

Thus, it is perfectly easy to imagine someone saying in response to my declaration of intellectual allegiance of eight years ago that, while agreeing with me that there's a lot of truth in historical materialism, *and* that the goal of an egalitarian, non-exploitative society is a good one, *and* that Marxism's focus on the problem of agency showed a commendable sense of social and political realism – nonetheless they do not subscribe to Marxism, preferring to identify with a radical left liberalism. Why they do not subscribe to Marxism is, let us say, that the insufficient attention of the tradition to ethical issues, and the lack of an adequate theory within it of political democracy, and the common dismissal by Marxists of the merits of liberalism, have all been seriously disabling features of the tradition, time and again leading its adherents astray. It is not by accident that I cite as weaknesses of Marxism features that I really do take to be such. I call myself a Marxist despite them. I can well understand why others might decline to call themselves Marxists because of them.

There is a sort of existential choice one makes. The choice is based on reasons, as I have tried to show, but the reasons are guiding rather than forcing ones, and other factors come into play, though I leave aside what those other factors are.

Intellectual

I turn to my second meaning of being a Marxist, the one that I have called the 'intellectual' meaning. What I have in mind here is that, as well as having some relevant combination of Marxist beliefs, a person can work – as writer, political publicist, academic, thinker, researcher – within the intellectual tradition begun by Marx and Engels and developed by later figures. They can work as Marxists, write as Marxists, by engaging with major themes or thinkers of the tradition, by wrestling with problems they perceive it to have left unresolved, by applying Marxist concepts in fresh domains, by doing new research to expand previously undeveloped aspects of Marxist thought and so on. Here, too, I would want to emphasize the breadth and variety we have seen in this way of being a Marxist.

For Marxist intellectual work embraces the work of historians who have seen themselves as applying the methods and insights of the materialist conception of history to the study of particular countries, social formations, historical periods; of political economists writing on the phases of capitalist development, today on globalization; political philosophers studying the ideas of Marxist thinkers, whether to clarify their meaning, take them further or remedy deficiencies they find there; literary and cultural theorists, interpreting literary texts and other cultural products in the light of Marxist concepts; sociologists of development; students of labour movements; those attempting to theorize the nature of fascism; etc. Whatever its weaknesses and its failures, one of the strengths of Marxism has surely been that it could animate the work of so many people across so many disciplines.

In this connection, also, however, I want to propose that one shouldn't think of Marxist intellectual work in too fixed and narrow a way – so that writing history or doing political economy can be seen as a straightforwardly Marxist type of activity; whereas, say, doing moral philosophy is not, because moral philosophy isn't something Marx himself engaged in and it has not been a notable feature of Marxist discussion since Marx. For suppose, as is in fact the case, that Marxism has been deficient in certain areas, saying nothing, or nothing useful, or not much, or the wrong things; and one wants to try and make good the deficiency, help to fill the gap. I shall suggest two examples: one from my own work and the other more speculative.

What does each of us owe to other people in the way of aid or rescue when their situation is dire – life-threateningly dire? What is the *extent* of our duty to others under such circumstances, assuming there is one? Now, one can ask of these questions: are they Marxist questions? They're obviously not *specifically* Marxist since anyone could ask them; they are of quite general philosophical and indeed human concern. But they *should* be questions of interest to Marxists, since the notion of solidarity, including international solidarity, has been important to Marxists. They are, in any event, questions that I asked in my book (1998) *The Contract of Mutual*

Indifference. They illustrate the fact that there are questions that have not been central in the Marxist canon, but that it is proper for Marxists to pursue – proper because they are questions that arise directly from what *are* more specifically Marxist concerns. That someone could raise and try to answer the very same questions without relating them to any Marxist context is true, but it isn't relevant to the point I'm making: which is that the development of Marxist thought must sometimes involve working in intellectual regions, such as moral philosophy, where its presence has hitherto been weak to non-existent.

My second example I will merely gesture towards, sweepingly, as being a general requirement if political Marxism is to thrive again in future – a prospect I no longer take for granted. Marxism has been characterized by a huge deficit with respect to democracy. The deficit has been both theoretical and practical. Theoretical because, envisaging the transformation of the world, no less, Marxism never adequately projected the theory of political democracy that would be adequate to cope with so far-reaching a task. And practical because, partly in consequence, Marxist movements have time and again fallen into anti-democratic and murderous ways. I will do no more than allude to the Stalinist experience, because it is definitive for many as a warning of what Marxism could become. Unless, today and tomorrow, Marxists show themselves willing to engage fully with the intellectual resources of liberalism – yes, liberalism, this so often maligned figure on the Marxist left – and to absorb everything that liberalism knows and Marxists have either derided or belittled or ignored; unless a Marxist political theory comes to terms with the truths of liberal political theory, acknowledging the normative force of human rights, the idea of judicial independence and separation of powers, exploring different forms of representation, insisting on free elections and an untrammelled freedom of speech and opinion, understanding the virtues of political pluralism; unless all of those, Marxism as a political movement might as well shut up shop.

Note that I do not say Marxism should be *uncritical* of liberalism. Liberalism in many variants is too accommodating of unjust inequalities. Yet, if it is not willing to learn from liberalism, Marxism is unlikely to be of any benefit to anyone politically. It will deserve to have had its day. A frankly, unashamedly *liberal* Marxism – this too might look unfamiliar to many in the way of Marxist intellectual work. But it is not merely a possible, it is a vital, area for future Marxist work if Marxism itself is to have a worthwhile future. That leads, so to say organically, into the last part of this paper.

Socio-political

The third meaning of 'being a Marxist' that I want to discuss – the socio-political meaning – concerns not just the would-be Marxist's beliefs or the content of his or her intellectual work. It's about being part of something larger. On this meaning, a person is a Marxist if they belong to the Marxist left. Here I could refer to the old theme of the unity of theory and practice, or to the idea that Marxism as well as being a theory was a mass movement. There is a well-known pedigree for these claims, starting with the eleventh of Marx's *Theses on Feuerbach* – 'the point is to change it' (Marx and Engels 1976: 3) – and taking in the idea of Marxism as the self-consciousness of the working class, a theory for the workers' movement. Whatever truth there may once have been in this notion of a theory providing guidance to a movement, however, it doesn't apply today. Politically, Marxism has become a very marginal presence.

Still, there is a Marxist left – both in an organized and in a looser sense. There are political organizations that profess Marxism; and beyond these there is a wider current of opinion formed by people who would call themselves Marxist or admit to being significantly influenced by Marxism; one might even count as on the periphery of the Marxist left people who would not acknowledge any direct Marxist influence on their thinking but who share with more avowed Marxists or semi-Marxists some important tenets of belief. Given what Marxism has now come to, it would surely be too strong to refer to this Marxist social presence as a *movement*. Despite that, I think we can continue to talk of a Marxist left of sorts. And one can be a Marxist in the sense of being part of this Marxist left.

At the risk of startling you, or some of you, but not just for that effect – rather in order to register my own conviction that here is a way of being a Marxist that no longer recommends itself – I am sorry to say that to be a member of the Marxist left today is to be part of something, a body of opinion, a political current, that is accursed. Steady on, you may think, that's a bit strong, isn't it? Accursed? Why that? And why now? In view of the history of the Soviet Union, or of the international communist movement that supported and excused it, or of China under Mao (to mention only those sorry examples of Marxism gone wrong), how has the Marxist left become accursed only today and not long before that?

I will not shirk the question, which is fair. This is my answer to it. It is partly personal, but also partly general. Like everybody else, I was – I am – of my generation. I was inducted into Marxism already knowing about Stalinism and all its horrors; but knowing also that that experience didn't exhaust the totality of Marxist thought or, as I thought and hoped, of Marxist possibility. Stalinism had been one grossly distorted realization of Marxism's anti-capitalist project, embarked upon under maximally unpropitious historical conditions, but other better realizations were still possible, and under the watchword this time of socialist *democracy*. Furthermore, what I knew in this regard, or at any rate hoped, I knew and hoped in the company of large numbers of others on the Western left, people not at all indulgent towards the crimes of Stalin. We were a part – for those who remember the 1960s and 1970s – of a *new* left, a left that had learnt the lessons of the historic tragedy that the Stalinist experience had been.

So, although there was even then a section of the Marxist left that one could aptly regard as compromised by an ugly past or indeed present, apologists for the crimes of Stalin and/or Mao, this was not the Marxist left as a whole, as we knew it.

Today, in the light of what has happened in the first decade of the twenty-first century, it is not so easy, if you believe in human rights and the importance of the fundamental civic and political freedoms that we owe to historical liberalism, to find a Marxist left that is worth belonging to or being broadly identified with. In both its organized and its looser, more amorphous forms the Marxist left is a place of the most disgraceful apologetics and ambiguous or worse than ambiguous alignments. What makes this a matter for especial regret and criticism today, by those of us who still think of ourselves as Marxists in either or both of my first two senses but feel no identification with, and eschew membership of, the Marxist left as such, is that this is a Marxist left that can make no further appeal to historical 'innocence'. It already knows the consequences of undemocratic organization, the absence of liberal safeguards, the elevation of the great leader; and of turning a blind eye to all this so as, supposedly, not to give comfort to enemies on the political right. It *should* know better, but it doesn't.

What am I talking about? I'm talking about a Marxist left from within which after 9/11 there came voices ready to make excuses for an act of mass murder that the whole left should have forthrightly condemned. And which, more generally, is always free with forms of 'understanding' of terrorism – by another name, murder of the innocent – in a shallow root-causes sociology of grievance, alienation, poverty or what have you. And from within which there have been people willing to march side by side with radical Islamists – that is, anti-democratic and reactionary theocrats – and to shout 'We are all Hezbollah' (also not an organization renowned for its commitment to Enlightenment or, for that matter, Marxian universalist values, to say nothing of liberal and democratic ones). And within which there are still those who will sing the praises of Cuba as a post-capitalist society, its harsh way with political dissent notwithstanding. And those who will turn out in Camden to give a warm welcome to Hugo Chavez, just the latest in a line of adored leaders whose merit seems to be that they are from somewhere else. And who will speak up even for the likes of Mahmoud Ahmadinejad or the Chinese leadership where there is a matter of some criticism directed at them by Western politicians who enjoy the moral advantage of being leaders of countries with free electorates and free elections.

And who have been so convinced that there was only one possible, one legitimate, viewpoint on the left about the war in Iraq that they have reacted to others on the left who didn't share that viewpoint as if they could no longer *be* of the left. These are often the same people, incidentally – these unswervingly convinced-of-one-viewpoint ones – as opposed the US-led response to 9/11 that overthrew Taliban rule in Afghanistan, as opposed Nato's intervention in Kosovo in 1999, as opposed the eviction of Saddam Hussein's armies from Kuwait in 1991 and as opposed the eviction of Argentina from the Falklands in 1982. They are, in any case, unable to accommodate the idea that someone on the left might favour the overthrow of a genocidal and fascistic tyrant.

They are also, some of them, people who have worked tirelessly to put in place in British universities a policy of boycotting the academics of one country – one country only – Israel; irrespective of what the Israeli academics to be boycotted (in fact blacklisted) by them may individually think about the policies of their government and irrespective of the historical pedigree of the idea of boycotts directed exclusively against Jews. And who, again some of them, treat the right of nations to self-determination as unproblematically to be recognized for many people but not, apparently, in the case of the Jews.[1]

This is a Marxist left that, in order to make its opposition to the Western military presence in Afghanistan more psychologically comfortable for itself, prefers not to talk about what the return of Taliban rule to that country would mean for its people, and its women and girls more especially, or when it does talk about it is not above mocking and belittling the genuine concern of others on that score. It is a Marxist left today which, in its Anglophone embodiment, is governed by one overriding impulse, 'anti-imperialism'; and, within this, opposition especially to any policy supported by the US or British governments, with all other considerations subordinate to that, if given any think-room at all.

I anticipate, as one possible response to all this, that these ideas and activities may be features of a small fragment, the 'far left', but that it is too quick a generalization on my part to treat them as any more widespread than that, or as typifying the Marxist left in general. I am familiar with this response and I don't accept it. To put it briefly and bluntly, I read. I read what goes on in the opinion pages of the national press, and so far from these tropes being confined to the far left, the SWP and its like, they extend even beyond what I have referred to as the more amorphous Marxist left, into broadly 'progressive' circles that would not willingly own to the name Marxist. This is, if you want, an ironic and distorted coming to fruition of the notion of Gramscian hegemony. Even with Marxism as a body of thought in overt political decline, some of the most lamentable apologetic tropes and moral compromises of Marxism's least glorious realization have taken hold more widely among the left-liberal intelligentsia.

I do not say, just to be clear about this, that there are no distinctions within the body of opinion that I have here evoked, no gradations. Distinctions and gradations there certainly are. There are the 'hard' crowd: the out-and-out 'we-are-all-Hezbollah'-niks; unashamed apologists for terrorism, dressed up this in the obscuring language of 'the right to resistance' and of 'revolutionary violence', as if either formula could justify murdering the innocent; the apologists for Cuba, or China, or Iran. But there is a softer version too, offered by the practitioners of the mumble and the evasion where authoritarian movements or regimes are up for assessment and possible condemnation; democrats to a man and a woman, and as insistent as anyone on the importance of basic rights when some misdemeanour of a Western government is under scrutiny, but much more 'nuanced' when patently undemocratic polities or organizations are the object of critical attention.

How to explain it, the continuing weakness, the persistent moral failure, of this sector of the left, with the Marxist left a substantial core of it? A full answer to the question would doubtless need to go much wider than I can on this occasion, but one part of the answer, I would suggest, is this. The failure has its source in a group of temptations regularly displayed by a section of the Western left when confronted by (a) the undemocratic practices of supposedly socialist or anti-imperialist or (in some assumed sense) 'progressive' states and (b) the claims made for the democracies of the wealthier capitalist countries. There is, first, a temptation to look for considerations mitigating the lack of democracy in the kind of states I have just referred to: considerations such as blockade, encirclement (of the young Soviet state), underdevelopment, the legacy of colonialism and so on. There is, second, an attempt to point to features compensating for that lack of democracy: principally social and economic achievements of one kind and another (rapid industrialization, Cuba's health care). Third, there are arguments to the effect that the democracies of advanced capitalist societies are themselves either flawed and limited as democracies or not really democracies at all but disguised forms of dictatorship.

Now, it is not that there is nothing at all to be said in support of these themes. In turn: (i) a country mired in poverty has fewer democratic resources than a wealthy one; (ii) where there are achievements to note, there is nothing wrong with noting them; (iii) the democracies of the capitalist world are indeed flawed in certain ways – differently, and some more than others, but invariably failing to offer all their citizens an equality of influence and rights. Nonetheless, there is a central piece of bad faith in the way that, for a section of the left, these three themes typically combine to enable their partisans to evade a single inescapable fact: namely that, flawed as they may be, the capitalist democracies are democracies, whereas none of the would-be anti-capitalist countries, anywhere, has managed to sustain comparably good or better democratic institutions over any length of time. I do not say that this means it could never happen. I do not believe that. What I do think, though, is that the democratic institutions that we are familiar with have yet to be improved on in any of those places that some leftists are given to casting an indulgent eye upon even while they seek to distance themselves critically from the political institutions of their own countries, institutions from which they benefit and which are superior. Unwilling to profess a clear allegiance towards what is democratically better, a certain type of leftist is always ready to make allowances for what is democratically worse.

This is a standpoint more attached to its own anti-capitalism than it is to the struggle against political tyranny or, if it comes to it, to the opposition (obligatory for any principled socialism) to terrorist murder. Some may be upset by such a characterization of the evaluative priorities of the left I'm talking about here, for it is not a ranking openly avowed as a rule. Yet, *practically*, in terms of the dominant polemical rhetoric coming from the relevant quarter, this is how it too often goes: the democracies of the West flawed, at fault, hypocritical, aggressors and so forth, while quite appallingly anti-democratic movements and regimes are made apology for, and bathed in the mitigation of that shallow root-causes sociology to which I earlier referred – root causes for which some proximate 'we' is always said to bear the ultimate responsibility. Tyranny, terrorism and even genocide almost cease to be horrors in their own right, evils to be opposed alongside economic exploitation, inequality, poverty and other byproducts of global capitalism. They are, as it were, 'levelled' by always being traced back in their turn to capitalism and imperialism so that they become lesser evils and their direct agents and perpetrators lesser enemies.

Conclusion

In conclusion, then, I have considered three meanings of 'being a Marxist'. They can go together or they can come apart. Marxists in the first and second meanings may also be Marxists in the third meaning; or they may not. However, unless a Marxism of personal belief and a Marxism of creative intellectual work both thoroughly renewed and wrested once and for all from the grip of anti-democratic and illiberal themes and concepts – unless *such* a Marxism can come to animate the Marxist political left, Marxism as a political force might just as well be dead and buried. A movement so slow to learn would have earned this fate.

Notes

1   As too often, responses to these points of mine at the January 2011 conference reached immediately for the easy convenience that I shouldn't confuse criticism of Israeli policy with anti-Jewish animus. As anyone can see for themselves, I took no exception, in what I said, to criticism of Israeli policy, an entirely legitimate activity. I took issue with (a) punitive actions directed against Israeli academics (which is not merely 'criticism'); and (b) the denial of the right to national self-determination of the Jews and the Jews alone, a denial implicit in the view that Israel is an illegitimate state (which, too, is not mere criticism, but a threat to the organized national existence of the Jewish people).

References

Collini, S. (2011), 'How to Change the World: Tales of Marx and Marxism by Eric Hobsbawm – Review', *The Guardian*, 22 January 2011. Available from: <http://www.guardian.co.uk/books/2011/jan/22/change-world-marx-eric-hobsbawm-review>.

Geras, N. (1998), *The Contract of Mutual Indifference: Political Philosophy after the Holocaust*, London: Verso.

Lenin, V. I. (1949), *The State and Revolution*, Moscow: Progress Publishers.

Marx, K. and Engels, F. (1976), *Marx/Engels Collected Works*, volume 5. London: Lawrence and Wishart.

CHAPTER TWO

An image in a curved mirror: Pareto's critique of Marxist science

Joseph V. Femia

Writing in *Capital*, Marx described himself as a scientist, who – like a natural scientist – seeks to penetrate beneath the surface appearance of things to reveal the essence of reality. In a famous passage, he asserted that 'a scientific analysis of competition is possible only if we grasp the inner nature of capital, just as the apparent motions of the heavenly bodies are intelligible only to someone who is acquainted with their real motions, which are not perceptible to the senses' (Marx 1976: 433). Marx's 'humanist' followers, notably Lukács and Gramsci, have chosen to play down Marx's scientific pretensions, almost as if the Great Man had not quite understood the implications of his Hegelian leanings. More generally, however, Marx's disciples have stoutly defended his credentials as a scientist, even comparing him to Copernicus and Darwin. Plekhanov, for example, characterized Marxism as 'objective truth, and no "fate" will move us any more from the correct point of view, discovered at last'. The science of man will of course 'make new discoveries' but these, according to Plekhanov, 'will supplement and confirm the theory of Marx, just as new discoveries in astronomy have supplemented and confirmed the discovery of Copernicus' (1956: 194–5).

Opponents of Marxism have found these claims laughable. Karl Popper, one of the more prominent critics, derided Marx and his followers as scientific imposters, whose vague and elastic terminology allowed them to 'explain away' whatever phenomena that might seem to render their theory erroneous. Consider the supposed tendency for the rate of profit to decline as capitalism progresses. Marx admits that there are countervailing factors which might cause the rate of profit to increase, though he insists that at some unspecified point in the future, the downward tendency will assert itself. This type of prediction is impossible to test, and testability is for Popper the key distinction between a scientific theory and a metaphysical one. It must be possible to state the exact conditions under which, through observation or experimentation, the theory can be *falsified*. Marxism, in his opinion, is an elaborate tautology, protected from refutation by its basic circularity. Once it is accepted that the 'essence' of history is to reveal its inevitable and final destination, communism, every apparently contrary fact can be subsumed in the general narrative, sometimes with the help of the dialectical method.

The arguments 'for' and 'against' Marxist science themselves suffer from a degree of circularity, as they are invariably based on contestable depictions of the scientific method. The debate is also polarized, with critics and defenders alike feeling that they must come down hard on one side or the other. It is therefore interesting to note that Vilfredo Pareto, the eminent economist and sociologist, whose attitude to Marxism was definitely oppositional, advanced a surprisingly measured evaluation of Marx's scientific claims. S. B. Finer has described Pareto's *magnum opus*, *Trattato di Sociologia Generale*, as 'a gargantuan retort to Marx'. This is more or less true, but we must also point out that the text rarely mentions Marx by name. Neither in his *Trattato* (translated into English as *The Mind and Society*) nor in his other works did Pareto present a systematic critique of his illustrious predecessor. For the most part, the Italian sets out his own ideas on methodology and society and refers to Marx only in passing. As Finer puts it, Pareto's strategy is not so much confrontation as 'envelopment'. Rather than contradicting Marx's concepts and categories, he 'transcends' them, or broadens them out so that Marxist propositions become special cases of a much more general theory (Introduction to Pareto 1966: 77–8). With respect to Marx's concept of ideology, Pareto expands it to include Marxism itself. Class exploitation is transcended by the more general concept of 'spoliation', which encompasses *all* cases in which one group of people (legally) acquires the wealth produced by others. Nor did he deny the Marxist proposition that people were motivated by economic interests – but he also drew attention to other, equally important sources of motivation that Marx ignored, such as human predispositions or sentiments.

To Pareto, Marx's mistakes, or 'blind-spots', fit into a pattern. While acknowledging that Marx aspired to a scientific analysis of society, and praising him for his ambition, he thought that Marx's admirable intentions were constantly being subverted by the 'essentialism' he inherited from Hegel, as well as by the intense moralism he inherited from the Utopian socialists. By way of preliminaries, it would be useful to outline what Pareto meant by science and the scientific method.

Like Marx, Pareto believed that the techniques of the natural sciences were appropriate to the study of society and history. A mechanical engineer by university training, he aimed 'to construct a system of sociology on the model of celestial mechanics, physics, chemistry' (Pareto 1935: para. 20). His views on epistemology and ontology were broadly positivist. Scientific theories are true or false by virtue of their correspondence to a mind-independent world. In a well-known passage, he summarizes his method rather starkly:

> We are following the inductive method. We have no preconceptions, no *a priori* notions. We find certain facts before us. We describe them, classify them, determine their character, ever on the watch for some uniformity (law) in the relationships between them. (Pareto 1935: para. 145)

Elsewhere he says that we 'start with facts to work out theories', the obvious implication being that we take 'only experience and observation as our guides' (1935: paras. 69, 6). Such statements make Pareto sound like a pure empiricist, but he accepted that theory construction required an element of deduction, and he also hastened to point out that 'abstraction is, for all the sciences, the preliminary and indispensable requirement for all research'. Abstraction, he notes, is used for purposes of simplification, to aid both analysis and computation. One form involves stripping away certain properties of a system in order to focus on those properties the scientist wants to study. In rational mechanics, for example, bodies are reduced to physical points, while in pure economics, we reduce real men, with all their passions and prejudices, to the calculating machine that is *homo economicus* (Pareto 1972: 12–13). Moreover, Pareto reminds us that the terms used in science are themselves abstractions and correspond to reality only within certain limits. Take 'clay'. We give the name of 'clay' to a compound of a number of chemical elements and the name 'humus' to a compound of a still larger number of chemical elements. The line drawn between the two compounds is obtained by abstraction (Pareto 1935: para. 2544). Positivism is sometimes caricatured as 'vulgar empiricism', but Pareto – as we can see – underlines the need for 'hypothetical abstractions' of one sort or another to enable scientists to uncover the regularities in complex systems where multiple categories of facts intermingle (Pareto 1935: paras. 2397, 144). He accepts that there is something 'subjective' and 'arbitrary' about such abstractions that our scientific theories are partly a human invention and not merely a mirror reflection of external reality (Pareto 1972: 12). Yet these theories will stand or fall depending on whether or not they conform to factual observation: 'Theories, their principles, their implications, are altogether subordinate to facts and possess no other criterion of truth than their capacity for picturing them' (Pareto 1935: paras. 69, 63).

The limitations of induction, as formulated by Hume, did not seem to trouble Pareto. According to the Scottish philosopher, there was no logical reason to believe that because the sun rose yesterday, and this morning, it would *certainly* do so tomorrow. The general point is that accumulated observations of empirical regularities can never establish the truth of a scientific theory. Popper was most exercised by this 'problem', claiming that it rendered positivism's 'verification principle' useless. Hence he offers his fallibilistic conception of science as progressing through 'conjectures and refutations'. What makes a theory scientific is its *falsifiability* – its ability to be stated with sufficient exactitude so that it can be clearly refuted by empirical evidence.

Although Pareto was long dead when Popper put forward his views, we can be sure that the older man would not have been impressed. In fact, Pareto shares Hume's scepticism about induction as a means to definitive truth, but he does not believe that this in any way discredits the inductive method. He insists on the 'relativity' of all scientific theories. Even in the experimental sciences, where controlled laboratory experiments are the norm, 'absolute certitude' does not exist: the physical or social scientist can speak 'only of greater or lesser probabilities'. In some cases, 'such probability is slight, for others great, and for still others so great as to be equivalent to what in ordinary parlance is known as certainty' (Pareto 1935: para. 540). The fact that no scientific law or theory can be verified in the *strictest* sense of the term is just a statement of the obvious, since science is, by its very nature, 'limited, relative, in part conventional'. Scientific laws 'imply no *necessity*'. They are just 'contingent' hypotheses, 'serving to epitomize a more or less extensive number of facts and so serving only until superseded by better ones' (Pareto 1935: para. 69n.3 and 69). However, Pareto is willing to use the language of 'proof' and 'verification' as long as it is understood that these terms do not denote mathematical certainty (Pareto 1935: paras. 69, 2398–9).

Because scientific laws are merely statements of probability, it is often hard to specify the conditions under which they would be 'falsified', in Popper's sense. The problem is especially acute in those sciences, such as celestial mechanics or sociology, where the use of experimentation is next to impossible, making it difficult 'to unravel tangles of many different uniformities' (Pareto 1935: paras. 100–1). When looking at human history, then, the best we can do is to 'determine the probable course of social development in the future' (Pareto 1935: para. 140). Historical movement, Pareto says, is especially difficult to predict because it takes on an 'undulatory form':

> You find a certain characteristic which . . . is more and more accentuated as time passes; you would be wrong to conclude therefrom that the

movement will continue indefinitely and that the society concerned will keep moving towards a certain objective. A reaction against the prevailing trend may well be in the offing, and the emergence of a movement in a contrary direction may not be long delayed. (*Les Systèmes Socialistes*, in Pareto 1966: 129)

Of necessity, any historical laws we discover will be laws of tendency only. The fact that such laws are too equivocal to admit of outright disproof would not be a matter of concern to Pareto. We do not abandon scientific theories because they generate a few inaccurate predictions. The laws of meteorology, for example, are not fatally contradicted by X number of mistaken weather forecasts. The acceptance or rejection of scientific theories is, to Pareto, a much more fluid process, where the boundary between 'proof' and 'disproof' cannot be defined in advance. Science, he believes, is a 'progressive' activity in the literal sense of the word. It is constantly adding to its fund of facts, 'so that sooner or later a lack of accord develops between the actual multiplicity of facts and the arbitrary multiplicity of the theory'. Eventually, the discrepancy becomes clear to everyone, though those who support the failing theory will at first make every effort 'to squeeze the facts into the theory', by the use of 'rescue hypotheses' of diminishing degrees of plausibility. In the long run, however, 'facts are tougher and more durable than theories'. A 'tipping-point' is reached, where the need to broaden or replace the old doctrine comes to enjoy near-unanimous agreement (Pareto 1935: para. 2400n.1). 'The logico-experimental sciences', in Pareto's memorable phrasing, 'are made up of a sum of theories that are like living creatures, in that they are born, live, and die, the young replacing the old, the group alone enduring'. Whereas faith and metaphysics aspire to an ultimate, eternal resting place, science 'knows that it can attain only provisory, transitory positions' (Pareto 1935: para. 2400).

The critique of Marx

Although he considered Marxist science to be deeply flawed, Pareto nevertheless thought that Marx had made great scientific discoveries, upon which a genuine science of society could be built. The key Marxist insight, according to Pareto, was to draw a distinction between the surface appearance of society, on the one hand, and the underlying reality, on the other. Individuals and groups are often unaware of the forces prompting their behaviour and ascribe their actions to imaginary causes which differ considerably from the real causes. Struggles between competing elites, for example, are often seen as struggles for justice or liberty, even by the elites in question. Theological dissensions, always couched in high principle, are mainly 'veils cloaking exclusively worldly interests'. Greed and self-aggrandizement lurk beneath the 'lofty declamations' of those who rule, or seek to rule, us (*Les Systèmes*

Socialistes, in Pareto 1966: 137). Indeed, terms such as 'justice' and 'morality' are historically contingent in their meaning, reflecting the needs of dominant social groups. When Pareto declares that 'most men make convictions of their interests', he is deliberately echoing Marx's point that 'most men' will justify actions that are advantageous to them with 'empty, high sounding, emotional formulas'. Ideas – that is to say – are weapons in the conflict between classes and groups, 'the tokens of which are to be found on every page of history' (*Les Systèmes Socialistes*, in Pareto 1966: 140–1). For him, Marx was 'entirely right' to emphasize class struggle and the centrality of exploitation: 'The struggle of some individuals to appropriate the wealth produced by others is the great factor dominating all human history' (*Cours d'Economie Politique*, in Pareto 1966: 117).

So what went wrong? Why was Marx's science of society only half-baked? Why did he fail to take his brilliant insights to their logical conclusions? Pareto's answer was fairly straightforward. Marx, mistrusting the evidence of his senses, ultimately betrayed the scientific (or 'logico-experimental') method and deduced facts about reality from abstract, *a priori* ideas: when the facts did not support his preconceptions, so much the worse for the facts. The supposed scourge of German metaphysics and French Utopianism could not in the end resist their seductive charms. To be more specific, Pareto concluded that Marx's scientific aspirations were thwarted by both essentialism (derived from Hegel) and moralism (derived from his socialist forebears). In examining Pareto's critique, let us take each category in turn.

Essentialism

Although Pareto was generally hostile to historical teleology, he did believe that science had progressed through the ages from the Aristotelian essentialism that saw reality as purpose-driven, either by divine providence or by a *telos* inherent in things, to 'modern science', whose principles are wholly 'subordinated to experience', and whose only 'purpose' is 'to replace figments of the imagination with the results of experience' (Pareto 1935: paras. 13, 2395). In medieval 'science', the facts had to accord with the inferences deducible from general principles – themselves the product of religious dogma or introspection rather than observation. It is often assumed that the growing prestige of the empirical method in the sixteenth and seventeenth centuries put an end to the influence of essentialism in scientific discourse. Pareto begged to differ. While theology has loosened its grip on the educated mind, it has been replaced, in some quarters, by a kind of metaphysical spiritualism, associated with the likes of Hegel and Kant, which gives 'the name of "science" to knowledge of the "essences" of things', to knowledge of principles and 'the necessary relations between facts' (Pareto 1935: paras. 19, 530). Even theories that aspire to logico-experimental status, that *claim* to be based on the facts of experience, sometimes betray a metaphysical bent, elevating principles to a 'quasi-independent subsistence' (Pareto 1935: para. 63). There is an approach to experimental sciences, says Pareto, that sees its task as identifying the 'higher principles' or 'essential relations' or 'inner necessity' that govern the workings of reality. For those who adhere to this approach, the statement 'Water solidifies at 0 degrees centigrade' contains 'something more than a mere epitome of experiments' – there must be some 'essence' or principle of necessity that makes the statement true for all time (Pareto 1935: paras. 528–31). Once established, these abstractions are allowed to determine the facts of the world rather than the other way round. The idea that science is fallible and cumulative, that theories are necessarily incomplete and constantly open to improvement, is abandoned in the search for 'absolutes' (Pareto 1935: paras. 106, 108).

This 'metaphysical' vision of science described (perhaps tendentiously) by Pareto clearly resembles what is now called scientific or 'critical' realism (see, e.g. Bhaskar 1978), and a convincing case can be made that Marx's method of analysis does indeed conform to its basic tenets (Walker 2001, Conclusion). As we have seen, Marx maintained that the goal of science was to discover the 'inner nature' or 'real motions' of phenomena, which are 'not perceptible to the senses'. This view of the scientific method has become rather fashionable – at least among philosophers. Pareto of course regarded it as backward and regressive. In what particular ways, according to him, did it lead Marx astray?

Pareto thought that Marx was right to stress 'the fact that economic factors modify social institutions and doctrines'. Too often human history is pictured as a logical progression of ideas, as if our material interests counted for nothing in the story of mankind. But Marx proceeds to strain the credulity of his readers by more or less ignoring other factors which 'are not reducible to purely economic categories'. In other words, the materialist theory of history has its point of departure in a principle which is true, 'but it errs in trying to claim too much: a claim taking it beyond the conclusions which are legitimately derivable from experience' (*Les Systèmes Socialistes*, in Pareto 1966: 126–7). Through a combination of observation and introspection, Marx thinks that he has uncovered the essential structure of human development. There is no way, however, that this type of reductionism could be verified by observation alone, for empirical evidence tells us that human events are 'determined by the concurrent action of large numbers of conditions' (Pareto 1935: para. 137). Social causation, says Pareto, 'is extremely complex and cannot be reduced to a single factor' (*Les Systèmes Socialistes*, in Pareto 1966: 137). Any objective consideration of economic interests, for example, would reveal that they are themselves modified by prevailing sentiments and ideas. Monism, according to Pareto, is abstract inference; pluralism is observational reality.

Having 'discovered' the hidden generative mechanism of social evolution, Marx then defines 'class' in purely economic terms and decides that only two – the bourgeoisie and the proletariat – matter in capitalist societies.

Never mind that, in the real world, there are an 'infinite number' of groups with different interests whose conflicts shape historical and social development. Ethnic and religious struggles, Pareto reminds us, are often far more intense than class (in the Marxist sense) struggles. Marx's theoretical priorities, however, dictate that all such struggles are reducible to esoteric economic cleavages, notwithstanding any evidence to the contrary (*Les Systèmes Socialistes*, in Pareto 1966: 140–1).

At this point, you may be wondering why a man who insisted that abstraction was central to the scientific enterprise should be so critical of Marx's use of abstraction. A defender of Marx might say that he was simply distinguishing 'essential' from non-essential properties of society in order to isolate causal chains, in much the same way as the neo-classical economist assumes perfectly rational and informed economic actors in order to analyse supply and demand. Yes, there is an element of simplification, but it helps us to demonstrate how fundamental properties of the system generate common patterns among disparate phenomena. For Pareto, however, abstraction is not the *goal* of scientific analysis – we are not searching for an 'essential structure' that defies sense perception. Abstraction is, instead, merely a heuristic device. Once it has done its work, we must, in his words, 'return to the concrete from the abstract', by filling in the missing details. Any economist who thinks that producers and consumers *really are* perfectly rational, or that markets *really are* perfectly competitive, would be a poor economist (Pareto 1972: 12–16). Abstraction is useful only if it helps to illuminate the facts of experience, not if it distorts them. For example, assuming that there are only two classes in capitalist society might enable us to identify an important dynamic of social change. While this could be useful as an initial approximation to reality, the complexity of the actual world can only be captured by 'the method of successive approximations', which gradually brings theory in line with multi-dimensional reality (Pareto 1972: 9). Marxist essentialism, in Pareto's view, disfigures reality, offering only 'an image in a curved mirror', where the form of the object is 'altered by refraction' (1935: para. 253).

For Pareto, the most egregious example of the inadequacy of Marxist essentialism is the theory of value. He thinks that 'value' is a 'mystical, metaphysical entity', which 'may mean anything' and has 'come to mean nothing at all'. He is quick to point out, though, that Marx and his followers are not the only guilty parties here. Classical and neo-classical economists – including Leon Walrus, his friend and mentor – also felt the need to distinguish 'value' from 'price'. But, to Pareto, saying that 'price is a concrete manifestation of value' is about as informative as saying that 'a cat is a concrete manifestation of "felinity"', whatever that might be. The concept of 'value' takes us into the nebulous realms of metaphysical abstraction, where empirical verification is rendered impossible (Pareto 1935: paras. 61n.1, 62, 62n.1). Even if value did exist as a distinct entity, it was completely arbitrary for Marx to say that it depended on human labour power alone. What about human tastes, limitations of supply, costs of production (apart from labour) (Pareto 1972: 177–9)? Of course, Marx could protest that Pareto's criticism is simply reflecting appearances – merely *describing* the external phenomena of life as they seem and appear, whereas his own theory of value identifies the hidden internal structure of capitalism, which is the extraction of surplus value. Pareto's rejoinder would be to ask how Marx arrived at this hidden structure. A proposition may be considered true either because it conforms to experimental reality, as confirmed by sense perception, or because it is in logical accord with some chosen standard situated outside objective experience – with divine revelation, or with concepts the human mind finds in itself (Pareto 1935: para. 16). Since Marx obviously ruled out divine guidance, we are left with introspection as the path to scientific truth. Having started from the premise that science was an observational form of human inquiry, Marx ended up with some quasi-Platonic notion of innate ideas allowing us to distinguish what is 'real' from what is only 'apparent'. In Pareto's scheme, there are no innate ideas, but there are innate human sentiments, or basic attitudes (Pareto calls them 'residues') which exert a powerful influence on the way we think and act. Human beings, he observes, are emotional rather than rational creatures, though the range and intensity of emotional responses may vary from one social context to another. Given its logico-experimental shortcomings, Marx's theory of surplus value must be construed as a reflection of underlying sentiments, including a desire to identify with the oppressed masses. It tells us something about the genesis of ideas and the evolution of social psychology; it tells us nothing objective about economics (Pareto 1972: 328–9). Nor, in Pareto's opinion, would refuting it actually refute Marx's socialist outlook, which like all ideologies is rooted in sentiment. No amount of factual analysis can refute articles of faith (Pareto 1935: para. 2316n.10). Because of its intense moralism and its refusal to dissociate faith from experience or reason, Pareto saw Marxism as a secular religion. Its essentialism originated in the religious impulse, which, in all its forms, aims to constrain human behaviour within a coherent framework of 'ought' demands.

Moralism

Pareto considers the desire to improve mankind as the enemy of social science. He scorns 'the mania for preaching to people as to what they ought to do . . . instead of finding out what they actually do' (1935: para. 277). Even those, like Comte and Marx, who purport to study society objectively, find it hard to resist the temptation to leave 'the scientific laboratory' and 'step over into the pulpit' (Pareto 1935: para. 253). Pareto is adamant that science deals only with propositions that are susceptible to experimental/ observational proof, and that this would exclude 'ought' propositions. In true positivist fashion, he insists on a dichotomy between facts and values, denying that an 'ought' proposition can be derived from a factual statement (Pareto 1972: 19–21). He recognizes that social scientists, like all human beings, will have preferences and prejudices. From the remotest times to the present day, commentators on society have wanted to believe that their value judgements have somehow been confirmed by experience. But this is simply mental laziness masquerading as objective analysis. Social scientists must put their personal values to one side, or at least make every effort to do so, and stop pretending that scientific analysis can issue or validate 'ought' propositions, 'as if it were a God' (Pareto 1972: 25).

Prima facie, Marx would seem to agree with Pareto's rigid separation of fact and value. When he informs us that historical laws are working 'with iron necessity towards inevitable results', he is, according to his own self-image, no more advocating those results than an astronomer is advocating the eclipses he predicts. At all times, Marx was insistent that his theory was explaining, not prescribing, and he dismissed other forms of socialism as Utopian moralizing. Yet his claims of scientific impartiality cannot be taken at face value. Even commentators who are sympathetic to Marx concede that his work 'seems to incorporate moral judgements throughout' (Walker 2001: 146; see, also, Geras 1983). The very language he uses, as Walker indicates, is often incompatible with a value-free approach. It is routinely observed that Marx equated the extraction of surplus value with 'theft' – but those looking for moralistic language need look no further than the word 'exploitation', which is value-laden and inherently negative in its connotations. If Marx had distinguished his moral judgements from his account of capitalism, then the Paretian standard of objectivity would have been preserved. It is by no means clear, however, that he made – let alone succeeded in – any such effort.

Pareto thinks that his interpretation of Marxism as a kind of religion can explain this baffling inconsistency in Marx's theoretical perspective. Religions uniformly embody the belief that all things good are, almost by definition, verified by experience and logic. Fact and value never contradict each other. Everything must fit into the narrative of struggle between 'light' and 'darkness'. Thus, in the Marxist religion, the labour theory of value, despite being empirically 'absurd', must be deemed scientifically true, because otherwise the capitalists would be justified in their extraction of profit (Pareto 1935: para. 2316n.10; *Les Systèmes Socialistes*, in Pareto 1966: 128). Such a discordant note would destroy the harmony of the theoretical framework.

The religion that Pareto perceives as closest to Marxism is Christianity. Both were, at least in their original forms, religions of the poor, which scorned material goods. Both exalt humanitarianism and altruism, and give objective form to the 'subjective sentiment of asceticism' (Pareto 1935: paras. 1799n. 1, 1859). And both had (and have) no chance of translating their ascetic, egalitarian vision into reality. Detachment from reality, according to Pareto, is a characteristic of all religions, as is deference to the authority of the 'Founder(s)'. Marxists, he points out, 'swear by the Word of Marx or Engels as a treasure-store of all human knowledge', in the same way that Christians defer to the Gospel (1935: para. 585). And much like the early Christians, there are Marxists who are willing to sacrifice their entire lives to become apostles of the new religion. To Pareto, this intense moralism, this desire to hold oneself and others to ideal standards of behaviour, is distinctly odd, given that Marxism, in its scientific guise, insists on the relativity of morality.

Conclusion

For Pareto, the verdict we pronounce on Marxism will depend on whether we view it as a science or as a religion. With regard to the former, Marx could lay claim to some important scientific breakthroughs in the understanding of society: the role of class conflict and economic forces in history, the demystification of so-called objective morality. But the development of these insights, Pareto argued, was subverted by preconceptions and *a priori* ideas. However, if we look at Marxism as a religion, then its scientific shortcomings do not really matter:

> As regards determining the social value of Marxism, to know whether Marx's theory of "surplus value" is false or true is about as important as knowing whether and how baptism eradicates sin in trying to determine the social value of Christianity – and that is of no importance at all. (Pareto 1935: para. 1859)

The Marxist socialist doctrine of solidarity, for example, has no scientific validity whatsoever, but Pareto (writing in 1916) acknowledges that its ultimate influence on mankind may be positive. The social functions of religion are very different from those of science. Of course, if you disagree with Pareto's conception of the scientific method, you will probably disagree with his critique of Marxist science. To my mind, however, Pareto made a powerful case for the proposition that Marx was trying, with limited success, to unify two contrary human impulses: the one that drives us to extend our knowledge of the external world and the one that impels us to seek the existential comfort of metaphysical postulates.

References

Bhaskar, R. (1978), *A Realist Theory of Science*. Brighton: Harvester.
Geras, N. (1983), *Marx and Human Nature: Refutation of a Legend*. London: Verso.
Marx, K. (1976), *Capital*, volume 1. Harmondsworth: Penguin.

Pareto, V. (1935), *The Mind and Society*, trans. A. Bongiorno and A. Livingston (4 volumes). London: Jonathan Cape. First published in 1916 as *Trattato di Sociologia Generale*.

—(1966), *Sociological Writings*, trans. D. Mirfin and ed. S. E. Finer. Oxford: Basil Blackwell.

—(1972) [1909], *Manual of Political Economy*, trans. A. S. Schwier. London and Basingstoke: Macmillan.

Plekhanov, G. (1956) [1895], *The Development of the Monist View of History*. Moscow: Progress Publishers.

Walker, D. (2001), *Marx, Methodology and Science*. Aldershot: Ashgate.

CHAPTER THREE

Slavoj Žižek's theory of revolution: a critique

Alan Johnson

Introduction

> there is that kind [of voluntarism] which . . . celebrates itself in terms which are purely and simply a transposition of the language of the individual superman to an ensemble of "supermen" (celebration of active minorities as such, etc) . . . one has to struggle against the above-mentioned degenerations, the false heroisms and pseudo-aristocracies. (Gramsci 1971: 204)

In 2000, when I was an editor at the Marxist journal *Historical Materialism*, the Slovenian cultural theorist Slavoj Žižek unveiled his new theory of revolution. Trotsky, he claimed, 'went as far as proposing . . . the universal militarization of life . . . That is the good Trotsky for me' (2000a: 196). In fact, in 1919 Trotsky called for the temporary, emergency militarization of *labour*. Žižek's slip, I suspected, was a case of what Freud called 'parapraxis', that is the revealing irruption of an unconscious wish. He has not repressed much since: '[t]here are no "democratic (procedural) rules" one is *a priori* prohibited to violate' because 'revolutionary politics is not a matter of opinions but of the truth on behalf of which one often is compelled to disregard the "opinion of the majority" and to impose the revolutionary will against it'. Revolutionary duty lies in 'the assertion of the unconditional, "ruthless" revolutionary will, ready to "go to the end", effectively to seize power and undermine the existing totality' (2000b: 177).

Having apparently learnt nothing from the historical record of the use of 'iron will' and 'ruthlessness' in the pursuit of utopia – Žižek admits his leanings are 'almost Maoist' in this regard (2002c) – he has argued that revolutionaries must 'act without any legitimization, engaging oneself in a kind of Pascalean wager that the Act itself will create the conditions of its retroactive "democratic" legitimization' (2002a: 153). He has identified a clear and present danger to this project: '*a priori* norms ("human rights", "democracy"), respect for which would prevent us from "resignifying" terror, the ruthless exercise of power, the spirit of sacrifice'. He has even glimpsed where his theory was taking him: '[I]f this radical choice is decried by some bleeding-heart liberals as *Linksfaschismus*, so be it!' (in Butler, Laclau, Žižek 2000: 326). Welcome to the 'New Communism'.

He need not have worried, for there has been very little decrying. Indeed, as Adam Kirsch pointed out in *The New Republic*, 'the louder [Žižek] applauds violence and terror – especially the terror of Lenin, Stalin and Mao . . . the more indulgently he is received by the academic left which has elevated him into a celebrity and the center of a cult' (2008). This chapter does not seek to explain that scandal, only to make the case that it is one.[1] In Part 1, I explain the roots of Žižek's theory of revolution and delineate its character as a *Wild Blanquism*. In Part 2, I try to make plain why that theory is totalitarian, drawing on two left-wing anti-totalitarians, Claude Lefort and Hal Draper.

Slavoj Žižek's theory of revolution

Žižek's theory of revolution is a grandchild of the disastrous nineteenth-century marriage between the philosophy of Hegelianism and the politics of Blanquism.[2] That marriage was consummated in the twentieth century within the Marxist movement when Lenin substituted a dictatorial conception of the 'Dictatorship of the Proletariat' for Marx's (ill-named but nonetheless) democratic original. Once unmoored from self-emancipation and democracy, Leninist 'Marxism' became a kind of *Organized Blanquism*: a party-elite seizes power by force in order to remake society and man from above, according to an Ideology, wielding the power of the modern state.

Žižek, I claim, spiritualizes and subjectivizes this already-dubious inheritance, creating a *Wild Blanquism*. His 'Hegel', like that of so many other Marxists, as Alain Finkelkraut has noted, is 'no longer contemplative' or 'inspired by the glow of twilight', but burns with 'the light of the morning . . . unrestrained and militant' (Finkielkraut 2001: 71). His 'Lenin' is an ultra-violent Schmittian decisionist (see Robinson and Tormey 2003). More: his readings of the Maoist Alain Badiou's concept of 'Fidelity to the Event' and Jacques Lacan's psychoanalytic notion of the 'Act' render 'revolution' at once *expressive* (an ungrounded act of pure desire) and *salvific* (a form of redemption from a banal existence). (see also Žižek 2002d)

The nineteenth-century marriage of Hegelianism and Blanquism: arbitrary construction and the cult of force

The German social democrat Eduard Bernstein was one of the first to raise the alarm. A coming together of Hegelianism and Blanquism within the movement, he warned, would transform Marxism into 'socialism from above' – an *Organized* Blanquism.[3] The connecting wires – both constitutive of Žižek's own theory of revolution – were arbitrary construction and the cult of force.

Social democrats were being lured from the 'solid ground of empirically verifiable facts' into an ethereal world of 'derived concepts' and 'arbitrary construction' by an '*a priori* deduction dictated by the Hegelian logic of contradiction' until 'all moderation of judgement is lost from view' and 'inherently improbable deductions' are embraced regarding 'potential transformations' (1993: 31).[4]

Although he accepted the general idea that societies developed through the resolution of antagonisms, Bernstein worried that Hegelian Marxists could not resist 'speculative anticipation of the maturation of an economic and social development which had hardly shown its first shoots'. A speculative philosophy of development encouraged a reckless politics to close the gulf between 'actual and postulated maturation'. Hegel's dialectic, thought Bernstein, '[t]ime and again got in the way of a proper assessment of the significance of observed changes' (1993: 34). In short, a properly strategic view of politics became impossible once reality was forced into a preconceived schema.

Bernstein warned that this 'almost incredible neglect of the most palpable facts' *had to be* partnered by 'a truly miraculous belief in the creative power of force' (1993: 35).[5] The chasm between the recalcitrant contingency of the world and the abstract idea of necessity could only be closed by a cult of force.[6]

Bernstein grasped that this was the great danger lying in wait for Marxism. He warned that commentary on Blanquism tended to stop at its externals (the absurdity of the secret societies, the tragi-comic putsches and so on). In fact, these were only the time-bound surface expressions of an underlying political *theory* concerning 'the immeasurably creative power of revolutionary political force and its manifestation, revolutionary expropriation' (1993: 38). A terrible destructive ardour was the fruit of the marriage between the Hegelian faith in 'absolute necessity' and the Blanquist faith in the transformational power of revolutionary violence. This marriage was 'the treacherous element' with Marxism fated to bend post-Marx Marxism into dictatorial shapes (1993: 46).

Ian Parker points out that Žižek's Hegel is actually the one who reappeared in France in the 1930s as 'a bit of an ultra-leftist' in the lectures of (the Stalinist agent) Alexandre Kojève (2004: 39). This Hegel is a 'figure of perpetual negativity' who supplies Žižek with a cluster of notions that decisively shape his own theory of revolution: that the revolution can retroactively constitute the grounds on which one acts, that redemptive repetition is the proper reaction to the failure of a revolution (this is the foundational idea of the so-called New Communism) and that 'abstract negativity' is the 'source and motor of revolutionary change' (see Parker 2004: 39–45). Taken together, these ideas license a view of revolution that is pretty close to the dictionary definition of *deus ex machina* – the god lowered by stage machinery to resolve the plot and extricate the protagonist from a difficult situation. Revolution, Žižek thinks, 'wipes the slate clean for the second act, the imposition of a new order' (quoted in Parker 2004: 43–5).

The Italian Marxist Sebastiano Timpanaro thought that when Marx decided the dialectic was a body of laws with an objective existence (and not merely a way of thinking), he created a difficulty for Marxists: how to 'establish the existence of these laws in reality through empirical means *without doing violence to reality in order to make it agree with pre-established laws*' (1975: 89, emphasis added). This was an existential danger to Marxism as a tradition of *emancipatory* thought for the simple reason that 'doing violence to reality' meant abandoning the values of freedom.

But Žižek treats this danger as an *opportunity*. His theory of revolution *is* the doing of violence to reality. It is also a brutal ethics of force because, as Milovan Djilas understood, for the Communist, '[i]n the forefront of facts marched the *a priori* truths; and the struggle for their realization stifled the ethical sense *and even became transformed into its own ethic, the highest ethic of all*' (1969: 72–3).

Žižek's *a priori* truth is not Hegel's, mind. Not pre-established laws but a ruthless and spiritualized will to power underpins his drive to do violence to reality. But it is *all the more* an arbitrary construction for that and *all the more* prone to turn to violence to close the gap between ideal and real. The 'achievement' of the mass murderer Mao was 'tremendous' to Žižek because Mao showed us that 'the victorious revolutionary subject is a voluntarist agent which acts against "spontaneous economic necessity", imposing its vision on reality through revolutionary terror' (2007b).

The twentieth-century consummation: Lenin's 'dictatorship of the proletariat'

We should stop the ridiculous game of opposing the Stalinist terror to the "authentic" Leninist legacy betrayed by Stalinism: "Leninism" is a thoroughly *Stalinist* notion. (Žižek 2002e: 193)

Žižek celebrates the moment when 'Lenin violently displaces Marx' because he believes that it is 'only through such a violent displacement that the "original" theory can be put to work' (2001b). Lenin consummated the marriage of Hegelianism and Blanquism when he substituted an anti-democratic concept of the 'dictatorship of the proletariat' for Marx's democratic original, thus 'Marxifying' arbitrary construction and the cult of force. Marxism was turned into an organized Blanquism, or, in Žižek's revealing phrase, Marx was 'put to work'.

The Marx scholar Hal Draper (1986, 1987) meticulously reconstructed the text and context of each and every use by Marx of the term 'dictatorship of the proletariat' to establish that the ill-starred term was invented by Marx as a way to re-educate Blanquists away from Blanquism. Marx was confronting the Blanquist notion of *revolution as elite putsch* with his own theory of *revolution as popular self-emancipation*. He did not have in mind a special dictatorial governmental *form* at all but was referring only to the class *content* of the state. Generally speaking, for Marx the 'rule of the proletariat' meant the working class leadership of an 'immense majority block', while the *governmental form* of that rule was the democratic republic: popular control over the sovereign body of the state, universal suffrage, representative democracy, a democratic constitution and truly mass involvement in political decision-making. Engels, in his 1895 critique of the Erfurt Programme, linked (social) form and (political) content thus: 'the working class can come to power only under the form of the democratic republic. This is even the specific form for the dictatorship of the proletariat' (cited in Draper 1986: 318).

Fatefully, Marx's democratic conception was soon replaced by a doppelganger within the Marxist movement. The 'dictatorship of the proletariat' came to mean specially dictatorial governmental forms and policies (1987: 44).[7] Plekhanov was the originator of this disastrous substitution, writing it into the programme of the Russian Social Democratic Labour Party in 1903 (1987: 39–41, 68–75). Lenin would later adopt Plekhanov's conception, not as an emergency measure but in principle, as a mark of revolutionary virtue. Sounding rather like Žižek, it must be said, Lenin argued that 'The scientific term "dictatorship" means nothing more nor less than authority untrammelled by any laws, absolutely unrestricted by any rules whatever, and based directly on force. The term "dictatorship" has no other meaning than this' (1987: 90). Draper points out that this formulation was 'a theoretical disaster, first class [with] nothing in common . . . with any conception of the workers state' held by Marx (1987: 91).

It is upon this Leninist-dictatorial formulation that Žižek grounds his theory of revolution (2000b: 176): 'Nothing should be accepted as inviolable . . . [not] the most sacred liberal and democratic fetishes. *This* is the space for repeating the Leninist gesture today' (2007a: 95).[8] He then spiritualizes Lenin's fateful substitution; in fact he renders it almost psychotic by foregrounding 'a double equation: divine violence = inhuman terror = dictatorship of the proletariat' (2008: 162). There is much Robespierrist talk; we could call it the Higher Thuggery: 'just and severe punishment of the enemies is the highest form of clemency', 'rigor and charity coincide in terror' and so on (2008: 159). He rescues the idea of egalitarian terror for 'today's different historical constellation' by citing Saint-Just ('That which produces the general good is always terrible'). He adds this menacing gloss: 'These words should not be interpreted as a warning against the temptation to violently impose the general good on a society but on the contrary, as a bitter truth to be fully endorsed' (2008: 160). Little wonder that Žižek can write of 'Stalinism's inner greatness' (2002e).

Wild Blanquism (1): revolution as Badiouian 'Event'

Sigmund Freud famously criticized '"Wild" Psycho-Analysis' in order to separate his creation from crude forms of analysis that had been picked up from books, short-circuited complexity and were practised by quacks (1910). Žižek's theory of revolution is 'wild' not just because his crude 'Leninism' short-circuits Marx's notion of working class self-emancipation, but also because he imports two theoretical resources, Badiou's concept of the Event and Lacan's concept of the Act, which (in Žižek's reading, at least) reduce the notion of revolution to an arbitrary, will-governed and expressive affair, ungrounded and astrategic, albeit personally salvific for its participants, even the dead ones.

Latterly, and especially in his 500-page warrant for totalitarianism, *In Defense of Lost Causes*, the decisive theoretical influence on Žižek has been the philosopher Alan Badiou. A member of the ultra-left group *L'Organization Politique*, Badiou resurrects 'the "eternal idea" of Communism' which Žižek reads as being composed of 'strict egalitarian justice, terror, voluntarism and "trust in the people"' (2008: 461). In Badiou's work, 'revolution' is less the descriptor of a substantive political overturn inaugurating a process of social transformation and more a plot point in what Terry Eagleton has astutely called a 'born-again narrative' (2003: 248). Casting politics in the apocalyptic mould, Badiou seeks a 'total emancipation' beyond both good and evil and serious political strategy. Substituting for both is unconstrained violence and pure will: 'extreme violence [is], therefore, the reciprocal correlative of extreme enthusiasm' (2007: 13).

The Badiouian concept of the Truth-Event – examples of which include the resurrection of Jesus Christ, the French Revolution and the Chinese Cultural Revolution – refers to the radically new irruption, alien to what is, which shifts history and thought onto new tracks. Žižek has adopted Badiou's conviction that the individual can only come alive, and is only constituted as a fully human subject, through their intense, faith-like commitment – Badiou's word is fidelity – to a particular Truth-Event (Eagleton 2009: 118).

Of course, what is being described here is *fanaticism* and it licenses within Žižek's thought what John Holbo has called Žižek's 'towering un-thoughtfulness' (2004: 440). After all, the enthusiastic Chinese Maoists in thrall to The Idea, who knocked the glasses off the head of an intellectual, mocked him, dragged him through a show-trial and then killed him, had fidelity to the 'Event' all right. Moreover, the concept of fidelity to the Event washes the blood from their hands and makes their stupid murders into ethical acts and a service to Truth.

Žižek finds in Badiou's concept a praiseworthy combination of 'voluntarism, an active attitude of taking risks, with a more fundamental fatalism: one acts, makes a leap and then one hopes that things will turn out all right'. Only it never has. Yet, 100 million Communist corpses later, Žižek still thinks that 'what we need today [is] the freedom fighter with an inhuman face' (2002a: 81–2).

McLaren points out that when Badiou's Maoist ontology is combined with a Žižek's 'Leninist' decisionism, revolution is reduced to an act of will (2002). Certainly, the Žižekian-Badiouian Truth-Event creates its own preconditions: 'a demand possesses, at a specific moment, a global detonating power . . . if we unconditionally insist on it, the system will explode' (2002b: 164). Žižek then tries to 'Leninize' (and 'Lacanize') his ultra-voluntarism:

> The Mensheviks relied on the all-embracing foundation of the positive logic of historical development; while the Bolsheviks (Lenin at least) were aware that "the big Other doesn't exist" – a political intervention proper does not occur within the co-ordinates of some underlying global matrix, since what it achieves is precisely the reshuffling of this very matrix. (1999)

Actually, political interventions *do* occur within an underlying global matrix, or what we might call 'circumstances not of our own choosing' or 'the conjuncture', as we choose. Žižek's wild theory of revolution rhetorically evades this brute and all-shaping fact in two ways. First, following Badiou, revolution is always thought under the political temporality of the 'future anterieur', or, as a brazen Žižek puts it, 'one acts now as if the future one wants to bring about is already here' (2008: 460). Second, revolution is spiritualized as personally *salvific* whatever the outcome. Win or lose, Žižek's revolution will force the individual to 'accept that his or her life is not just a stupid process of reproduction and pleasure-seeking but that it is in service of a Truth' (2002a: 69–70). Win or lose, participation redeems: only when we act with 'excessive intensity', risking all and being willing to die for this Truth are we truly alive, anything less being only an 'anemic spectacle of life dragging on as its own shadow' (2003).

Wild Blanquism (2): revolution as Lacanian-Antigonian 'Act'

Žižek's wild Blanquism is also heavily influenced by his reading of Lacan's psychoanalytic concept of the 'Act'. There is a moment in Lacanian psycho-analytic clinical practice when the desperate analysand makes a ruthlessly honest self-assessment, gathering up all her courage and ignoring all her fears, even despite herself and beyond her conscious control, in order to make a therapeutic breakthrough. Parker argues that Žižek's mistake has been to turn the 'psychotic "passage à l'acte" . . . into something that is the model of proper political action' (Parker 2004: 80).

In consequence, Žižek's theory of revolution floats free of institutional, ethical or strategic constraints. Ernesto Laclau noted that even when ostensi-bly talking politics, Žižek's is 'not . . . a truly *political* reflection' but is rather 'a psychoanalytic discourse which draws its examples from the politico-ideological field' (in Butler et al. 2000: 289). Terry Eagleton has criticized Žižek for being 'startlingly causal, almost naive in the way he moves directly from the psychoanalytic to the political' (2003).[9] Parker points out that Žižek treats psychoanalytic change 'as the model of social transformation' when it plainly isn't, 'individual self-questioning in a clinic' being incom-mensurable with 'political strategies in public collective space' (2004: 63).

Lacan's concept of the Act is influenced by Sophocles *Antigone*, and there is a sense in which Žižek's theory of revolution is *Antigonian*. Antigone is deranged by the denial by the King, Creon, of a proper burial to her brother, and so sacrifices her life to secure that rite. Maybe she even longs for death ('And if I die for it, what happiness!'). Žižek takes this as an exemplar of a properly political act: driven and excessive, pursued to the end, ignoring the consequences. He dismisses critics of such violent excess and astrategic absolutism as people who 'effectively oppose the act *as such*' (2002a: 153). His belief that a genuine ethico-political 'Act' must not just risk death but embrace it is then projected onto politics in the form of the claim that a '1794' is an inevitable and necessary corollary of each and every '1789' (2008: 393; 486–7n10).

Stavrakakis (2007) has argued that Žižek's reading of *Antigone* distorts Lacan's original notion of the Act by valorizing pure desire and parading indifference to the consequences of Antigone's unhinged behaviour for the polity. He also claims that Žižek *misreads* Antigone who doesn't actually 'risk' anything, as any genuine notion of risk must involve a bare minimum of calculation and strategy. She does not so much act (or even Act) as 'act out' desire – and this is a particularly poor model for political action.

In the end, though, Žižek's Antigonianism is really a fraud. 'Antigonian rage' is only for the foot-soldiers of the revolution, not for Žižek. 'All suc-cessful socialist revolutions [have] followed the same model', he tells us. First, the revolutionaries exploit some local form of Antigonian 'rage capital' in order to climb to power. But second, the revolutionaries anticipate the moment when the rage capital will dissipate, so they 'build . . . up repressive apparatuses' to ensure that, whatever is the will of the people, it is 'too late to reverse things, for the revolutionaries are now firmly entrenched' (2009: 90).

Žižek 'Marxifies' this cynicism by talk of a 'Leninist' outburst followed by a 'Stalinist obscene underside'. In Sophoclean words, an Antigonian moment is manipulated to climb to power, and a Creonian moment is embraced to retain it, the revolutionary taking 'the heroic attitude of "Somebody has to do the dirty work, so let's do it!"' (2002a: 30).

Žižek's theory of revolution, then, is marked by a politics-shaped hole. Before the putsch we can only find the *Žižekian-apocalyptic* (the revolutionary elite is on the prowl for 'rage-capital' to exploit: a decisionist ultra-politics). After the putsch is only the *Žižekian-administrative* (the elite engages in repressive measures and deploys the power of organization: a non-democratic meta-politics). From the first moment to the last, the lonely hour of the *Žižekian-political* never comes.

Two sources for an anti-totalitarian critique

Two anti-totalitarian thinkers, Claude Lefort and Hal Draper, offer resources for a radical democratic critique of Žižek's theory of revolution.

The 'anonymous intentionality' of the totalitarian regime of thought and language: the critique from Claude Lefort

Claude Lefort argues that the totalitarian *regime of thought and language* common to fascism and communism is the bearer of an *anonymous intentionality* that ensures not only the 'vast efficacy' of totalitarianism, but also its criminality, whatever the desires of the militants (1998: 2–3). Lefort identifies four bearers of this anonymous intentionality and Žižek's theory of revolution I claim, is in thrall to each. I believe he realized this during his debate with Laclau and Butler ('if this be linksfaschismus') but decided to exult in that fact (so be it!').

The dream of a society unified and transparent to itself

The first bearer of anonymous intentionality lodged within the totalitarian regime of thought is the dream of a society unified and transparent to itself. Lefort warns that '[w]ith the demand for . . . a concrete community freed from the reign of abstraction, is attached the endless elimination of the enemy' (1998: 22). Despite his public image as a free spirit, largely based on his demeanour and his jokes, Žižek actually yearns for closure; he wants a world with a 'point'. The name of his desire is not freedom but 'final victories and ultimate demarcations' and he wants to secure them by a 'radical and violent simplification'. He dreams of the 'magical moment when the infinite pondering crystallizes itself into a simple "yes" or "no"' and he seeks a life lived in the service of a 'Truth' understood not as Istina (truth as adequacy to the facts) but as (Badiou's) Pravda – 'the absolute Truth also designating the ethically committed ideal Order of the Good' (2002a: 70, 80). Wanting 'definitive Solutions' he sneers at the 'merely pragmatic temporary solutions' the democratic way of life relies upon (2002a: 78).

Because the vision of a society wholly unified and transparent to itself is *impossible to realize*, a host of crimes and pathologies flow from the attempt to impose it, staining the hands of the best-intentioned (and Žižek is not exactly well-intentioned to begin with, as we have seen). Lefort describes the dynamic at work:

> the representation, which should be called phantasmal, of a society unified in all its parts, released from the opaqueness which derived from the division of interests and passions, mobilized by the task of self-realization and the aim of eliminating all those who conspire against the power of the people . . . does not this representation imply the position of someone who is detached from everyone, all-powerful, all-seeing, omniscient, thanks to whom the people calls itself One . . . the image of a man who considers obedience to legality as a simple prejudice, who is constantly proving his will of iron who presents himself as invested by Destiny, elucidates the character of the regime. (1998: 10)

The individual subject is submerged in 'Necessity' which is as expressed in 'The Idea'

The second bearer of anonymous intentionality in the totalitarian regime of thought is its submergence of the individual beneath 'The Idea'. Lefort argues that totalitarianism never offers a novel idea but rather *transforms an existing doctrine into a total ideology* through 'the intensification of the belief into a comprehensive intelligibility and predictability of the processes of history' forcing the internalization of necessity and the surrender of the individual subject (1998: 14).

The doctrine that Žižek has transformed into a total ideology is, as we have seen, a crude mish-mash of one-dimensional Leninism, spiritualist Maoism and psychoanalytic Stalinism. His recent writing is saturated with the idea that the only authentic life is one given up in self-sacrificial fidelity to the 'Event'. Inevitably, this has led Žižek to valorize and aestheticize martyrdom. For example, Robespierre's 'sublime greatness' lies in the fact that he was 'not afraid to die' and viewed his own death at the hands of the revolution as 'nothing'. Žižek has plainly come to find death more interesting, authentic and meaningful than (merely bourgeois) life. Again and again his gaze falls lovingly on death. Thus, Mao's insouciance in the face of the threat of nuclear war is lauded, as is Che Guevara's willingness to risk nuclear war during the Cuban Missile Crisis. 'There is definitely something terrifying about this attitude', Žižek admits, 'however, this terror is nothing less than the condition of freedom' (2008: 170).

The revolutionary's role is to adopt the 'proper attitude of a warrior towards death' as illustrated by, of all people, the Zen Priest Yamamoto Jocho. Žižek quotes Mr Jocho approvingly: 'Every day without fail [the warrior] should consider himself as dead ... This is not a matter of being careful. It is to consider oneself as dead beforehand'. Žižek even praises those Japanese soldiers who, during World War II, performed their own funerals before they left for war. It is tempting to laugh at this and assume Žižek is joking. Resist; he isn't. He tells us this 'pre-emptive self-exclusion from the domain of the living' is 'constitutive of a radical revolutionary position' (2008: 170). *Linksfaschismus* indeed.[10]

Lefort points out that totalitarian ideology establishes the *supreme* law which is exalted far above law-as-such, which shrinks to mere command, indistinguishable from terror (1998: 14). Because Žižek's revolution is a 'magic moment of enthusiastic unity of a collective will' then even mass murder can be justified when carried out in the name of that enthusiasm, in a spirit of fidelity to the Event. Mao's Red Guards, for example, may have killed half a million people during the Cultural Revolution, but for Žižek all is redeemed because ... it 'sustained revolutionary enthusiasm'; indeed, it was 'the last big installment in the life of this Idea' (2008: 207). Žižek invites his readers to 'heroically accept this "white intellectual's burden"', observing that Heidegger was great 'not in spite of, but because of his Nazi engagement' (2008: 107, 119) while Foucault's support for the Iranian Islamists is to be applauded because '[w]hat matters is not the miserable reality that followed the upheavals ... but the enthusiasm that the events in Iran stimulated in the external (Western) observer, confirming his hopes in the possibility of a new form of spiritualized political collective' (2008: 108).

'Organization' to control and regulate behaviour in every sphere of life

The third element of the totalitarian regime of thought that bears an anonymous intentionality is the use of organization to 'place the doctrine at the service of a plan for total domination' and to ensure the end of the distinction between the political and the non-political (1998: 14). The ideology is grounded in a 'single source, that of power materialized in the party' and that party presents its unity as 'untouchable'. Thus, in totalitarianism, 'the power of discourse and the discourse of power become indistinguishable' (1998: 3–4). The most shocking example of this *erasure of the gap between might and right* in Žižek's own writings is this ugly piece of braggadocio.

> To be clear and brutal to the end there is a lesson to be learned from Hermann Goering's reply, in the early 1940s, to a fanatical Nazi who asked him why he protected a well-known Jew from deportation: "In this city, I decide who is a Jew!". (2008: 136)

Žižek admits that he would love to *mimic* Goering and say 'In this city we decide what is left' in a future in which he can 'simply ignore liberal accusations of inconsistency' (2008: 136).

Lefort understood that unlike mass parties in democratic societies, the entire point of organization in totalitarian ideology is 'to control and regulate behaviour in all spheres of social life . . . all situations where human relations are formed outside institutional frameworks . . . to render everything organizable, everything [a] matter for party organization' (1998: 16). Erasing the distinction between the political and the non-political renders suspect *all* social ties forged by 'a spontaneous mode of socialization'. And as spontaneity can never be fully repressed, the active minority must stand perpetual guard over the 'maleficent adversary who is everywhere active [and] conspiratorial' (1998: 17).

On cue, Žižek yearns for a time when 'terms like "revisionist traitor" were not yet part of the Stalinist mantra, but expressed an authentic engaged insight' (2000b: 177), and he is nostalgic for the days when GDR workers would have their marriage raked over by co-workers because, after all, 'private problems themselves (from divorce to illness) are put into proper perspective by being discussed in one's working collective' (2001a: 133). As for Žižek's vision of the post-revolutionary society, it is captured in his conviction that 'Lenin was right: after the revolution, the anarchic disruptions of the disciplinary constraints of production should be replaced by an even stronger discipline' (2000b: 177).

Embracing the totalitarian politico-aesthetic of the 'substantialist idea'

The fourth bearer of anonymous intentionality within the totalitarian regime of thought is its aestheticized incorporation of all individuals in one social 'body': the 'substantialist ideal'. The price is the constant replication and representation of the state-unified people not only functionally but also in a host of state-run front organizations, as well as a bloody aesthetics: an endless drama of the healthy social body fighting off parasites in pursuit of purity.

Badiou wishes the revolutionary to view the world as 'an ancient world full of corruption and treachery. One has to constantly start again with purification' (2007: 14) and he looks forward to 'the advent or commencement of man: the new man . . . a real creation, something that has not come into existence because it arises out of the destruction of historical antagonisms' (2007: 14, 16). Man is to be drilled – Žižek himself is attracted by the aesthetic of 'the new man who gladly accepts his role as a bolt or screw in the gigantic coordinated industrial Machine' – and when out of step, forced to be free. Little wonder that Žižek flirts with talk of the individual being 'crushed, stamped on, mercilessly worked over, in order to produce a new man' (2002f).

Žižekian hatred for the Enemy, expressed in his thuggish Goering-talk for example, saturates his writings. In 'The Leninist Freedom' he reports gleefully on Lenin's response to the Menshevik defenders of democracy in 1920: 'Of course, gentlemen, you have the right to publish this critique – but, then, gentlemen, be so kind as to allow us to line you up against the wall and shoot you!' (2001b).[11] (Actually, Lenin said 'Do your job, gentlemen – we too will do our job', but Žižek captures his meaning well enough.)

The adoption of the tone of the commissar and the aestheticizing of murder are two signs that the anonymous intentionality of the totalitarian regime of thought is eating its way through a thinker. Since his break with Laclau in 2000, Žižek has often sung in this leather-booted register, abusing anti-totalitarians as 'conformist liberal scoundrels' who denounce 'every attempt to change things' (2001a: 4) and traducing anti-totalitarian thought as 'a worthless sophistic exercise, a pseudo-theorization of the lowest opportunist survivalist fears and instincts, a way of thinking that is . . . reactionary' (2008: 4).

No socialism without democracy:
the critique from Hal Draper

Žižek's call for a 'left alternative to democracy' has not given his many admirers pause, and nor has his praise for those philosophers, from Plato to Heidegger, who have been 'mistrustful of democracy, if not directly anti-democratic' (2008: 102). On the first page of *In Defense of Lost Causes* Žižek announced that there is no difference between three statements: 'the Church synod has decided', 'the Central Committee has passed a resolution' and 'the people have made clear its choice at the ballot box' (2008: 1). Praising Alain Badiou's view that 'Today, the enemy is . . . called Democracy' (in Žižek 2008: 183) Žižek argues that democracy is 'in its very notion a passivization of the popular Will' (2009c: 135), a form of 'corruption'

(2009c: 136), and – an echo of Plato, the original totalitarian – a political system that is unable to provide a 'place for Virtue'. He scorns liberal-democratic politics as a void and its partisans as 'the party of the non-Event' (2002a: 151) and cracks a tendentious joke hints at his alternative. 'You've had your anti-communist fun, and you are pardoned for it – time to get serious once again!' (2009: 157).

While democracy is wholly external to Slavoj Žižek's theory of revolution, Hal Draper established that it was wholly internal to Karl Marx's. Marx was a democratic extremist – 'the first socialist figure to come to an acceptance of the socialist idea through the battle for the consistent expression of democratic control from below'. Uniquely, he 'came through the bourgeois-democratic movement: through it to its farthest bounds, and then out by its farthest end. In this sense, he was the first to fuse the struggle for consistent political democracy with the struggle for a socialist transformation'. Seen through this optic, Marx's true revolution in thought was not Capital, but the idea that *only* on the social ground of *self-emancipation* could the *integration* of political democracy and the 'social question' be worked out:

> Marx's theory moved in the direction of defining consistent democracy in socialist terms and consistent socialism in democratic terms. The task of theory . . . is not to adjudicate a clash between the two considerations . . . but rather to grasp the social dynamics of the situation under which the apparent contradiction between the two is resolved. (1977: 283)

Draper argues that democracy is the sine qua non of self-emancipatory socialism. Not 'merely of sentimental or moral value . . . nor is it merely a preference', democracy is 'the only way in which the rule of the working class can exist in political actuality' (1962). While Marx thought in terms of the maturation of the working class through reform-fights ('We say to the workers: "You will have to go through fifteen, twenty, fifty years . . . to change yourselves and fit yourselves for the exercise of political power"'.),[12] Žižek offers sound bites: 'We are the ones we have been waiting for' (2009: 154). While Marx believed the *first* step was 'winning the battle of democracy' because the encroachment of a new social logic is impossible without untrammelled democracy; civil liberties, a culture of pluralism, with maximum space for initiative from below and for enforcing the accountability of the government representatives. Žižek prefers to 'resignify terror'.

The other lesson of the Stalinist experience ignored by Žižek and Badiou is that *without democracy, statification equals totalitarianism*. They both desire to give a fresh existence to the communist hypothesis but only in the form of a *redemptive repetition*. They seek new conditions for its existence, but *the hypothesis itself* is placed beyond criticism as the Eternal Event to which one must have fidelity.

Žižek's 'Wild Blanquism' functions to protect the project of a redemptive repetition of the communist hypothesis by shielding it from a confrontation with its historical nemesis: real people (who are never to be confused with Badiou's totalitarian category 'The People'). The true purpose of 'resignifying terror', mocking as 'liberal scoundrels' all who warn of the totalitarian temptation, rehabilitating the educational dictatorship and grounding politics in a Truth that must be imposed against the people in the name of 'The People', is precisely to wall-off the Communist hypothesis from that very 'independent movement of the immense majority' in which Marx placed every hope.

Conclusion: why we must keep saying totalitarianism

Today, the project of the Left desperately needs theoretical resources that help it to do two things: deepen and extend the democratic revolution begun in the eighteenth century while completing what the French anti-totalitarian writer Pierre Rosanvallon calls the 'reconceptualization of the political in the light of the totalitarian experience' (2006). Slavoj Žižek's theory of revolution sunders the political project of the left from both. It reprises as an academic farce in this century what was a genuine tragedy in the last, when, in the plangent words of Albert Camus, 'The great event of the twentieth century was the forsaking of the values of freedom by the revolutionary movements. Since that moment, a certain hope has disappeared from the world and a solitude has begun for each and every man' (quoted in Howe 1982: 132–3). Žižek may make us laugh. But he does not restore that hope, nor lift that solitude.

Notes

1 Žižek's diagnosis of the crisis of late modernity – whatever criticisms one may make of it – is not a scandal, of course. He is a penetrating critic of a range of maladies that have swept the globe since the Thatcher–Reagan revolution, and by treating those maladies as indicators of 'what is wrong in the very structure of the system' (2007a: 81) Žižek has held open the question of a global alternative to capitalism. And he can be brilliant in forcing us to adopt strange angles of vision on a vast array of familiar cultural objects, high and low, making us see them afresh as forms of meaning in the service of this 'system'-in-crisis. No, the scandal does not lie in his insistence that a global alternative be held *open*, but in how he proposes to *realize* it. In 2000 – somewhere in the middle of his debate with Ernesto Laclau and Judith Butler – he decided to give up on democracy, 'radical' or otherwise. That exchange began with

a declaration of their shared anti-totalitarianism and radical democracy but ended with Žižek embracing terror, dictatorship and *linksfaschismus* (Butler, Laclau and Žižek 2000).

2   The French conspirator and revolutionary Louis-Auguste Blanqui (1805–81) opposed universal suffrage and believed that the revolution would be made by a ruthless elite band organizing a putsch. After the seizure of power the Blanquist believed that '[t]he revolutionary band of idealistic dictators alone would exercise the transitional dictatorship' (Draper 1987: 13). In a meticulous account of the Marx-Blanqui relationship, Draper concluded that 'Marx did vigorously reject Blanquist (Jacobin-Communist) putschism . . . from his earliest known writings to his last, with unusual consistency' (1986: 145). Blanquism, thought Draper, has always been 'the "left" way to reject self-emancipation' (1986: 162).

3   'Marxism and the Hegelian dialectic', the second chapter of Bernstein's 1899 book *The Preconditions of Socialism*, was not translated by Edith C. Harvey in *Evolutionary Socialism* (1961), but was included in Henry Tudor's 1993 translation, which also restored the original title.

4   Bernstein thought Hegelianism a 'treacherous element in Marxist doctrine' (1993: 36). In Germany, after 1848, Marx and Engels, as a result of 'working on the basis of the radical Hegelian dialectic, arrived at a doctrine very similar to Blanquism' (1993: 37). By thinking the proletariat as the 'antithesis' they expected a proletarian revolution in Germany *in 1848* and '[t]his position led directly to Blanquism' (1993: 38). It has not only been the devil Bernstein who has raised this alarm. Sebastiano Timpanaro thought that 'the intrinsically idealist character of the dialectic was not clearly recognized by either [Marx or Engels]' and that 'Hegel has had certain negative effects on the thought of Marx and Engels which cannot be brushed aside' (1975: 89, 129n82).

5   In a very different language, Laclau and Mouffe repeat Bernstein: '"dialectics" exerts an effect of closure in those cases where more weight is attached to the necessary character of an a priori transition, than to the discontinuous moment of an open articulation' (1985: 95).

6   Sidney Hook argued that over the course of the twentieth century the Marxist ideal of revolution degenerated into 'the cult of revolution'. The cultist 'rejects the processes of democratic social change as hopelessly ineffective or deceptive or both' and gives up on the working class as hopelessly corrupted. Bizarrely, in societies that have welfare states and mass reformist social democratic parties and elected governments, the cultist fastens on notions of violence, revolutionary myth, 'emancipatory terror' and dictatorship (2002: 204–7). Hook might have been describing Žižek.

7   The idea that Marx's concept of 'the dictatorship of the proletariat' was systematically misunderstood by his followers can also be found in Hook (1934) and Laurat (1940).

8   Parker argues that Žižek is not really a Marxist, but only 'uses Marxism tactically against other political and theoretical systems' (2004: 96). Laclau has criticized Žižek's 'insufficiently deconstructed traditional Marxism' (in Butler et al., 2000: 204–6). See also Homer (2001).

9   See also Ebert (1999).

10 See Johnson (forthcoming).

11 Listening to the giggling of tenured faculty and their affluent students as Žižek jokes about the murder of the party of Julius Martov is enough to make one reconsider the virtues of terror.
12 Norman Geras makes the case for thinking of self-emancipation as 'central, not incidental, to historical materialism' (1986: 134).

References

Badiou, A. (2007), 'One divides itself into two' in S. Budgen, S. Kouvelakis and S. Žižek (eds), *Lenin Reloaded: Towards a Politics of Truth*. Durham, NC: Duke University Press, pp. 7–17.

Bernstein, E. (1993), *The Preconditions of Socialism*. Cambridge: Cambridge University Press.

Butler, J., Laclau, E. and Žižek, S. (2000), *Contingency, Hegemony and Universality: Contemporary Dialogues on the Left*. London: Verso.

Djilas, M. (1969), *The Unperfect Society: Beyond the New Class*. London: Unwin Books.

Draper, H. (1962), *Transcript of a talk to Centre for Study of Democratic Institutions*. Santa Barbara, CA, (unpublished, May 4).

— (1977), *Karl Marx's Theory of Revolution: Volume 1: State and Bureaucracy*. New York: Monthly Review Press.

— (1986), *Karl Marx's Theory of Revolution: Volume III: The 'Dictatorship of the Proletariat'*. New York: Monthly Review Press.

— (1987), *The 'Dictatorship of the Proletariat' from Marx to Lenin*. New York Monthly: Review Press.

Eagleton, T. (2003), *Figures of Dissent. Critical Essays on Fish, Spivak, Žižek and Others*. London: Verso.

— (2009), *Reason, Faith and Revolution*. New Haven, CT: Yale University Press.

Ebert, T. (1999), 'Globalization, internationalism, and the class politics of cynical reason', *Nature, Society and Thought*, 12, (4), 389–410.

Finkielkraut, A. (2001), *In the Name of Humanity: Reflections on the Twentieth Century*. Pimlico London.

Freud, S. (1910), '"Wild" psycho-analysis', *The Standard Edition of the Complete Psychological Works of Sigmund Freud*, 11, 219–27.

Geras, N. (1986), *Literature of Revolution. Essays on Marxism*. London: Verso.

Gramsci, A. (1971), *Selections from the Prison Notebooks*. London: Lawrence and Wishart.

Holbo, J. (2004), 'On Žižek and trilling', *Philosophy and Literature*, 28, 430–40.

Homer, S. (2001), '"It's the political economy stupid!" On Žižek's Marxism', *Radical Philosophy*, 108, 7–16.

Hook, S. (1934), 'On workers democracy', *Modern Monthly*, 8, (October), 532.

— (2002), 'The cult of revolution', R. B. Talisse and R. Tempio (eds), *Sidney Hook on Pragmatism, Democracy and Freedom*. New York: Prometheus Books, pp. 202–22.

Howe, I. (1982), *A Margin of Hope, An Intellectual Autobiography*. New York: Harcourt Brace Jovanovich.

Johnson A. (forthcoming), 'Communism without self-emancipation: a critique of
   Žižek's concept of "divine violence"', *Studies in Marxism*, 13, 2012.
Kirsch, A. (2008), 'The deadly jester', *The New Republic,* December 2. Available
   from: http://www.tnr.com/article/books/the-deadly-jester.
Laclau, E. and Mouffe, C. (1985), *Hegemony and Socialist Strategy: Towards a
   Radical Democratic Politics.* London: Verso.
Laurat, L. (1940), *Marxism and Democracy.* London: Left Book Club.
Lefort, C. (1998), 'The concept of totalitarianism', *Papers in Social Theory,*
   Warwick Social Theory Centre, Coventry. Available from *Democratiya,* 9,
   (Summer 2007): http://dissentmagazine.org/democratiya/article_pdfs/d9LeFort.
   pdf.
McLaren, P. (2002), 'Slavoj Žižek's naked politics: opting for the impossible, a
   secondary elaboration', *Journal of Advanced Composition Quarterly*, 21, (3),
   614–37.
Parker, I. (2004), *Slavoj Žižek: A Critical Introduction.* London: Pluto.
Robinson A. and Tormey, S. (2003), 'What is not to be done! Everything
   you wanted to know about Lenin, and (sadly), weren't afraid to ask
   Žižek', unpublished manuscript. Available from: http://web.archive.org/
   web/20061207054738/http://homepage.ntlworld.com/simon.tormey/
   articles/Žižeklenin.pdf.
Rosanvallon, P. (2006), *Democracy Past and Future.* New York: Columbia
   University Press.
Stavrakakis, Y. (2007), *The Lacanian Left.* Edinburgh: Edinburgh University Press.
Timpanaro, S. (1975), *On Materialism.* London: Verso.
Žižek, S. (1999), 'When the party commits suicide', *The Human Rights Project,*
   http://www.bard.edu/hrp/Žižekessay2.htm.
— (2000a), 'An interview with Slavoj Žižek', conducted by Matthew Beaumont
   and Martin Jenkins, *Historical Materialism*, 7, 181–97.
— (2000b), 'Postface: Georg Lukács as the philosopher of Leninism', in G. Lukács,
   A Defence of History and Class Consciousness: Tailism and the Dialectic.
   London: Verso.
— (2001a), *Did Somebody Say Totalitarianism? Five Interventions on the (Mis)use
   of a Notion.* London: Verso.
— (2001b), 'Can Lenin tell us about freedom today?', *The Symptom*, 1. Available
   from: http://www.lacan.com/freedomf.htm.
— (2002a), *Welcome to the Desert of the Real.* London: Verso.
— (2002b), 'A cyberspace Lenin: why not?', *International Socialism*, 95, 87–100.
— (2002c), *Interview with Doug Henwood,* http://bad.eserver.org/issues/2002/
   59/Žižek.html.
— (2002d), *The Fragile Absolute. Or, Why is the Christian Legacy Worth Fighting
   For?.* London: Verso.
— (2002e), *Revolution At The Gates: A Selection of Writings from February to
   October 1917.* New York: Verso.
— (2002f), 'Welcome to the desert of the real', *The Symptom*, 2. Available from:
   http://www.lacan.com/desertsym.htm.
—(2003), 'Homo Sacer as the object of the discourse of the university', *Lacan.com,*
   http://www.lacan.com/hsacer.htm.
— (2005), 'Revenge of global finance', *In These Times*, May 21, http://www.lacan.
   com/Žižekfinance.htm.

— (2007a), 'A Leninist gesture today: against the populist temptation', in S. Budgen, S. Kouvelakis and S. Žižek (eds), *Lenin Reloaded: Toward a Politics of Truth*. Durham, NC: Duke University Press.
— (2007b), 'Mao Zedong: the Marxist lord of misrule', Lacan.com, http://www.lacan.com/zizmaozedong.htm
— (2008), *In Defense of Lost Causes*. London: Verso.
— (2009), *First as Tragedy, Then as Farce*. London: Verso.

CHAPTER FOUR

How to not read Žižek

Paul Bowman

[N]ote how many texts in the present volume follow a similar argumentative strategy. First, they impute to me a ridiculously caricaturized position; then, when they are forced to admit that many passages in my work directly contradict the described position, they do not read this discrepancy as what, prima facie, *it is, a sign of the inadequacy of* their *reading, but as* my own *inconsistency.*

(ŽIŽEK 2007: 201)

My propositions are elucidatory in this way: he who understands me finally recognizes them as senseless, when he has climbed out through them, on them, over them. (He must, so to speak, throw away the ladder after he has climbed up on it.)

(WITTGENSTEIN 1922/2005: 189)

Reading the romance

Slavoj Žižek's work is theoretically dense, deft, racy, fast-paced. At the same time, he is a theorist who seems to court controversy with his writings, who seems to try to provoke, by making outrageous declarations about all manner of subjects, no matter how delicate. Nothing is off-limits, it appears, to Žižek's analytical, diagnostic, polemical gaze. He seems to delight in breaking academic taboos. Surely this is at least part of the reason why he is so widely read (see also Belsey 2003; Bowman 2006). However, to fearlessly speak out, to heroically break taboos (academic taboos, though: so, mock-heroically) and to unashamedly make diagnoses, judgements and denunciations without worrying about offending sensibilities is one matter. The ethics and politics that one actually puts forward is quite another. It is with this problematic issue that this chapter will primarily be concerned.

More and more commentators have noted the problematic character of Žižek's 'targets' – the objects of his critique and even scorn and ridicule (see for instance Bowman 2006 and the contributors to Bowman and Stamp 2007, especially Leigh Claire La Berge and Jeremy Gilbert). Others focus on the problematic character of Žižek's politics and ethics, and especially his specific political proposals (or lack thereof). Alan Johnson's new reading of Žižek, included in this present volume, is an example of one such extremely important response to the problem of Žižek. For what Johnson demonstrates in 'Žižek's theory of revolution: a critique', is not only that the nuts and bolts of Žižek's political theory are highly problematic in many respects. (People have been saying this for some time.) It is also that it is in a sense a scandal that anyone who places themselves on any kind of progressive political left could continue to read Žižek as if Žižek's work could be placed on any kind of progressive political left.

Johnson concerns himself with a demonstration of the key features of Žižek's political pronouncements over the last decade and more, in order to reveal the bare bones of the political theory that Žižek expounds. Žižek's politics are scandalous, he argues:

> the scandal does not lie in his insistence that a global alternative be held *open*, but in how he proposes to *realize* it. In 2000 – somewhere in the middle of his debate with Ernesto Laclau and Judith Butler – he decided to give up on democracy, 'radical' or otherwise. That exchange began with a declaration of their shared antitotalitarianism and radical democracy but ended with Žižek embracing terror, dictatorship and *linksfaschismus*. (Johnson 2012: 64n1)

'This essay does not seek to explain that scandal', writes Johnson at the start of his essay, 'only to make the case that it is one'. To my mind it is clear that he does so in order to demand from us an engagement with the even more scandalous fact that people seem to be reading Žižek in such a manner as to not notice his unpalatable politics. It is clearly a concern with this situation that animates Johnson's project. For, in this case, as in all others, the issue is surely not simply that someone's politics may or may not be scandalous. The serious issue relates rather to what is done with it, and by whom. In other words, the impetus behind Johnson's excavation of Žižek's political thought must involve an intention to precipitate a wider engagement with – a facing up to – the problematic fact that scholars, researchers and academics generally are continuing to read Žižek in often affiliative manners in light of the elaboration that Žižek himself has given of his own political theory over the last decade. Ultimately, that is, the problem animating Johnson's work – which he elucidates by quoting from Adam Kirsch – is that 'the louder [Žižek] applauds violence and terror – especially the terror of Lenin, Stalin and Mao . . . the more indulgently he is received by the academic left which has elevated him into a celebrity and the center of a cult'. What I would like to do in response to Johnson's illuminating reading of the letter of Žižek's political theory of revolution is to try to make some headway in an engagement with the ongoing modes of reading (or not-reading: consuming, enjoying) Žižek by an academic community that tends to conceptualize itself as more or less left and more or less radically or progressively democratic.

Blindness and insight

One possible interpretation, one way to make sense of this reading formation or this general discursive context and its uncritically hospitable reception, would be to suggest that Žižek's readers have simply not noticed precisely *how* scandalous Žižek is, or that they have not identified and isolated exactly *why* Žižek is scandalous, and have not 'therefore' come ineluctably to the conclusion that perhaps Žižek should no longer be read in a straightforwardly supportive way. Of course, this would be a slightly barbed interpretation – because it would imply that Žižek's primary readers are not really *reading* Žižek thoroughly, or are not being attentive or paying attention to the implications of what Žižek is actually saying, either in his many digressions, asides and virtuoso vignettes, or in the general reiterated and consistent points that he regularly makes and returns to again and again.

Now, to be clear, I do not want to suggest that Žižek's most hospitable readers are simply uncritical fans. For, even though it is inevitable that some surely will be, I know many 'Žižekian' scholars to be extremely sharp, perceptive, insightful and analytical readers. Nevertheless, I still want to propose that, given the style of his writing – particularly the way it jumps around from one topic and one theorist to another topic and another theorist and then another theorist on another topic and so on, in an apparently chaotic manner – that given this, there is always going to be a degree of difficulty in stating with absolute certainty exactly what Žižek is actually saying; and perhaps not because of any '*prima facie*' lack or failure on the reader's part, nor because of the effects of that old chestnut called 'textual excess' and the play of the signifier, but perhaps because the consistency and coherence that Žižek adheres to is an effect of his investment in his own reading of the Lacanian 'Real', one of the effects of which will be the effect of consistent inconsistency.

I will return to this suggestion later. But for now, I'd merely want to suggest that an inevitable effect of the range and apparently ramshackle nature of Žižek's texts will be conducive to the establishment of some disagreement between readers – especially, perhaps, because Žižek combines his readings of a wide range of theorists, philosophers and psychoanalysts in such a way as to suggest that they are each confirming what the others are saying. As Michael Walsh puts it:

> In other words, there's no arguing with a thoroughgoing Hegelian; this is a position that always-already anticipates (or sometimes just 'implies') any-thing of value that is subsequently voiced. So it is with characteristic relish that Žižek comments after quoting some paragraphs of Hegel: 'Every-thing is in this marvellous text: from the Foucauldian motif of disciplinary micro-practice as preceding any positive instruction to the Althusserian equation of the free subject with his subjection to the Law' .... Žižek's enthusiasm is infectious, so that one feels almost churlish in saying that 'from the Foucauldian motif' to 'the Althusserian equation' can scarcely be described as 'everything', is in fact no great distance – Foucault was Althusser's student, and is cited by his former teacher in the first footnote to *Reading Capital*. This sense of a pre-ordained inevitability is reinforced by Žižek's other favourite formulations, the paradox . . ., the 'nothing but' ('Lacan's whole point is that the Real is *nothing but* this impossibility of inscription' . . .) and the rhetorical question – 'Is not the supreme case of a particular feature that sustains the impossible sexual relationship the curl-ing blonde hair in Hitchcock's *Vertigo*?' . . .; 'Do we not find the ultimate example of this impossible Thing . . . in the science-fiction theme of the . . . Id-Machine?' . . .; 'Is it not clear already in Kant that there is transcenden-tal self-consciousness?' (Walsh 2002: 391)

Žižek does and does not court consistency, in equal measure. In the face of the wide range of assertions within Žižek's work, and consequently the wide array of responses to his work, Žižek always has one or more lines of flight open to him in defending himself or claiming to have been misread. A clear case of this occurs in the pages of a book of essays I co-edited on Žižek's work, a book of essays which concluded with Žižek's response – a long afterword called 'With defenders like these, who needs attackers?' (Žižek 2007). In response to over a dozen essays offering various criti-cisms of his analyses, methods and conclusions, Žižek concedes very little, almost nothing, and not one of the many substantive criticisms made of his work in the book; claiming instead that all of the contributors have misread and misrepresented him, that they have been aggressive, abusive, 'smash and grab', unscholarly. Similarly, the ensuing reviews and discussions of the book online often restated Žižek's sentiments, albeit sometimes in considerably less measured terms: the contributors to our book were incompetent readers, they said, each of whom had read Žižek entirely wrong[1] . . . Consequently, it strikes me that if over a dozen academics from all over the world, each working independently and with no particular anti-Žižek axe to grind, could each spend protracted periods of time researching, analysing and assessing Žižek's work, and could each come up with critical interpretations which were then received as complete misreadings, then anyone can.

All texts are, after all, essentially open. But does that mean that finding one's way through reasons and arguments and analyses and evidence must be an interminable process of ongoing error – all blindness and no insight? Is disentangling Žižek impossible? Perhaps. Certainly, the range of poststructuralist or 'deconstructionist' paradigms all propose different versions of this. Of course, Žižek himself rejects such paradigms and persistently uses a mode of address that implies that truth and insight can be directly apprehended and clearly stated by the scholar. Our own choice of title for our book – *The Truth of Žižek* – was, in this context, ultimately a playful jibe at Žižek's own favourite rhetorical formulation: 'Is this not precisely the truth of [x, y, or z]?' – a rhetorical (non)question which more than implies that there is a 'truth' or, indeed, an 'essential truth' to this, that or the other, that can be known and stated. In the wake of our immersion in poststructuralism and the textual paradigm of deconstruction, as well as the discourse approaches of Foucault, not to mention Žižek's own early post-Marxist and poststructuralist allies and collaborators, Ernesto Laclau and Chantal Mouffe, this kind of Žižekian proposition about 'truth' inevitably struck us as both engaging and problematic. It was one of the reasons we decided to compile a book of critical appraisals and responses to Žižek in the first place. For, given the textual ontology of deconstruction and of Laclauian discourse theory, how could one claim access to or knowledge of truth? John Mowitt's contribution to our book, 'Trauma Envy' (Mowitt 2007), suggested that Žižek's claim to be able to access the truth – a truth that would trump all others – could be understood in terms of the status he accords to the Lacanian Real, a status that allows him to regard his particular paradigm as superior to all others currently available, insofar as the (post)poststructuralist discursive formation cannot countenance the possibility of context-free 'truth'.

In a sense, this possibility opens a way to confer upon Žižek's work a different kind of consistency or coherence. Nevertheless, whenever Žižek has been accorded a 'position' by interpreters, and particularly when this has been used as the basis for a critique of his work, this has always been something Žižek has been able to sidestep, by claiming that the position attributed to him is not in fact his (true) position and that that was not what he was actually saying. In other words, maybe, as with the Real, there is no consistent Žižekian position. This is a possibility that deserves to be taken seriously. Another possibility would be to consider that, given the sheer proliferation of his writings on equally proliferating subjects, one should not really expect to find any consistency at all: pure, regular, repetitive consistency in an author's works through time and space would surely constitute evidence of an inflexible, sedulous non-reading of any unique thing, text, issue, problem or debate. So perhaps the inconsistencies to be found could be taken as the great strength and virtue of Žižek's work. Perhaps Žižek is performing either the chaotic eruption of the Real or (more pragmatically) Foucault's argument that the historical and entrenched idea of the existence of a singular consistent coherent author is a social fiction (Foucault 1977). Perhaps 'Žižek the author' should be regarded as a Barthesian 'figure in the carpet' of the texts that bear his name. Perhaps the best way to read Žižek, then, would be always to forget, anew, each time, whatever it was he may have seemed to have said the last time you read him, and to dive in and enjoy your Žižek for reasons other than overarching consistency – perhaps purely for the range of examples, anecdotes and witty and suggestive deployments of theory and philosophy, rather than for anything consistent. Perhaps Žižek is all suggestion, all provocation, all critique with no consistency . . . Perhaps.

But still, there does seem to be consistency to Žižek's writings. The same sorts of arguments regularly recur. The same sentiments, the same connections, often even the same passages and paragraphs and pages moving from one publication to the next. And these consistencies can be enumerated, elaborated, interpreted. In light of this, I genuinely wonder how Žižek and his primary readership will respond to the challenging consistencies that Alan Johnson has revealed in the political theory Žižek has produced in the last decade. Will Johnson's interpretation be accorded the status of a persuasively *systematic reading*, or will it be consigned to the category of a *symptomatic misreading*? (Once one is inclined to start regarding *some* things as symptoms, it seems to become very hard to prevent that tendency turning into regarding *everything* as a symptom.)

The reading of Žižek

Johnson is at pains to demonstrate that what is most scandalous about Žižek is not merely his apparent delight in breaking putative academic taboos. Nor is it even that the main targets of Žižek's harshest judgements are invariably his own primary readership – those involved in cultural studies, film studies, cultural theory, continental philosophy, political theory (see Bowman 2006, Gilbert 2007 and Le Berge in Bowman and Stamp 2007). Rather, what makes Žižek so scandalous, in Johnson's reading, is the fact that his political theory is based first on a deeply problematic misreading of both the spirit and the letter of certain historical events and second that his political pronouncements are explicitly anti-democratic, authoritarian, totalitarian, crypto- and not so crypto-fascist. Johnson meticulously and persuasively elaborates his evidence for arguing this. As such, I do not need to retread the same ground. So, rather than reiterating or recapitulating Johnson, I would prefer to start from the same initial observation that he makes about Žižek's typical method, and from there to strike out on an equivalent but different tangent, into the matter that animates Johnson but that he leaves largely implicit: the problem of the reading of Žižek.

'Žižek's Theory of Revolution: A Critique' begins from a clarification of Žižek's most typical manner of proceeding: namely, the fact that Žižek so often starts from a misreading (or *partial* reading) and moves immediately into an amphibology, or, that is, a skewed argument, in order to arrive at conclusions that are, as such, faulty. So, typically: first Žižek misrepresents or caricatures something. He then runs with this chimera into a hyperbolical all-or-nothing argument in which straw men are set up to be struck down by the violent actions of zealous 'free radicals' – characters/caricatures that Žižek often represents as heroic (and violent) phallic heroes. This is a regular occurrence in his writings. Johnson begins from the example upon which Žižek bases his theory of revolutionary politics, but many equivalent examples on various topics could be provided. I will discuss one: one of the most frequent: Žižek's reading of his favourite object of scorn, 'cultural studies'.

Žižek almost invariably uses the term 'cultural studies' as a short-hand way of conjuring up everything academic that he holds in contempt. In Žižekian, 'cultural studies' is short-hand for the cutting edge of the entire field of social, cultural and political studies, the arts, humanities and social sciences. This is because Žižek believes cultural studies to be exemplary of the leading tendencies both of academia and (hence) of capitalist ideology. This is why he so often singles out cultural studies for particular scorn (Bowman 2006). However, the problem with Žižek's reading of cultural studies is that he persistently fails to engage with the object of his criticism on any level at all.

Some of the stakes and drama of this are played out most clearly in an essay by Jeremy Gilbert, again in *The Truth of Žižek*.[2] In his essay 'All the right questions, all the wrong answers' – a title which encapsulates the overarching consensus about Žižek that emerged within the pages of *The Truth of Žižek* – Gilbert takes issue with Žižek's frequent declarations and assertions about cultural studies. Gilbert takes Žižek to task on a factual level – pointing out various ways in which most, if not all, of the claims that Žižek makes about cultural studies are demonstrably false, caricatural, mendacious, ill-informed, smacking of all the biases associated with the most right-wing of conservative reactionaries (Gilbert 2007: 61–80), and, I would add, palpably imbued with the stench of a resentment and hostility that – should *any* of the things that Žižek claims about this 'cultural studies' object that he represents as weak, soft, feminized, deluded and impotent have *any* basis in fact whatsoever – would put Žižek firmly in the position of a kind of school bully, of the sort who singles out the most naïve and gentle boy for attack, precisely because he is the one least likely to fight back. (I am supplementing my paraphrase of Gilbert's argument with some of my own imagery here.)

It is worth looking at one aspect of the Gilbert-Žižek exchange, at some length, not least because it also connects Žižek's criticisms of cultural studies with his interest in totalitarianism (the object of Johnson's attention), as well as relating directly to the question of reading (Žižek's reading and reading Žižek). So, allow me to quote Gilbert at length:

> Let us take as one exemplary text, Žižek's *Did Somebody Say Totalitarianism?*. For a start, this book opens by promising to address the 'problem' of the fact that accusations of 'totalitarianism' have become unanswerable and automatically condemnatory charges in the context of a certain post-structuralist intellectual climate. It proceeds to do *nothing of the kind*, instead offering a more or less stream of consciousness set of reflections on certain uses of psychoanalytic theory to address a disparate and frequently disconnected set of intellectual issues. At no point does the book make *any attempt* to engage with the complex intellectual history which leads to the blanket condemnation of 'totalitarianism' – the disillusion with party communism after 1968, the rigorous scholarship of Lyotard and Lefort, the influence of anarchism on the 'new social movements', etc. In place of any such thing, we get remarks such as this one: 'If at a Cultural Studies colloquium in the 1970s, one was asked innocently "Is your line of argumentation not similar to that of Arendt?" this was a sure sign that one was in deep trouble' (Žižek 2001: 2).
>
> On the one hand, this is a remark intended to illustrate a general point about the changing fashionability of Arendt's work during recent decades, to be read quickly and passed over. On the other, it sets up Žižek's entire case that there is something 'wrong' with 'cultural studies' that can be registered in terms of its changing attitude to Arendt. As such, if Žižek's initial assertion about this change is not substantiable then it raises severe questions as to the whole premise of this argument – never mind the substance of the argument itself. So wait. Read the remark again. Pause and reflect. Only one of two responses is really possible here: either silent acquiescence from someone who assumes that the remark must be reasonable (because it is made in a book by a famous authority on cultural theory published by a renowned publisher of esteem and quality), or a protesting query from anyone who knows anything at all about Cultural Studies and its history. Locating myself in the latter category I have to ask: what the hell is Žižek talking about? How on earth would Žižek *know* what 'would have happened' (with enough certainty to know that anything would have been a *'sure sign'* of anything else) at a 'Cultural Studies colloquium in the 1970s'. There was only one place in the world where one might have attended a 'Cultural Studies colloquium in the 1970s': at the University of Birmingham – and to the best of anyone's

recollection (I have asked a number of people who were there), Slavoj Žižek never made it along to one.

Žižek may be right and he may be wrong about his substantive point. That isn't the immediate issue, although we will come back to it. The important point for now is that Žižek is making an authoritative comment on something – Cultural Studies colloquia in the 1970s – without offering the slightest reason for the reader to put aside their justifiable scepticism as to Žižek's authority so to comment. Let's be clear about the implicit assumption here: the reader is assumed (or hoped, at least) to know even less about the subject than Žižek, and to take his word for it. Such a reader is being misled for the sake of a polemical point on Žižek's part. (Gilbert 2007: 63–4)

Žižek responds to Gilbert at some length in his afterword to *The Truth of Žižek*, 'With defenders like these, who needs attackers?' (Žižek 2007). In response to Gilbert's key point about cultural studies 'as such', all Žižek says is this:

> Well, Birmingham definitely was not the only place 'in the world' – being born in 1949, I am old enough to have followed the scene around Europe from the early 70s, where, in the aftermath of the 1968 events, a Leftist critical analysis of cultural products was flourishing, especially in Germany and France, but also in Latin America. And, unfortunately, from that time, I remember clearly incidents where stating similarity to Arendt functioned as an act of ominous accusation.

With this, Žižek confirms the first half of Gilbert's reading ('On the one hand, this is a remark intended to illustrate a general point about the changing fashionability of Arendt's work during recent decades, to be read quickly and passed over'). But it does so as if Gilbert had not already said this, and at exactly the same time as it *misses everything else* that Gilbert goes on to say – *all* of the important points, all of the essential critique that Gilbert is making. Žižek's response to Gilbert's taking of him to task about his incessant polemicizing against cultural studies (*specifically*: cultural studies *specifically*, and not some vague intellectual 'scene'), takes the form of ignoring the essential point of the criticism that Gilbert is clearly, insistently, deliberately and unequivocally making.

The manner in which Žižek misses the point is very precise. Let us take note of its features. First, note that Gilbert is obviously not claiming that Birmingham was the 'only place in the world' in the 1970s. He is stating the institutional–historical fact that there was 'only one place in the world where one might have attended a "Cultural Studies colloquium in the 1970s"'. For cultural studies as a named institutional disciplinary entity – that is, cultural studies *as such* – the *thing* called 'cultural studies' was baptized in the 1960s at Birmingham University in the United Kingdom. It was not until the 1980s that it spread widely, through the institution of degree programmes, departments, centres, schools, conferences, associations, publishers' categories and so on; and it was not until the 1990s that a quick evocation of 'cultural studies' could be taken as shorthand for the general tendencies of the intellectual scenes of the arts and humanities – that is, not until *after* the institutional transformation of the arts and humanities precipitated in large part by the institutional proliferation of centres and sites of cultural studies.

In other words, the question is this: before cultural studies *as such*, was there cultural studies 'as such'? In a very general sense, one might say, yes, perhaps, sort of. But should one wish to answer this kind of question with any kind of precision or rigour, one would have to say, no, not really, not as such, and surely it could only look like there was 'cultural studies before cultural studies' from an un-self-reflexive post-cultural studies position. Alternatively put, before the paradigms, approaches, questions, orientations and discourses of cultural studies hegemonized the intellectual scene, had the paradigms, approaches, questions, orientations and discourses of cultural studies hegemonized the intellectual scene?

I have argued before – indeed, in the same book containing the Gilber–Žižek exchange – that this tendency in Žižek to quickly introduce something (whether a debate, issue, entity or complex problematic) by using sweeping statements and short-hand is both a strength and a weakness of his work (Bowman 2007). For, on the one hand, it allows him to conjure up, quickly and dramatically, any entrenched and ongoing debate. That is, rather than re-inventing the wheel, Žižek assumes that we know what he is talking about. But on the other hand, this wreaks all the conceptual and representational violence of any other reductive representation or account. So, on the one hand, this accounts for some of the appeal of Žižek's work; it quickly maps out historical polemics, disciplinary disagreements and ways to read philosophers and theorists against each other. But on the other hand, it often proceeds, as in the case Jeremy Gilbert points out here, according to an *entirely* problematic manner of *not* reading, *not* engaging, *not* reflecting and *not* seeking or digging to find out whether things are actually as Žižek says they are, in a quick synopsis.

In this case, then, Gilbert's specific point is that, in the 1970s, there really was a cultural studies scene, but that it is not what or where Žižek says it was. On the one hand, again, this merely reconfirms the fact that Žižek uses the term 'cultural studies' to refer to the general tendencies or discursive formations of left discourse in and around the arts and humanities disciplines – which takes us directly back to the point Gilbert concedes from the outset, that 'this is a remark intended to illustrate a general point . . . to be read quickly and passed over'. But, on the other hand, it still leaves entirely unaddressed Gilbert's *actual* challenge to Žižek – his questioning of his (persistent mis)reading and representation of 'cultural studies', specifically his *ad hominem* and *ad nauseum* insistence 'that there is something "wrong" with "cultural studies"'. In other words, if Žižek is *never* actually referring to 'actually-existing' cultural studies, then why does he *always* refer to cultural studies?[3]

Over and above the specific issue of Žižek's long-running misreading and compulsive defamation of cultural studies, my main reason for drawing attention to this matter again here is to add further fuel to the fire that Alan Johnson is surely lighting in his critique of Žižek's theory of revolution. For, as we see in these and other equivalent cases, Žižek has a tendency to take only a fraction of the salient information about an issue or entity, to miss the essential issue and to run with what amounts to a reduced or reductive stereotype into an all-or-nothing argument. In this, we may say, Žižek's manner of reading amounts to a formalizable or formulaic mode of misreading. And I would suggest that it happens on all scales: from the scale of the phrase to the scale of the book, at least. On the level of the phrase, we see this in Žižek's reduction of the essential thrust of Gilbert's sentence about cultural studies in the 1970s ('There was only one place in the world where one might have attended a 'Cultural Studies colloquium in the 1970s': at the University of Birmingham . . .' – This is not the entire sentence, but it is the essential thrust of it). Žižek reduces this to 'Birmingham definitely was not the only place "in the world"'. On a larger level, on the scale of a whole book, we see it in the following: Simon Critchley wrote a brief Preface to *The Truth of Žižek*, entitled 'Why Žižek must be defended'. With this title Critchley stakes out his own generous position vis-à-vis Žižek's efforts (which, as I mentioned above, takes its best expression in the proposition of Gilbert's title: namely, that Žižek asks all the right questions but comes up with all the wrong answers). However, no one else in the book purported to operate under Critchley's title. It was Critchley's own. Everyone else had different titles. Yet what Žižek picks up and runs with throughout his entire response to the book is the sentiment announced in Critchley's title. Hence Žižek's own title, 'With defenders like these, who needs attackers?' Hence also the problem residing here: no one except Critchley even suggested that they were bent on defending Žižek. Yet, Žižek proceeds as if this were everyone's brief. Hence, Žižek's contribution keeps returning to and playing with this presupposition, as if his critics were failing in their stated mission of defending him. For instance:

> Gilbert 'defends' me by way of raising against me two main reproaches: my books 'display a level of scholarship which would be considered pitiable in the work of an undergraduate student'; and, I am 'a writer whose main stock-in-trade is demonstrably ill-informed and frequently inaccurate diatribes against the legacies of the New Lefts'. (Žižek 2007: 216–17)

It may be needless to say by now that these reproaches were not actually Gilbert's defences of Žižek at all. There were some points on which Gilbert sought to defend Žižek. But these are quite different to the ones Žižek refers to here.

Laughing at Žižek

In following the structure that they so regularly do, Žižek's arguments could be said to be rather like jokes. Indeed, maybe this is another reason why people enjoy Žižek so much. For, rather than being as concerned as the likes of myself, Jeremy Gilbert or Alan Johnson with the characteristics that Žižek imputes to such matters as 'cultural studies', 'politics', 'revolution' and so on, presumably some readers may be more casual (disinterested?) and may simply enjoy or laugh along with Žižek's ridiculing of such huge social problems as naïve 'liberal tolerant multiculturalists', wishy-washy 'postmodernist deconstructionists', hapless 'cognitivists and positivists', the credulous 'new social movements', spoilt-brat consumerist feminists, narcissistic gays and blacks or indeed any of the bugbears Žižek so frequently singles out for scorn – bugbears, it deserves to be noted, that are typically the bugbears of choice of reactionary right wing and conservative thought, rather than those of any left other than the most tyrannical. So surely some people simply laugh. And surely Žižek's lampooning of things like minority groups and positions may inevitably come as a breath of fresh air, or release a certain pressure, built up inside leftist readers, caused by their always having to maintain a serious and sober respect for so many 'worthy' things so much of the time. . . Presumably also there will be some readers who hold some version of the platitude 'it's funny 'cos it's true'. While there will be others who believe that Žižek is simply telling it like it is.

Before we get to the question of taking Žižek seriously, perhaps we need to ask the question: if we're laughing along or nodding along with something, what does this signify or portend? In Freud's theory, 'getting' a joke is evidence of what Freud calls a 'far reaching psychic conformity'. In other words, if we laugh at the racist joke, it is because we are racist, or at least have been made to become so momentarily insofar as we become involved in the setting up and elaboration of the joke. For, in Freud's characterization of 'tendentious jokes' – namely, sexist, racist or otherwise hostile and aggressive jokes – the listener is recruited (interpellated) as a co-conspirator in the fantasy belittlement or victory over the object of the joke – an object that Freud argues is actually an object of desire, resentment, fear or preoccupation (Freud 1976).

In other words, any enjoyment of the 'tendentious' joke derives from a normally unspoken desire to 'get' something that we can't otherwise 'have'. Hence, blondes are rendered stupid and thereby beaten symbolically because they cannot be 'had' in reality, blacks are punished symbolically because they won't go away and so on. Any laughter that bursts out from us signals the release of our pent-up 'inhibitions' (to use Freud's word). These 'inhibitions' arise within us (if they are going to arise at all) as soon as someone leans closer to you and says 'Did you hear the one about the blonde who went to see the ventriloquist's show?', or suchlike. On hearing this, if the listener has indeed been successfully interpellated or recruited to the drama, certain 'inhibitions' and an accompanying sense of excitement, anticipation, nervousness and even appetite all arise – because we recognize that this is going to be a bit 'naughty', a little bit 'taboo' – and we become primed, like a coiled spring, to release all of this in a burst of laughter. As Adorno and Horkheimer famously put it: laugher always occurs when some fear passes. There are lots of reasons why fear arises in the build up of jokes: jokes are conspiratorial, disrespectful, naughty. We are fearful in the face of talk about blondes or blacks because we worry that we might be reprimanded or, more fundamentally, that our enjoyment of socially unacceptable desires and wishes may become the target of reprimand. So, the punch-line comes both as a release and a relief.

What, then, are we signing up to when we laugh along, or smile, or nod, with Žižek's 'insights' into the 'truth' of this or that aspect of, say, 'tolerant liberal multiculturalism', when this topic or group is rendered by Žižek as a symptom of some kind of evil ideology? Perhaps nothing. Perhaps puncturing the perceived prohibitions of 'political correctness' by pointing out that exponents of political correctness themselves are not free from the contaminations of their own prejudices (tolerance cannot tolerate intolerance, for instance); and perhaps pointing out the 'ideological' uses and dimensions of the ostensibly worthy world of 'political correctness' (its use in the macropolitical repression of 'true' otherness, for example; as when the norms of 'tolerant' societies are used to criminalize the norms and practices of 'intolerant' cultures and societies); perhaps enjoying this and other sorts of Žižekian 'ideology critique' will not necessarily make one into an *opponent* of political correctness as such. Surely, we can all laugh at ourselves from time to time, and this does not mean that we are somehow opposed to or hostile to ourselves or our own activities through and through. So perhaps enjoying Žižek's critique of the left, the liberal, the postmodern, the tolerant, the multicultural and the like does not mean that we are *opposed* to any of these things. But, is Žižek?

To echo Johnson, the short answer would seem to be yes. There does seem to be a plethora of evidence within Žižek's texts to demonstrate this – especially in the form of quips, jokes, anecdotes, diagnoses (as 'ideological') and so on; even if there is also evidence of Žižek occasionally dropping the smile and offering straight-faced reassurances to the effect of, 'obviously, folks, I am not against these others that I may seem to have spent so much time apparently attacking here' – in a manner reminiscent of the two white students in the Hollywood comedy *Soul Man* who have a habit of exchanging racist jokes in earshot of blacks before quickly turning to them and saying 'Hey! Joke! No offence! Right?'

The asymptotic sinthome of ideology

Alan Johnson follows one strand in Žižek's thinking: his theory of revolution, as it has developed since it was first explicitly announced over a decade ago. Johnson reads Žižek's statements about political revolution in such a way as to argue that what Žižek is championing is ethically and politically aligned with totalitarianism. What I am adding here is that, given this, the fact that a certain readership regards Žižek as 'one of us' suggests that Žižek's readers are, in effect, *not* reading Žižek. The fact that what Johnson represents as the scandal of Žižek's politics has not been received *as a scandal* by his primary readership is the problem that animates Johnson's work.

The existence or dominance of such a non-reading is scandalous to Johnson because Žižek remains so widely 'read' in academic and intellectual circles by people who are overwhelmingly avowedly democratic, left-leaning, liberal, progressive, tolerant and theoretically informed. For, Žižek is widely read by cultural critics, researchers, scholars and students of film, culture, society, race, gender, class, ethnicity, subjectivity and so on – by academics working within the traditions of leftist cultural, political and identity studies. Yet, Žižek makes no bones of his contempt for this leftist position – what he often denounces as a pathetic and contemptible 'resigned and cynical' liberal tolerant deconstructionist, multiculturalist stance. Indeed, Žižek often openly pours scorn on actually-existing struggles and movements of the democratic left, and particularly on the entire formation and orientation of cultural and political thinking and theory associated with it. So, just as Johnson elaborates the extent to which, for over a decade now, Žižek has openly embraced an anti-democratic position of hard authoritarian voluntarism, one could easily construct an even longer list of his denunciations of everything associated with progressive left theory and politics. And yet many associated with precisely such a left seem to love him. His lecture tours sell out. His books go like hot cakes – bought by the very people who one would expect to be repelled by his declarations and denunciations. Us. Why does this happen?

In forensic mode, Johnson deftly lays bare the key coordinates of Žižek's politics. Stripping away the many digressions, anecdotes, 'jokes', asides and scattershot diagnoses, declarations and denunciations that constitute the core of Žižek's texts (and which surely help fuel his popularity), Johnson reveals the structure of Žižek's politics: it is 'wild Blanquism', he argues, and it is totalitarian. It is, in other words, contrary to the overwhelming impetus and orientation of contemporary cultural, political, humanistic and social thinking in general and of cultural studies in particular.

I have already gestured to the peculiarity of the ongoing situation in which on the one hand you have the massive popularity of Žižek within cultural studies while on the other hand you have Žižek's manifest and enduring contempt for cultural studies (Bowman 2006). Another peculiar feature of this situation is that, alongside the fact that Žižek almost invariably singles out cultural studies for the strongest criticism in the opening pages and paragraphs of his books and articles (and that these books and articles are consumed by people working in and around cultural studies), there is a contrary movement in which Žižek frequently writes endorsements for the back of books claiming, time and again, that 'finally' we have a book which 'redeems cultural studies'. But the question remains one of why Žižek remains so frequently read in the disciplinary field he holds in such contempt.

Žižek *vis-à-vis* cultural studies is equivalent – perhaps even structurally identical – to the situation Johnson lays out regarding Žižek *vis-à-vis* political theory. His method is to start from a misreading, to move into a caricature, to construct an all-or-nothing binary and then to slay the chimerical straw bogeyman he has invented. And yet he remains read. My speculation is that this is because Žižek deals with all the 'big' subjects in a lively and fast-paced manner. Everything from the Holocaust to cybertechnology to politics to the most arcane aspects of theology and continental philosophy are engaged by Žižek, and often by way of contemporary popular cultural and often filmic examples. So, to a readership used to much more measured and meticulous scholarship, this is quite exhilarating. As such, Žižek's actual animosity to cultural studies or democratic politics either becomes secondary to the liveliness of his texts or becomes something that can be forgiven because he offers so much more besides.

In other words, the fundamental consistencies which subtend Žižek's work are either overlooked or forgiven because of the assortment of stimulating examples and vignettes he produces. But surely the fundamental orientation, or the overwhelming tendency of someone's discourse, *matters*. Surely, it makes a difference – that is, if anything about academic reading and writing makes any difference. Surely, at least, such forgiveness or forgetting, on the part of the generous reader, amounts to a species of misreading, non-reading, or under-reading. Holding such a view is what moves Johnson to elaborate Žižek's frequently reiterated contentions about political action: because surely it *matters* that this stuff is passing into academic and intellectual circulation without being clearly marked as what it is: problematically voluntarist, violent, anti-democratic and totalitarian.

In offering us this reading, I think that Johnson adds weight to a growing response to Žižek, of which I like to think *The Truth of Žižek* was an important early instalment. There are now numerous types of increasingly critical response to Žižek. Some of these include the following. First, that Žižek can be shown to be predominantly concerned with the ongoing 'multicultural' transformation of the sociopolitical world. As a white male academic, it seems to be primarily the deconstruction of this traditional seat of power that bothers him – hence his spleen against LGB, non-white, nontraditional intellectuals (see Leigh Claire la Berge's contribution). Another is that Žižek's political position is unable to distinguish or disentangle itself from one which may justify terrorism. Another, as we have seen, is that despite the fact that Žižek asks 'all the right questions', the problem is that he invariably comes up with 'all the wrong answers'. This is because, as Johnson similarly observes (as have others, including Critchley, Laclau and Chow), Žižek reads sociopolitical reality as if a 'body politic' simply exists, and as if psychoanalytic insights into (or dogmas about) subjectivity and behaviour can be directly mapped onto the macropolitical world. It is certainly the case that Žižek anthropomorphizes and Lacanianizes everything, including processes without a subject. But even though he does this, it is not the case that he interprets the world through a consistent psychoanalytic paradigm. Rather, Žižek uses inconsistent, mutually incoherent and incompatible terms and concepts, which do not map smoothly or consistently and produce clear and compelling insights in the way he tries to persuade us they do. Specifically, for instance, Žižek piles Lacan on top of Marx who he puts on top of Hegel, as if these all click together smoothly and with no remainder or contradictions in order to produce an analytical machine that produces truth-insights that the righteous cultural critic can point out in order to speak truth to power. Moreover, in seeing his task as speaking truth to power Žižek arguably identifies too closely with the power that is his object and perhaps seeks to occupy, become or possess, himself. Whether or not this is literally true, it certainly seems to be the case that, with his investments in the primacy of the Lacanian Real, Žižek stakes a claim to a register of truth that he believes trumps all others: the chaotic Real.

It certainly seems to be the consistencies in Žižek which cause so much difficulty. Readers who try to find consistencies in Žižek, whether by way of identifying the tendencies, reiterations and repetitions that populate Žižek's otherwise ramshackle works, or by attempting to follow the letter of Žižek's argumentative constructions and scenarios (see Valentine 2007, for an excellent example), either 'reveal' a Žižekian position that is so simple as to appear caricatural, or to tie themselves up in knots. I place my own work and Johnson's work in the former category. And I know that this leaves me – if not Johnson – wide open to the accusation of another type of misreading.

Žižek himself has long forwarded the idea that the very idea that there should be consistency is a kind of structuring fantasy, or Lacanian sinthome. So, given this, to accuse Žižek of inconsistency might be no real criticism. Conversely, perhaps identifying consistencies may amount to a real problem. It is certainly the case that readings which attempt to establish a consistent or coherent reading of Žižek encounter problems. But *not* attempting to do this – even if any attempt to read Žižek for coherence or consistency always ends up proving to be wide open to the accusation that it is not a complete, coherent or consistent reading, but rather something that can at best be asymptotic to a reading of Žižek – may be a much more serious issue.

Notes

1 Initial reactions on the blogosphere in 2007–8 suggested that people had not only read Žižek's Afterword *first*, but that their readings of the book had stopped there. At the time of writing this draft of this present paper (19th May 2011), I have again become embroiled, all over again, in a strangely familiar and entirely predictable (symptomatic?) argument with members of a facebook group called *Žižek Studies*, who argue that they are 'with Žižek' and against the rest of the contributors to *The Truth of Žižek* because not only do the contributors attack Žižek on a 'personal' level, but these contributors are also 'fetishists'. I have tried to point out the irony/self-contradiction of their replaying of the accusation they make, and also that therefore they must be against Žižek because in his Afterword Žižek himself rejects any and all 'characteriological' analysis. But to no avail, it seems.

2 I am making so much use of 'my own' book not in order to boost sales – the entire book is now online for free – but because it is something of a one-stop-shop to find a range of key criticisms of Žižek and to see Žižek's response to them.

3 I have answered this question at length on a few occasions (Bowman 2006, 2007, 2008). As does Jeremy Gilbert in the essay we are discussing here (Gilbert 2007).

References

Belsey, C. (2003), 'From cultural studies to cultural criticism', in P. Bowman (ed.), *Interrogating Cultural Studies*. London: Pluto, pp. 19–29.

Bowman, P. (2006), 'Cultural studies and Slavoj Žižek', in C. Burchall and G. Hall (eds), *New Cultural Studies: Adventures in Theory*. Edinburgh: Edinburgh University Press, pp. 162–77.

— (2007), 'The Tao of Žižek', in P. Bowman and R. Stamp (eds), *The Truth of Žižek*, London: Continuum, pp. 27–44.

— (2008), *Deconstructing Popular Culture*. London: Palgrave.

Bowman, P. and Stamp, R. (eds), (2007), *The Truth of Žižek*. London: Continuum.

Foucault, M. (1977), 'What is an author?', *Language-Counter-Memory, Practice: Selected Essays and Interviews*. Ithica, NY: Cornell University Press.

Freud, Sigmund (1976), *Jokes and their Relation to the Unconscious*. London: Penguin.

Gilbert, J. (2007), 'All the right questions, all the wrong answers', in P. Bowman and R. Stamp (eds), *The Truth of Žižek*, London: Continuum, pp. 61–80.

Johnson, A. (2012), 'Slavoj Žižek's Theory of Revolution: A Critique', in, M. T. Johnson (ed.) *The Legacy of Marxism*. New York: Continuum, pp. 50–69.

Mowitt, J. (2007), 'Trauma envy', in P. Bowman and Richard Stamp (eds), *The Truth of Žižek*. London: Continuum, pp. 117–42.

Valentine, J. (2007), 'Denial, anger and resentment', in P. Bowman and R. Stamp (eds), *The Truth of Žižek*. London: Continuum, pp. 179–98.

Walsh, M. (2002), 'Slavoj Žižek (1949–)', in J. Wolfreys (ed.), *The Edinburgh Encyclopaedia of Modern Criticism and Theory*. Edinburgh: Edinburgh University Press.

Wittgenstein, L. (1922/2005), *Tractatus Logico-Philosophicus*. Abindgon: Routledge and Kegan Paul.

Žižek, S. (2001), *Did Somebody Say Totalitarianism?: Five Interventions in the (Mis)Use of a Notion*. London: Verso.

— (2007), 'With defenders like these, who needs attackers?', in P. Bowman and R. Stamp (eds), *The Truth of Žižek*. London: Continuum, pp. 197–254.

CHAPTER FIVE

Marxism and development: a search for relevance

Ronaldo Munck

Introduction

As capitalism develops so does Marxism as a means to understand it and to create a new order. For Marx and Engels, put at its simplest, capitalist development was to be encouraged as it would create the conditions for a socialist or communist order. Then, after the first actual Marxist-led revolution occurred in Russia in 1917, Marxism–Leninism as it became known, began to act in the non-Western world as an ideology of development. From the ambiguity of Marx–Engels, we passed into a phase of unambiguous Marxist–Leninist endorsement of development as progress and modernization from the 1930s to the 1950s. In the 1960s and 1970s, Marxism took a new stance against the dominant theory of modernization with 'dependency theory' stressing the deleterious effects of capitalist development in what was then called the 'Third World' (the first being capitalist, the second communist). The flourishing of capitalist development in Southeast Asia and later China and India soon laid this particular Marxist approach to rest. Then, in the 1990s, we had the era of globalization as a new paradigm for development. Marxist responses were quite diverse: for some, this was simply 'globaloney' and capitalism was still capitalism, others became quite enthusiastic about the possibilities under this new order, while some imagined actually seeking 'another' globalization. I will focus first, however, on the revival of interest in imperialism as an optic on global development from a Marxist and a liberal perspective, which responded to the renewal of global tensions following the end of the Cold War. Finally, I examine the possibilities of Marxism finding a relevant and radical engagement with development today through a dialogue with postcolonialism and post-development approaches. Perhaps we can regain some of the dialectical subtlety of the founders of Marxism and develop guides to action rather than proclamatory critiques.

Marx and modernity

For Marx, development and capitalism were almost synonymous and this vision of development was set in the context of modernity. In the Communist Manifesto, we are told that 'everlasting uncertainty and agitation distinguish the bourgeois epoch from all earlier ones. All fixed, fast-frozen relations ... are swept away' (Marx and Engels 1967: 222). The insatiable drive of bourgeois development would tear up all obstacles in its way. Nature would be subjected to the human will, chemistry would transform agriculture and the railway/telegraph would transform communications. Markets would constantly expand, capitalist social relations would break down and supersede all pre-capitalist remnants and productivity would increase by leaps and bounds. The relentless pressure towards growth and progress would continue until a big global market emerged.

Marx and Engels were aware, of course, of colonialism, but even in that context capitalism was seen as the harbinger of development and modernity whatever its costs. Marx paid handsome tribute to the progressive role of British colonialism in India for example: 'England has to fulfill a double mission in India: one destructive, the other regenerating – the annihilation of old Asiatic society, and the laying of the material foundations of Western society in India' (Avineri 1969: 132). The railway system and modern production methods would drag the inert Indian village into the modern era. Marx recognized that the Indians would not reap the benefits of this modernization. That would only happen when the industrial proletariat supplanted the bourgeoisie in Britain or 'till the Hindus themselves shall have grown strong enough to throw off the English yoke altogether' (Avineri 1969: 137). The latter was seen as unlikely and hopes were pinned on the Western front.

There was no theory of imperialism even implicit in the work of Marx and Engels, except perhaps in relation to Ireland. When they wrote on the war between Mexico and the United States they did not hesitate to back the 'industrious Yankees' against the 'lazy Mexicans'. If capitalist imperialism spread capitalist relations of production and created an industrial proletariat, then this was positive from a socialist perspective. In Ireland there was some hesitation, perhaps due to closer familiarity – especially from Engels – and the direct impact of the Fenian question in British labour politics. Whereas previously there was a simple repetition of the phrase that the advanced countries simply showed the more backward ones what the future held, now Marx and Engels were able to proclaim that 'a country which enslaves another cannot itself be free'. Ireland problematizes the teleological or logocentric Marxist perspective on development (and the national question of course).

Towards the end of his intellectual trajectory, Marx did begin to question more broadly historical materialism as a theory of unilinear modernization. In 1881 Marx struggled to answer one of the Russian Marxists, Vera Zasulich, who questioned him on the nature of the Russian peasant commune. Was it a symptom of all that was archaic or was it a harbinger of a communist future? Marx replied that there were two options: state capitalism could penetrate and destroy the commune or it could become 'the fulcrum of social regeneration in Russia' (Shanin 1983: 124). In other words, the commune could act as springboard for a new mode of social organization, a position Lenin would soundly criticize as 'populist'. Marx, however, was clear and rejected any attempt 'to metamorphize my historical sketch of the genesis of capitalism in Western Europe into a historico-philosophic theory of the general path every people is fated to tread' (Shanin 1983: 59).

Marx left an ambiguous legacy in relation to development. He would probably have agreed with Geoffrey Kay's provocative statement that 'capital created underdevelopment not because it exploited the underdeveloped world, but because it did not exploit it enough' (Kay 1975: x). Put another way, if there is something worse than exploitation it is not being exploited at all. A mechanistic Marxist development theory certainly finds some support in the oeuvre of Marx and Engels. However, an engagement with development from an open or creative Marxist perspective would produce something quite different. It would focus on the contradictory nature of capitalist development, the diversity of political forms which could accompany capitalist development and the importance of social agency in making development, albeit under conditions not of our own making.

Leninism and development

Lenin began his intellectual engagement with the particularities of Russia with a detailed rebuttal of the 'populists' who saw the rural commune as a possible route to bypass the horrors of capitalist development. For Lenin, following Engels more than Marx's late writings, 'only the higher stage of capitalist development, large-scale machine industry creates the material conditions and social forces necessary for . . . victorious communist revolution' (cited in Bideleux 1985: 72–3). We see here a return to a quite unilinear and mechanical view of development. Lenin's conception of capitalist development centred around the process of social differentiation among the rural population. He tended to overestimate the degree of capitalist development and subsumed economic structures which Marx had seen as clearly pre-capitalist. The main point, though, is that Lenin focused on the internal process of capitalist development in Russia rather than its setting within the global economy at first.

Lenin is best known, however, for his theory of imperialism which lies at the heart of all subsequent theories of global capitalism as a centre-periphery system. While it was not intended to be a major or innovative investigation, it soon acquired iconic status. Lenin's political objective was to counter Kautsky's notion of 'ultra-imperialism' as a smooth and peaceful carve-up of the world by the colonial powers. Lenin, instead, showed the inevitable trend towards a world war implicit in the increased worldwide competition between the colonial powers. Lenin was not really concerned with the social or economic impact of imperialism in the colonial world. Ironically he moved towards the under-consumptionist arguments (the need for markets) which he had criticized in his earlier work. The Leninist model of imperialism could thus be seen as the precursor to the underdevelopment theories of the 1960s, with an emphasis on 'the tendency to stagnation and decay, which is characteristic of monopoly' (Lenin 1963: 745).

As the Soviet Union became consolidated so did the influence of the Third (Communist) International. With the proletarian revolution in the West becoming a non-starter by the mid-1920s, hopes were pinned on peasant revolts in the East. Imperialism was now portrayed as retrogressive economically and foreign investment as a drain on national resources. Development would henceforth become synonymous with national development and not the development of the forces of production under capitalist relations of production. Capital was acquiring a political colouring so that the same social relations of production were seen as healthy if under the control of the national bourgeoisie, but not when foreign capital was involved. This shift away from basic Marxist principles would in due course feed into the dependency and 'development of underdevelopment' perspectives.

By the 1950s, Soviet leaders had codified a new 'non-capitalist' development path which would supposedly characterize regions where they were influential. This perspective built on Lenin's notorious 1920 definition of communism as 'Soviet power plus electrification'. This economistic–productivist approach gained traction in the Third World as an alternative to Western development models. The Soviet development model took root in a number of countries, particularly in Africa, encouraged by a Soviet Union not keen to promote socialism abroad. In legitimizing many authoritarian Third World industrializing regimes, this hybrid developmentalist 'Marxism–Leninism' helped stabilize capitalist rule worldwide and allowed Western imperialism to rid itself of some of the failures of colonialism now deemed to be an impediment to capitalist expansion.

In retrospect, Lenin's and the Leninist engagement with development left a contradictory legacy. On the one hand, Lenin clearly recognized, for example, that 'the export of capital affects and greatly accelerated the development of capitalism in those countries to which it is exported' (Lenin 1963: 718). This is a view that would prove little comfort to Gunder Frank and the dependency tradition in Latin America. Yet, Lenin could also be seen as the forerunner of the neo-Marxist underdevelopment school in his emphasis on imperialism and monopoly capitalism as a fetter on development and a cause of stagnation. For Bill Warren, 'Lenin set in motion an ideological process that erased from Marxism any trace of the view that capitalism would be an instrument of social progress even in pre-capitalist societies' (Warren 1980: 48). Development would henceforth become synonymous with national development and the effect of engagement with the global economy would be under-development.

Dependent development

Mainstream development ideology from the 1950s onwards focused on what became known as modernization theory. In the shape of Walt Rostow's (1960) classic stages of economic growth, with the significant subtitle 'A Non-Communist Manifesto', it provided a dominant narrative on how development worked. These stages of economic growth – from traditional society, through a take-off phase and then a drive to maturity – were quite similar in some ways to the orthodox Marxist models of production, from antiquity, through feudalism, on to capitalism and then, of course, communism. The main driver of development, for Rostow, was the diffusion of Western values and investment which would create a society in its own image in the rest of the world. This was an evolutionary model of development, heavily marked by the Cold War context in which it emerged and one which would condone authoritarian methods to achieve modernity.

The Marxist, and more broadly radical, critique of modernization theory was comprehensive and persuasive. It was not hard to show that history was not unilinear and that paths to modernity were diverse. Nor could Britain's industrial revolution be elevated to universal model ignoring its pre-eminent hegemonic role, its empire and the slave trade. The US-centric vision of Walt Rostow was also quite transparent, with US consumer society presented as the apogee of civilization as we know it. Also the so-called traditional societies in Latin America and elsewhere could easily be shown to be part of a capitalist world system. And the diffusion model, based on the civilizing impact of General Motors and Readers Digest, was clearly at odds with reality. Finally, modernization brought most often not democracy but authoritarian or military regimes of various unsavoury types.

The dependency approach articulated a new Marxist perspective on development, building on some of Lenin's comments on dependent countries which were situations where there was political independence but economic dependence. Argentina's role pre-1914 as part of Britain's 'informal empire' would be an exemplar of this category. The dependency approach went further and eventually sought to create a new category of capitalism, dependent, or non-autocentric capitalism. Dependency was variously presented as a soft 'conditioning situation' or as a determinant of development in all its economic political, societal and cultural aspects. Non-dependent development would require de-linking from the global capitalist economy although how autarchy could create development was never really spelt out. Ultimately, at least in Latin America, the alternative model dependency theorists had in mind had a simple name: Cuba. This hard pressed and internally stressed society could not carry that weight.

Not all Marxists went along with the dependency approach and the emphasis on underdevelopment. Thus Bill Warren carried out a spirited attack on this approach seeking to revive Marx's original vision. For Warren capitalist imperialism had clearly fostered development in the Third World and the obstacles to development had to be located in its internal social structure and not in external constraints. His view was that socialists had been misled by romantic Third Worldist notions and nationalist myths around economic self-reliance and so on. At one level Warren is clearly correct that, for Marxism, capitalist expansion creates development. However, he ends up in a teleological position quite similar to Rostow's stages of economic growth as a universal pattern based on the West's history and a Panglossian belief that 'capitalism and democracy are . . . linked virtually as Siamese twins' (Warren 1980: 28). The bloody history of colonialism cannot really be so easily dismissed however.

While in the North the dependency versus orthodoxy confrontation was not really very productive, in the global South there was a continued engagement with the reality of dependent development. Nowhere more so than in Latin America, where Gunder Frank had not actually been such an important player in the Marxist debates around dependency and development. Much more important was the 1969 work by Brazilian sociologist F. H. Cardoso and Chilean historian Enzo Faletto 'Dependency and Development in Latin America'. To the structuralist perspective of the Economic Commission for Latin America on Latin America's role in the global economy they added a strong historical dimension. They did not propose a theory of dependent capitalism but, rather, sought to describe the various 'situations of dependency' which had emerged in the postcolonial era. It is a structural–historical methodology focused on capitalist development in the periphery and its interaction with social and political structures. Cardoso and Faletto, and many others across disciplines and countries in Latin America, did not conceive of dependency as something external. Indeed, as they argued, 'it is through socio-political structures sustained and moved by social classes and groups with opposed interests that capitalism . . . is realized in history' (Cardoso and Faletto 1979: xx). Their focus is on the internal struggles within Latin America and not on external dependency as the explanatory variable. Where this approach also departs from the common image of dependency was in the total acceptance that 'a real process of dependent development does exist in some Latin American countries' (Cardoso and Faletto 1979: xxiii). This development is of course uneven, both regionally and socially, and is accompanied by much exploitation and inequality, but it is undoubtedly real and it has changed the face of Latin America.

If these debates from the 1970s and 1980s have largely run their course we should note the more recent revival of interest in the Marxist theory of imperialism. This occurred in the context of an unabashed positive reappraisal of imperialism on the right in the context of US interventions in Iraq, Afghanistan and Libya. Arguably one of the most interesting and original approaches emerging is the historical–geographical materialist approach of David Harvey who distinguishes between the logic of territory and the logic of capital and shows that the two are not always coterminous. The spaceless universalization of endless capital accumulation has learnt to mask the territorial aspect under the guise of globalization. Most interesting – from a global South perspective – is Harvey's re-centralizing of 'accumulation through dispossession' in an overdue recognition of Rosa Luxemburg's insight that capitalism always required a non-capitalist periphery.

Marxism and imperialism

If in the year 2000 we had wanted to analyse the world around us in terms of the Marxist theory of imperialism we would have been swimming against the globalization current, a new paradigm that seemingly swept all before it. The last substantive review of Marxist theories of imperialism would have been that carried out by Anthony Brewer in 1980. Since 2000, on the other hand, there has been an explosion of interest in imperialism (in its historical and current forms) from both the left and the right of the political spectrum. On the one hand, a resurgent neoliberal capitalism gave many establishment intellectuals the confidence to articulate an open and unapologetic case for the 'new imperialism'. Thus senior British diplomat Robert Cooper could argue that 'what is needed is a new kind of imperialism, one compatible with human rights and cosmopolitan values' (Cooper 2002). Then, after the Third or 'majority' World made itself felt forcefully in the very heart of global corporate power in September 2001, Max Boot (2001) explicitly made 'The Case for an American Empire'. Bestselling historian Niall Ferguson followed his 2003 study of British imperialism in *Empire* with

Colossus: The Rise and Fall of the American Empire, both of which argue that, warts and all, imperialism was no bad thing. From the ranks of mainstream development economists Deepak Lal published his 2004 *In Praise of Empires, Globalization and Order* which threw his pro-liberal globalization arguments behind the new positive reconsideration of empire as strategy for domination.

From the other side of the political spectrum, Antonio Negri – a long-standing Italian autonomist activist and philosopher – teamed up with US cultural critic Michael Hardt to produce the publishing event known as Empire (2000). Within what they still consider to be a Marxist framework, they incorporated the insights of poststructuralism as method, and globalization as new frame of reference, to produce an end of millennium–millenarian text. Globalizing the Deleuze and Guattari (2003) poststructuralist view of the world they theorized a new form of power (bio-power) under a regime of imperial sovereignty characterized by a 'smooth space' very much in the idiom of Thomas Friedman's (2005) recent thesis that 'the world is flat'. Though clothed in progressive rhetoric (and probably intent) the Hardt/Negri rendering of Empire viewed the turn-of-the-century expansiveness of US power as a positive historical moment, to put it in Hegelian terms. Even as it was being launched, Empire became less plausible as a new (post) capitalist manifesto insofar as the 'easy' phase of globalization came to an end and the so-called war on terror was unleashed by the United States on the majority world after 2001.

Formal political empires are, of course, quite distinguishable analytically from broader economic or political forms of imperialism. Empire came back into fashion partly due to the success of Hardt and Negri's Empire, but since then it has been taken up by a number of progressive analysts. Ellen Meiksins Wood, who had previously railed against the failings of 'globaloney', took a somewhat different and rather more nuanced tack in *The Empire of Capital*. She contrasts the new capitalist imperialism to the historical forms of the Roman and Spanish empires. Interestingly, this contemporary form is traced back to Britain's domination over Ireland, from the late sixteenth century onwards. This was designed not just to impose English law on the rebellious Irish, but to transform their society to make it a useful adjunct to the 'industrial revolution'. The British Empire subsequently carried capitalism to many quarters of the world, but the need for direct political and military control of these lands was to be its ultimate undoing as anti-colonialism developed. Today, however, 'the objective of US imperialism is economic hegemony without colonial rule' (Wood 2005: xi). The United States depends on its economic and military supremacy and the empire it creates is not a vague post-territorial network, but a hegemonic order based on subordinating other states through brute force and/or economic vulnerability. In a striking phrase reflecting on current US military aggression, Wood writes: 'This war without end in purpose or time, belongs to an endless empire without boundaries, or even territories' (Wood 2005: 167–8).

The current US turn from multilateralism to militarism brings force back to the centre of global affairs, as Rosa Luxemburg's original theory of imperialism would have predicted. Postmodern globalization and a nebulous supra-territorial empire cannot account for the chaos, conflict and increasing contradictions within the world order. A study of the history of empire and imperialism might just help us understand these though and make Marxist accounts relevant for a new era of inter-imperialist competition.

While for Hardt and Negri in Empire the current world order of globalization marks a totally new phase in capitalist development, for more orthodox Marxists it is simply the latest phase of imperialism. Jan Nederveen Pietersee (2004) in Globalization or Empire? helps us move beyond such simple binary opposition. From the Leninist strain within Marxism there has always been a reductionist tendency to argue that imperialism is but the latest/highest stage of capitalism. So the early twentieth century gave us monopoly capitalism, and now the early twenty-first century is producing neoliberal globalized capitalism. However, empire has never been simply about economic gain, with this economic reductionism long since disproven. Furthermore, following Nederveen Pietersee, 'Equating capitalism = imperialism = globalization = neoliberal globalization creates a trans-historical soup in which nothing essentially changes over, say, two to five centuries. If nothing really changes, then why bother to analyze at all' (Pietersee 2004: 37). To argue that globalization should be called 'empire' as Hardt and Negri do is also not particularly helpful, especially when they define it in contrast to imperialism that, for them, died in the 1970s. That terms such as imperialism and empire will be used as metaphors – thus the popularization of the 'imperialism of human rights', the 'US Empire' – is understandable but not too helpful. We can and should analyse neoliberal globalization without invoking the term 'imperialism' and thus target it more precisely. Nor is the difference between imperialism and globalization simply that the first is directional and economic, while the latter is diffuse and multi-directional. I would argue that contemporary globalization represents a paradigm shift in the way accumulation on a world scale occurs. There are multiple globalizations and these processes are intrinsically decentred and deterritorial. Following Nederveen Pietersee, 'from taking a historical angle on globalization it follows that empire is a phase of globalization (as is decolonization)' (Pietersee 2004: 39). That US hegemony of this process is currently taking an imperialist turn is not, of course, in doubt.

Looking to the future contribution Marxism might make to our understanding of development in the era of globalization, I would take three main areas for consideration: 1) the Rosa Luxemburg position on the continued presence of non-capitalist modes of production; 2) the relevance of the theory of uneven and combined development associated with Lenin and Trotsky and 3) the unequal exchange perspective on world trade developed in the 1970s by Emmanuel and Bettelheim (see Emmanuel 1972 for both).

Marx 'consistently and deliberately assumes the universal and exclusive domination of the capitalist mode of production as a theoretical premise of his analysis' (Luxemburg 1971: 348), wrote Rosa Luxemburg in 1913 during the first wave of Marxist theorizing around imperialism. Although Marx saw colonialism and primitive accumulation as 'incidental' processes in this story, for Luxemburg, the reality was that 'capitalism in its full maturity also depends in all respects on non-capitalist strata and social organizations existing side by side with it'. If that was not clear enough, Luxemburg goes on to say that 'the accumulation of capital becomes impossible at all points without non-capitalist surroundings' (Luxemburg 1971: 365). Capitalism needs the means of production and labour power of the whole world and will seek to bring non-capitalist sectors under its control. To do so, it will use force and not just in the original or primitive accumulation when it emerges dripping in blood, according to Marx. Luxemburg ends with words that sound contemporary in the era of neoliberal globalization: 'Force, fraud, oppression and looting are openly displayed without any attempt at concealment, and it requires an effort to discover within this tangle of political violence and contests of power, the stern laws of the economic process' (Luxemburg 1971: 452).

What then would be the implications today of taking up Luxemburg's radical revision of Marx? David Harvey is quite clear that 'accumulation by dispossession' means quite simply 'the continuation and proliferation of accumulation practices which Marx has treated as 'primitive' or 'original' during the rise of capitalism' (Harvey 2005: 159). My own impression is that, from the perspective of 'metropolitan Marxism', the implications of such a revision have not yet been fully realized. If capitalism is not (or is no longer) seeking to transform the world in its image, this has huge implications for the politely dubbed 'developing world'. The other aspect neglected by Harvey is the vital gender dimension of current accumulation by dispossession. As Nancy Hartsock puts it in a friendly critique of Harvey, 'the contemporary moment of globalization should be retheorized as a moment of primitive accumulation, which is simultaneously a moment of the feminization of the labour force wherein workers are denigrated, made powerless, invisible and unreal' (Hartstock 2006: 178–9).

An overarching theoretical framework for an understanding of these processes within historical materialism was, historically, the 'uneven and combined development' theory or 'law'. Though Lenin had earlier referred to the 'unevenness' of capitalism in Russia, it was Trotsky who argued most coherently that the backward and advanced elements (or) nations are inextricably combined. With the rise of imperialism, it would become impossible for the backward countries to follow mechanically the path of those now advanced. Thus, Marx's famous dictum that 'The country that is more developed industrially only shows to the less developed, the image of its own future' was no longer seen as valid. The idea of uneven and combined development thus decisively breaks with any lingering evolutionism within Marxism and provides a possible insight into the shape of the world-historical process. In political terms, it breaks with the post-Lenin orthodoxy of 'stages' in the revolutionary process and further assists us in the analysis of revolutionary situations and ruptures.

In terms of current attempts to create a theory of globalization, might the uneven and combined development approach be of use? Does this approach represent a revision of Marx's understanding of the development of capitalism? We can certainly detect a return of interest in this topic (see van der Linden 2003). In its contemporary version, uneven and combined development has been shorn of its earlier law-like rendering and any illusion that it can act as a forecasting tool. What it might help us to do, however, is to better theorize the 'international' and the 'global' within Marxism. As an intellectual paradigm, it might allow us to discern the dynamics of the global order in a manner more cognizant of complexity than globalization, or counter-globalization, proponents allow for. The complex causality of combined capitalist development requires more sustained attention to the inter-societal dimension, bearing always in mind the 'combined' nature of global development which cannot be reduced to the unfolding of economic laws.

In spatial terms, unevenness has been associated with theories of 'unequal exchange' on the world market. The term was coined by Arghiri Emmanuel (1972) in his novel theorizing of trading relationships between 'core' and 'periphery' that sought to place the then current dependency approach on a firmer economic footing. Essentially the 'unequal exchange' theory represented a rebuttal of the Ricardian and neoclassical theories of comparative advantage and their assumptions that the market has egalitarian effects, rather than accentuating the market position of the strong. Emmanuel, in a deceptively simple move, applied Marx's transformation problem to international trade. Given the equalization of profit rates across national boundaries due to capital mobility and the non-equalization of wages due to labour's (relative) lack of mobility and their determination by historical factors, the developing countries with low wages suffer a disadvantage in trade as their imports include the higher wages of workers in the industrialized countries, as well as the equalized profit rates. Subsequently, Emmanuel was challenged by Charles Bettelheim (in Emmanuel 1972) and by other more orthodox Marxists (Brolin 2006) which led his insights to be more or less set aside.

Today we find a renewed interest in the theory of unequal exchange, again seeking to put on a firmer footing the radical critique of 'free trade' orthodoxy. Thus James Heintz argues persuasively that 'the unequal exchange tradition remains relevant today. Many of the characteristics of modern international production and trade networks reflect the conditions identified in the unequal exchange literature' (Heintz 2003: 7). The problem, of course, is that the original unequal exchange approach was developed when the international division of labour pitted an industrialized North against a primary goods exporting South. With the latter now a major exporter of manufactured goods, does the unequal exchange theory still hold true? There is some evidence of a negative trend in the commodity terms of trade for manufactured goods, but this is contested. I would argue that if we are interested in developing a contemporary theory of imperialism, we would need to go back to the element of 'unequal exchange' to examine where it fits in, and whether it can be used to demystify the fetishism of 'free trade' approaches.

Post-development

For a renewed Marxism to take advantage of the current openings for an oppositional politics, it does, really, need to come to terms with its own limitations and the real possibilities of the new critical emancipation theories (Munck 2007). As Cindi Katz (2007: 245) puts it in a friendly critique of Harvey's project: 'refusing his synoptic but singular vision, these critics . . . might be more convinced by the power of a Marxist analysis if Harvey were more open about its limitations, its contradictions, its indeterminacy rather than repeatedly demonstrating its all-encompassing power'. If the critical analysis of imperialism was always one of classical Marxism's stronger points, its renewed relevance would be even more significant if it could relate positively to the various currents, such as postcolonialism, post-development studies and the feminist critique of development. It is precisely an epistemological challenge to imagine a genuinely postcolonial future taking us beyond the false promises of globalization discourse (Kapoor 2008). Decolonization also entails a new power/knowledge paradigm fit for purpose in the era of globalization, at least for those who see the need to overcome its grip and seductive power. It is also a strategy for power because it recognizes the continuities of North/South economic disparities and refuses the iron grip it imposes on the life prospects of the world's majority populations. Certainly postcolonialism in its Western academic guise has tended towards a form of culturalism, but there is nothing intrinsic in its makeup that prevents it considering the overwhelming reality of the economic factors that continuously make and reproduce underdevelopment. Nor do we necessarily need to romanticize the knowledge of the subaltern that is ultimately a refusal of, but not an alternative to, falsely universal economic prescriptions and a blind faith in Western science and progress as antidotes to underdevelopment.

The clash between modernization and dependency theories led to what was widely received as an 'impasse' in development theory. Some Marxists took this as a cue to return to the mainstream (e.g. Booth 1985) arguing that Marxism was simply too necessitarian to serve as a useful theory and practice for development. Others (e.g. Gunder Frank 1977) carried on insisting that they were right long after real-world developments had belied the basic tenets of dependency theory and the belief that capitalism could only lead to the 'development of underdevelopment'. On the whole though, the collapse of an alternative non-capitalist development model in the 1990s and the rise of neoliberal globalization as hegemonic development model led to certain quietism. But Marxists in the global South could not afford the luxury of defection and new approaches began to be generated.

In a parallel development to the post-Marxism scenario opened up by the 'crisis of Marxism' of (1968, 1979 or 1989 according to taste) so there was a move towards a 'post-development' paradigm in the 1980s–90s. Arturo Escobar, for example, argued forcefully that 'not only does the deployment of development contribute significantly to maintaining domination and economic exploitation but the discourse itself must be dismantled if the countries of the "Third World" want to pursue a different type of development' (Escobar 1984: 378). Marxism, as we have seen above, is not immune to this critique insofar as it shares a belief in the modernist 'grand narrative' and a teleological view of history. It allows us to theorize the close links between power and knowledge and the inter-relations between different forms of oppression, be they class, gender, race or spatially based. It also breaks decisively with the dominant economic bias of development theory.

What the postcolonial approach allows us to do is to engage productively in the creation of a de-colonized, postcolonial knowledge. The whole post-war 'development project' is deconstructed persuasively as a dominating universalizing discourse of the affluent North. The problem of underdevelopment is seen to be a construction of the very same hegemonic powers which constructed it in the first place through imperialism, colonialism and neo-colonialism. Of all the social divides in the post-war period (class, gender, race, region) the one that is most enduring (and indeed deepened) is that between North and South. As with the postmodern critique of modernism (and that includes Marxism), the postcolonial lens profoundly destabilizes Eurocentric forms of knowledge, brings to the fore the subaltern perspective and reintroduces the possibility of radical social transformation.

One of postcolonialism's most influential texts asks 'Can the subaltern speak? (Spivak 1993) and its dominant idiom is cultural and literary. It rarely asks 'Can the subaltern eat? and, if not, why not?' Mainstream development theory focuses almost exclusively on the technical impediments to the subaltern eating: better seeds, better management, more perfect markets, better governance, etc. It would not be overly concerned with 'voice', notwithstanding all the World Bank documents on 'empowerment'. It certainly does not want to look too closely at the power differentials in the global political economy; there are taken as a given. Marxism could serve as bridge, perhaps, between the real-world problems addressed by the mainstream (poverty is not just a discursive construction) and the critical Southern oriented concerns of the postcolonial approach.

Marxism needs to be living and under constant development if it is to be relevant to the development challenges of the twenty-first century.

I have suggested an engagement with the postcolonial current but there are many other paths that could be taken. What relevance might the 'unequal exchange' theories of the 1960s have today to explain uneven development in the global era? What is the Marxist take on 'development aid' and the rise of development NGOs beyond proclamatory denunciation? How do we analyse the role of Marxists (or socialists of some sort) such as F. H. Cardoso and 'Lula' as Brazilian presidents, beyond saying that they 'sold out' to 'neoliberalism'? Marxism has a rich theoretical arsenal at its disposal and a dramatic historical record of engagement with development from Ireland/India in the mid-nineteenth century, to Russia 1917, China 1945 and across the so-called developing world. It should be centre stage again, not consigned to a footnote of history, or the language of bystander critics.

References

Avineri, S. (ed.) (1969), *Karl Marx on Colonialism and Modernization*. New York: Anchor.

Bidelux, R. (1985), *Communism and Development*. London: Methuen.

Boot, M. (2001), 'The case for American empire', *Weekly Stand*ard, 7, (5), 15 October. Available from: http://www.weeklystandard.com/Content/Public/Articles/000/000/000/318qpvmc.asp.

Booth, D. (1985), 'Marxism and development sociology: interpreting the impasse', *World Development*, 13, (7), 761–87.

Brewer, A. (1980), *Marxist Theories of Imperialism: A Critical Survey*. New York: Monthly Review Press.

Brolin, J. (2006), *The Bias of the World: Theories of Unequal Exchange in History*. Sweden: Uland University.

Cardoso, F. and Faletto, E. (1979), *Dependency and Development in Latin America*. California: California University Press.

Cooper, R. A. (2002), 'Why we still need empires', *The Observer*, 7 April. Available from: http://observer.guardian.co.uk/worldview/story/0,11581,680117,00.html [Accessed 02 July 2011].

Deleuze, G. and Guattari, F. (2003), *A Thousand Plateaus: Capitalism and Schizophrenia*. London and New York: Continuum.

Emmanuel, A. (1972), *Unequal Exchange: A Study of the Imperialism of Trade*. London and New York: Monthly Review Books.

Escobar, A. (1984), 'Discourse and power in development: Michael Foucault and the relevance of his work in the Third World', *Alternatives*, 10, 377–400.

Friedman, T. (2005), *The World is Flat: A Brief History of the Twenty-First Century*. New York: Farrar, Strauss and Giroux.

Gunder Frank, A. (1977), 'Dependence is dead, long live dependence and the class struggle: an answer to critics', *World Development*, 5, 355–70.

Hardt, M. and Negri, A. (2000), *Empire*. Cambridge and London: Harvard University Press.

Hartstock, N. (2006), 'Globalization and primitive accumulation: the contribution of Harvey's dialectical Marxism', in N. Castree and D. Gregory (eds), *David Harvey: A Critical Reader*. Oxford: Blackwell, pp. 167–90.

Harvey, D. (2005), *A Brief History of Neoliberalism*. Oxford: Oxford University Press.

Heinz, J. (2003), 'The new face of unequal exchange: low-wage manufacturing, commodity chains, and global inequality, *PERI Working Paper Series No. 59*. Amherst, MA: University of Massachusetts Press.

Kapoor, I. (2008), *The Post-Colonial Politics of Development*. London and New York: Routledge.

Katz, C. (2007), 'Messing with "*the project*"', in N. Castree and D. Gregory (eds), *David Harvey: A Critical Reader*. Oxford: Blackwell, pp. 234–46.

Kay, G. (1975), *Development and Underdevelopment: A Marxist Analysis*. London: Macmillan.

Lal, D. (2004), *In Praise of Empires: Globalization and Order*. London and New York: Palgrave.

Lenin, V. I. (1963), *Imperialism, The Highest Stage of Capitalism: V. I. Lenin, Selected Works*, voiume 1. Moscow: Progress Publishers, pp. 667–766.

Luxemburg, R. (1971), *The Accumulation of Capital*. London: Routledgc.

Marx, K. and Engels, F. [1848] (1967), *The Communist Manifesto*. London: Penguin.

Munck, R. (2007), *Globalization and Contestation: The New Great Counter-Movement*. London and New York: Routledge.

Nederveen Pietersee, J. (2004), Globalization or Empire?, New York and London: Rouledge.

Rostow, W. (1960), *The Stages of Economic Growth: A Non-Communist Manifesto*. Cambridge: Cambridge University Press.

Shanin, T. (ed.) (1983), *Late Marx and the Russian Road*. London: Routledge.

Spivak, G. (1993), 'Can the subaltern speak', in C. Williams and L. Chirsman (eds), *Colonial Discourse and Post-Colonial Theory*. Hemel Hempstead: Harvester.

Van der Linden, M. (2003), *The 'Law' of Uneven and Combined Development: Some Underdeveloped Thoughts*. Amsterdam: Mimeo.

Warren, B. (1980), *Imperialism: Pioneer of Capitalism*. London: Verso.

Wood, E. M. (2005), *Empire of Capital*. London: Verso.

CHAPTER SIX

Progress, anti-isms and revolutionary subjects: the importance of transcending liberalism

Matthew Johnson

Introduction

In his *Theses on Feuerbach* [1845],[1] Karl Marx states that '[t]he philosophers have only interpreted the world, in various ways; the point is to change it' (McLellan 2000: 173). At present, the world is experiencing unprecedented levels of economic, social, political, demographic and environmental change. Most of this change is being directed by states, organizations and institutions committed, in some measure, to the expansion of capital. Since the demise of the Soviet Union, Marxists have increasingly been associated with opposition to this change, becoming subsumed among broader anti-globalizaion, anti-imperialism and anti-war movements.[2] This has reached an apogee in recent years in efforts to oppose US-led interventions in Afghanistan and Iraq. The Socialist Workers Party (SWP), badged 'an anti-capitalist, revolutionary party', has epitomized the movement towards opposition by seeking and forming tactical alliances in the Stop the War Coalition (StWC)[3] with groups apparently opposed fundamentally to orthodox Marxist goals, such as the Muslim Association of Britain (MAB) which has links to the Muslim Brotherhood (Phillips 2008: 102).[4] Although expressing progressive, internationalist values, the likes of the SWP have adopted an 'enemy of my enemy is my friend' approach, believing that the capitalist West is their enemy with their enemy's enemy, Islamist groups in both the West and beyond, their friend (Bassi 2010).[5] Such opposition to Western expansion has developed to such an extent that it has been seen almost as an integral, defining feature of contemporary Marxism.

Many commentators, particularly those on the left, such as Norman Geras, in this collection, and Nick Cohen (2004) in his various columns, have challenged this instrumentalist tactic, demonstrating the ideological inconsistency in analysis, goals and methods. The tactic is doubly contentious since classical Marxism, through such key texts as *The German Ideology*, *Communist Manifesto* and *Capital*, is associated with a stagist account of historical development along with a core conception of progress which gave rise to qualified, instrumentalist support for the development and expansion of capital into non-Western or pre-capitalist areas. In recent years, some Marxists, such as Kevin Anderson (2010), have sought to rehabilitate Marx from accusations derived from these positions of ethnocentrism, racism and bigotry. These authors have highlighted Marx's later thoughts on Ireland and India in order to suggest that his support for Western imperialism waned or disappeared in his 'mature' phase, and expounded his late thoughts on Russia to suggest a 'multilinear' account of development and progress. This development has appeared to give credence to the sorts of approaches adopted by the SWP.

In this chapter, I shall trace the development of Marx's positions on development and imperialism to challenge this conclusion. I do not wish, though, to put forward a single, rigid, all-encompassing Marxian position on development, Western expansion or political instrumentalism – there simply is not one. Marx's writings constitute nearly five decades and millions of words of work. Within these writings are developments, inconsistencies, ambiguities and, of course, errors. The notion of an entirely consistent, timeless Marx is surely as fanciful as the notion of an entirely consistent, timeless Holy Book. As is well known, there are numerous developments with regard to conceptualization, theorization and, even, terminology, with circumstance and political concerns as well as intellectual maturation influencing various shift in stance (see Adamson 1981). What I do wish to show is that there is, in Marx, a core conception of, and commitment to, progress which persists throughout his various positions on development, imperialism and non-Western/non-capitalist societies. This, along with his approach to tactical alliances, suggests that there is little justification in Marx for the coalitions formed by such groups as the SWP. By positing possible explanations for this apparent divergence from Marx, I wish to show that the approaches adopted are misguided and serve to smother potential avenues for Marxist contributions to humankind. The conclusion I draw is that, if Marxism is going to mean and to contribute anything positive and progressive to the world, it will be necessary for its proponents to abandon 'enemy of my enemy is my friend' approaches and put forward a practicable, concrete vision of human flourishing – a task with which Lawrence Wilde, without necessarily agreeing with my arguments here, engages in the next chapter.

Before I begin, it is necessary to clarify my position with regard to the controversial groups to whom the anti-imperialist left has offered support. Those concerned with the rise of regressive alliances within the left are often dismissed as 'Islamophobic', on the grounds that they are seen to harbour an irrational, ethnocentric fear of Islam and Muslims. In this chapter, I oppose alliances with certain groups which profess to be Islamic, not because of a singular, irrational fear of Islam, but because of what I consider to be reasonable concern regarding the desire of certain messianic, anti-modern, monotheists to attain positions of cultural and political power (see Bhatt's 2006 discussion of the relationship between 'the left' and faith groups).[6] The capitalist world has experienced the horrors of religious fervour and inter-faith conflict. Only by stripping religious authorities of power and subjecting faith and dogma to criticism, opposition and, at times, ridicule, has the modern world begun to develop the secular, egalitarian, universal tenets to which the Marxist left has traditionally been tied. I treasure the fact that racism, gender segregation and homophobia are being challenged and do not wish to live in a society in which the likes of Monty Python, Chris Morris and Stewart Lee are condemned as heretics, rather than treasured for their progressive satire. Of course, bigotry, chauvinism, racism and dogma persist in a range of faiths and secular belief systems. However, until anti-imperialist Marxists form alliances with Christian fundamentalists, such as the Lord's Resistance Army and the Westboro Baptist Church, Jewish extremists, such as Kach and Kahane Chai, or bigots belonging to any number of other faiths or belief systems, it is necessary to focus on this particular approach towards regressive forces which profess belief in Islam. As I argue throughout this chapter, Marxism that lacks antipathy towards opponents of progress may neglect core features of its very being. I begin by discussing the 'stagist' approach to history.

The stagist conception of history

In the traditional, stagist model of history, advanced particularly in *The German Ideology* [1846], Marx suggests that human societies begin life curtailed and suppressed by nature. All efforts and actions are directed towards satisfying the most basic of needs. In this state, 'relations are purely animal', with humans 'overawed like beasts', possessing 'a purely animal consciousness of nature . . . because nature is as yet hardly modified historically' (Marx and Engels 1974: 51). Humans are drawn naturally to achieve emancipation from natural constraints by directing nature and resources rationally, 'with the least expenditure of energy and under conditions most worthy and appropriate for their human nature' (Marx 1981: 959; see also Nordahl 1986: 7–9).

In striving towards this, humans 'distinguish themselves from animals' by developing technological 'means of production' (Marx and Engels 1974: 42). Initially, these means amount to basic tools (also employed by certain other great apes), such as spears and digging utensils which extract, with greater ease than by hand, sustenance from the environment. Over time, the combination of human labour and technological innovation – the 'forces of production' – enables an increase in productive efficiency, the creation of a surplus of raw materials and a growth in population. Additional materials and group members enable agricultural innovation and, in turn, larger scale trade between groups. These developments pose new problems to society, requiring new solutions (see Spier 1996: 5), such as means of transit. The increase in the complexity of the means of production dictates the growth of specialization in the forces of production, with 'a division of material and mental labour' (Marx and Engels 1974: 51) emerging along the lines of natural physical diversity (Marx 1976: 471–2).

The division of labour enables those engaged in mental labour to direct production to their own ends, appropriating surpluses as private property and creating class-based 'relations of production'. The expropriators perpetuate their position within the relations through the creation of 'Morality, religion, metaphysics' or, more perniciously, 'ideology' (Marx and Engels 1974: 47). As Marx explains in his preface to *A Critique of Political Economy* [1859], these cultural devices engineer 'false consciousness' by presenting life, and indeed nature, in terms that obscure exploitation by representing particular, subjective interests as universal and objective. The combination of the forces and relations of production – the 'mode of production' – is then enshrined in 'a legal and political superstructure' (McLellan 2000: 425), aimed at maximizing productivity and the surplus and stifling the development of alternative orders. However, these means of conserving an order are not insurmountable.

Within each mode of production lie the seeds of dialectical change. The increased efficiency, productivity and rationality that the development of a superstructure brings, enable further increases in population and the development of new needs, requiring new technologies for their satisfaction. While these technologies emerge from within the existing mode of production, once matured they require new skills and forms of organization in order to function and develop. These emerging means of production are operated by groups outside the expropriator class. These groups gradually accumulate power as the utilization of their 'forces of production' increases until they become the dominant productive force of the society. At this point, 'the material productive forces of society come into conflict with the existing relations of production . . . within which they have been at work hitherto. From forms of development of the productive forces these relations turn into their fetters' (McLellan 2000: 425).

Because of the immanent species desire for emancipation from natural and historically contingent social constraint, the antithetical forces emerge dominant from the conflict, having the capacity to satisfy needs more effectively (McLellan 2000: 426). As Marx claims in his *Letter to Annenkov* [1846], in 'order that [people] may not be deprived of the result attained, and forfeit the fruits of civilization, they are obliged, from the moment when the form of their commerce no longer corresponds to the productive forces acquired, to change all their traditional social forms' (McLellan 2000: 210) and enable new relations of production to emerge and, with them, a new complementary form of consciousness enshrined in a new superstructure.

This account of socio-cultural development is grounded analytically in the determinacy of technology. Humans need to satisfy needs. They do so using technologies. In order to employ those technologies effectively, they need to create specific forms of organization. In order to perpetuate these forms of organization, and in order to justify, preserve and enforce the appropriation of surpluses, exploitative classes create particular ideologies and particular forms of legal-political structure. As Marx puts it in *The Poverty of Philosophy* [1847],

> The hand-mill gives you society with the feudal lord; the steam-mill, society with the industrial capitalist. The same men who establish their social relations in conformity with their material productivity, produce also principles, ideas, and categories in conformity with their social relations. Thus these ideas, these categories, are as little eternal as the relations they express. They are historical and transitory products. (McLellan 2000: 219–20)[7]

This does not mean that humans are mere automatons, with every action determined by an all-powerful causal relationship between need satisfying humans, the environment, the means of production used to satisfy needs and the superstructure used to reproduce the society. Rather, it means that environments, means of production and superstructures are parameters which shape the possibilities for human beings. Some structural parameters are more constrictive than others.

In the West, humans are seen to have progressed, through technological development, via primitive communism, ancient slave society, feudalism, to contemporary capitalism with mastery over nature increasing at each step (McLellan 2000: 425). Corresponding to these steps of mastery over nature has been a rise in the desire for liberation from the ideological constraints which emerged through the division of labour during the struggle with nature (Marx and Engels 1974: 51–2). Through the conquest of nature, humans create the technological conditions for the dissolution of these temporal, human obstacles to freedom. Highly developed industrial or post-industrial production requires a complex, skilled society with a free, quasi-meritocratic labour force equipped with scientific understandings of nature and proto-egalitarian social norms. These principles, combined with the inherent instability and 'irrational' in egalitarianism of capital, stimulate revolutionary sentiment. By creating an international market, industrial capital 'presupposes the universal development of the productive forces and the world intercourse bound up with communism' (Marx and Engels 1974: 56), leading to the eventual overthrow of the market and the realization of, first, state directed socialism and, ultimately, universal communism. For Marx, it is in this *telos* of communism that humans 'bring their "existence" into harmony with their "essence"' (Marx and Engels 1974: 61) in a condition of freedom from natural and social constraints.

By bringing their 'existence' into harmony with their 'essence', humans are able, finally, not simply to satisfy their needs for food, water and shelter but, also, to develop fully their extensive range of capabilities for love, reason, thought, discourse and recognition of beauty. As he argues in one of his many *Economic and Philosophical Manuscripts* [1844],

> Only through the objectively unfolded wealth of human nature can the wealth of subjective *human* sensitivity – a musical ear, an eye for the beauty of form – be either cultivated or created . . . . *Sense* which is a prisoner of crude practical need has only a *restricted* sense. For a man who is starving the human form of food does not exist, only its abstract form exists; it could just as well be present in its crudest form, and it would be hard to say how this way of eating differs from that of *animals*. The man who is burdened with worries and needs has no *sense* for the finest of plays; . . . thus the objectification of the human essence, in a theoretical as well as a practical respect, is necessary both in order to make man's *senses human* and to create an appropriate *human sense* for the whole of the wealth of humanity and of nature. (Marx 1992: 353–4)

By liberating humans from their material anxieties, advanced modes of production enable people to flourish.

Technological progress as an evaluative device

This materialist account of human progress presents a means of comparing and evaluating societies with claims to objectivity, universality and transhistoricity. For Marx, societies can be judged according to the extent to which they have the *potential* to satisfy needs and enable humans to develop their species-specific capabilities (Nordahl 1986: 11). The transhistorical goodness of a society increases as its productive forces develop the capacity to bend the natural world to human ends, such that capitalist societies are superior *in potential* than feudal societies, even where socio-economic inequalities deprive individuals of the benefits of labour. As Marx (1973: 706) puts it in *Grundrisse* [1858],

> Nature builds no machines, no locomotives, railways, electric telegraphs, self-acting mules etc. These are products of human industry; natural material transformed into organs of the human will over nature, or of human participation in nature. They are *organs of the human brain, created by the human hand*; the power of knowledge, objectified. The development of fixed capital indicates to what degree general social knowledge has become a *direct force of production*, and to what degree: hence, the conditions of the process of social life itself have come under the control of the general intellect and been transformed in accordance with it. To what degree the powers of social production have been produced, not only in the form of knowledge, but also as immediate organs of social practice, of the real life process.

It is because of this that Marx described certain non-capitalist societies in the *Communist Manifesto* [1848] as 'barbarian', 'backward', 'stagnatory' and 'vegetative' (Marx and Engels 1967: 222–4).[8] In these societies, Marx saw parallels to the historical condition of capitalist societies, in which people were subjugated, and sometimes enslaved, by 'their natural superiors' in stultifying, hierarchical slave, and then feudal, relations of production (Marx and Engels 1967: 222). He believed that the consciousness engendered by pre-industrial modes of production was conducive to fanaticism, intolerance and communitarian oppression. These tendencies were, according to Marx, overcome by the development of industrial modes of production and the emergence of capital, with

> National differences and antagonisms between peoples ... daily more and more vanishing, owing to the development of the bourgeoisie, to freedom of commerce, to the world market, to uniformity in the mode of production and in the conditions of life corresponding thereto. (Marx 1976: 488)

Marx saw in capitalism not only 'naked self-interest', and 'shameless, direct, brutal exploitation' (Marx and Engels 1967: 222), and alienation from the products of their labour, of proletarians (e.g. Marx and Engels 1974: 82–6 and McLellan 2000: 127–32), but also the kernels of liberation. According to Larrain (1991: 187), he believed that 'the progress brought about by the new humanistic and scientific rationality in capitalist Western Europe [was] inherently superior and must finally prevail in the world against opposing forces', affirming 'the superior relevance, the more advanced stage and historical priority of these social processes occurring in Europe' (see, also, Halliday 2002: 79).

The objectivity and universality of this approach, and its emphasis on immanent capabilities and desires for the conquest of nature, has been challenged on account of the marked international disparity in levels of development, with Chakrabarty (1993), Hardt and Negri (2001: 120), Katz (1990) and Lim (1992) levelling serious accusations of ethnocentricity (cf Antonio 2003: 177). One possible Marxian response to these accusations may be to suggest that, as Marx argues in *Capital I* [1867], developmental disparity emerges, not as a result of differences in innate potential or cultural trajectory but, rather, through environmental unevenness and particularity: 'Different communities find different means of production and different means of subsistence in their natural environment. Hence their modes of production and living, as well as their products, are different' (Marx 1976: 472). In some areas, environmental resources permit and stimulate rapid technological development and societal expansion. In others, environmental conditions constrain opportunities for development. At the same time, rigid superstructures can constrain whatever opportunities do exist. In the case of nineteenth-century India, for example, the likes of Avineri (1969: 10–13), Krader (1975: esp. pp. 140–75) and Lefort (1978: 93–6) argue that Marx held the relations of production and the lack of landed property to be the prime inhibitors of change, with caste and slavery precluding free labour (see also Katz 1990: 150–2). Lichtheim argues, however, that 'the non-existence of private landed property . . . [was] due to climatic conditions', with '[C]entralized Oriental despotism [arising] from the need to provide artificial irrigation' (Lichtheim 1963: 38). Different environments and different means of production produce different parameters within which societies develop. Within these parameters, humans have the capacity to stunt or promote development through the pursuit of class interests. Therefore, the less constrictive the environment and the more powerful the means of production, the greater the potential for human liberation.

The uneven development of societies due, in this account, to environmental contingency creates a series of normative quandaries in Marxian thought. Humans are seen potentially to benefit from development of the mode of production. In order to realize communism, all societies must be developed, and an international working class must act together, with the same consciousness, in order to overthrow capital. What, then, should be done with regard to societies trapped in unfavourable circumstances?

Capitalism and consequentialism

Marx's normative response to uneven development is consequentialist. In his writings on colonialism for the *New York Daily Tribune* in the 1850s he suggests, as Avineri (1969: 19) puts it, that non-Western society is 'non-dialectical and stagnant . . . the only impetus for change has to come from the outside . . . European bourgeois civilisation is thus the external agent of change in non-European societies'. Marx's faith, at this point, in the consequentialist value of bourgeois society lies in his analysis of its dynamic and expansionist economic foundations.

In the *Communist Manifesto*, Marx argues that, technologically, capitalism is unique in that, unlike previous class orders, competition dictates that 'The bourgeoisie cannot exist without constantly revolutionising the instruments of production, and thereby the relations of production, and with them the whole of society'. Consequently, needs develop rapidly in a dialectical relationship, which ensures that capitalism 'has created more colossal productive forces than all preceding generations together'. These forces require centralized, urban populations for their efficient operation, dictating the building of 'enormous cities . . . and . . . thus rescu[ing] a considerable part of the population from the idiocy of rural life'. The need for a 'free', unencumbered and flexible labour force dictates the dissolution of old, pre-capitalist relations, tearing 'asunder the motley feudal ties that bound man to his "natural superiors"' leaving 'no other nexus between man and man than naked self-interest, than callous "cash payment"'. In turn, this undermines and revolutionizes the old 'ideologies', destroying 'the most heavenly ecstasies of religious fervour, of chivalrous enthusiasm, of philistine sentimentalism, in the icy water of egotistical calculation' (Marx and Engels 1967: 222; 224–5; 224; 222; 222). From this historical base, capitalism expands and changes all before it:

> The need of a constantly expanding market for its products chases the bourgeoisie over the whole surface of the globe . . . The bourgeoisie has through its exploitation of the world market given a cosmopolitan character to production and consumption in every country . . . In the place of the old wants, satisfied by the productions of the country, we find new wants, requiring for their satisfaction the products of distant lands and climes . . . National one-sidedness and narrow mindedness become more and more impossible, and from the numerous national and local literatures, there arises a world literature. The cheap prices of its commodities are the heavy artillery with which it batters down all Chinese walls, with which it forces 'the barbarians' intensely obstinate hatred of foreigners to capitulate. It compels all nations, on pain of extinction, to adopt the bourgeois mode of production . . . In a word, it creates a world after its own image. (Marx and Engels 1967: 223–4)[9]

In his speech on free trade to the Democratic Association in Brussels in 1848, Marx claims that, in creating an international, free trade economy, the domestic division of labour is mirrored, with powerful, advanced capitalist nations growing rich at the expense of subordinated nations. Marx is clear, however, that communists should reject the 'conservative' system of protectionism and support the advance of the destructive system of free trade on the grounds that it 'breaks up old nationalities and pushes the antagonism of the proletariat and the bourgeoisie to the extreme point' hastening 'the social revolution' (McLellan 2000: 295).

In some cases, capital expands and penetrates non-capitalist society without the support of state-level 'hard power'. In other cases, however, expansion is facilitated by direct, military intervention and appropriation – that is, through imperialism and colonialism. For Marx, the merits of these actions are judged primarily according to their contribution to the notion of progress outlined above. In relation to his writings for the *New York Daily Tribune*, Avineri (1969: 19–20) concludes that 'Marx would have to welcome European penetration in direct proportion to its intensity: the more direct the European control of any society in Asia, the greater the chances for the overhauling of its structure and its ultimate incorporation into bourgeois, and hence later into socialist, society'. Indeed, were socialist revolutions to be achieved in the West prior to the globalization of capital, proletarian imperialism may be necessary to complete the developmental process in pre- or non-capitalist countries (Avineri 1969: 21–2; 473; Warren 1980: 44–5). It is this sort of logic which led Marx to the following conclusion with regard to British imperialism in India:

> Now, sickening as it must be to human feeling to witness those myriads of industrious patriarchal and inoffensive social organizations disorganized and dissolved into their units, thrown into a sea of woes, and their individual members losing at the same time their ancient form of civilisation, and their hereditary means of subsistence, we must not forget that these idyllic village communities, inoffensive though they may appear, had always been the solid foundation of Oriental despotism, that they restrained the human mind within the smallest possible compass, making it the unresisting tool of superstition, enslaving it beneath traditional rules, depriving it of all grandeur and historical energies. We must not forget the barbarian egotism which, concentrating on some miserable patch of land, had quietly witnessed the ruin of empires, the perpetration of unspeakable cruelties, the massacre of the population of large towns, with no other consideration bestowed upon them than on natural events, itself the helpless prey of any aggressor who deigned to notice at all. We must not forget that this undignified, stagnatory and vegetative life, that this passive sort of existence evoked on the other part, in contradistinction, wild, aimless, unbounded forces of destruction and rendered murder itself a religious rite in Hindostan. We must not forget that these little communities were contaminated by distinctions of caste and by slavery, that they subjugated man to external circumstances instead of elevating man to be the sovereign of circumstances, that they

transformed a self-developing social state into never changing natural destiny, and thus brought about a brutalising worship of nature, exhibiting its degradation in the fact that man, the sovereign of nature, fell down on his knees in adoration of *Hanuman*, the monkey, and *Sabbala*, the cow. England, it is true, in causing a social revolution in Hindostan, was actuated only by the vilest interests, and was stupid in her manner of enforcing them. But that is not the question. The question is, can mankind fulfil its destiny without a fundamental revolution in the social state of Asia? If not, whatever may have been the crimes of England she was the unconscious tool of history in bringing about that revolution. (Avineri 1969: 93–4)

Despite, or rather as a result of, being motivated 'only by the vilest interests', Britain was unconsciously performing a double, almost Hegelian,[10] World-Historical 'mission in India: one destructive, the other regenerating – the annihilation of old Asiatic society, and the laying of the material foundations of Western society in Asia'. Among the benefits Marx saw in these processes were the enforcement of unity on a divided, tribal society through coercive centralization, the organization of a national army, which 'was the *sine qua non* of Indian self-emancipation, and of India ceasing to be the prey of the first foreign intruder', the development of the free press 'for the first time into an Asiatic society' and, vitally, the introduction of modern industry to enable global commerce, telecommunications, urbanization and the mastery of natural obstacles to progress, such as desert and drought (Avineri 1969: 90; 131–5; see, also, Marx 1976: 477–9). Although the full benefits of these goods could not be gleaned until India had overthrown colonial rule and engaged fully and on a roughly even footing with international revolutionary societies, the stimulus for development remained, in Marx's eyes, external (Avineri 1969: 131–5).

At present, attempts are being made by the US-led coalition to introduce and expand certain features in Afghanistan. Many billions of dollars and thousands of people have been employed in Afghanistan to introduce centralized government, a national army,[11] a more independent press (as part of a general push to increase the power of civil society) and modern infrastructure. In this account of Marx, there is no intrinsic reason to reject outright imperialism or to believe that external oppression is any worse than internal forms. The goodness or badness of an intervention is determined by the extent to which, rather than the way in which, oppressive, communitarian practices, parochial identities and national boundaries are dissolved and modern goods implemented – all of which are regarded as contingent consequences of specific productive activities. However, in recent years, some Marx scholars have sought to rehabilitate Marx from this contingent endorsement of 'imperialism', emphasizing a trend of opposition to imperialism in other parts of his work.

Instrumentalist opposition to imperialism and the possibility of skipping stages

Throughout Marx's work on imperialism and non-Western societies is recognition of a) the harm of imposing the instruments of capitalism even where, as above, he concludes that such imposition leads to net benefit and b) the subordination of subject peoples by imperialist societies through an international division of labour which has the capacity to hinder the development of capitalism in non-capitalist areas (McLellan 2000: 295). In particular places, especially in his late writings, however, Marx suggests that certain forms of imperialism should be opposed. This opposition shares, though, the instrumental considerations evident in his support for other imperial projects and actions. In his treatment of Ireland in a letter to Engels in 1867, for example, Marx invokes instrumentalist objection to British colonialism on three grounds: first, that the British were unable and unwilling to introduce successfully the advances in industry capable of raising Ireland to a capitalist level of development; second, with Leninist undertones, that the holdings of the English landed aristocracy in Ireland served to entrench their position in England and, third, that the Irish worker served the English ruling classes as the bogeyman against which to rally English proletarians behind their oppressors (McLellan 2000: 638–40). Similarly, in *Capital Volume 3*, written between 1863 and 1883, Marx (1981: 451–2) notes the resistance of Indian 'Asiatic' social forms to capital, in which deficiencies in imperial experiments combined with indigenous social conservatism meant that the destructive and regenerative capacity of capital was inhibited, leaving communities with damaged and dysfunctional traditional modes of production in lieu of efficient capitalist industry.

Some scholars, such as Shanin (1983) and Anderson (2010), have highlighted elements of Marx's writings on the failure of capitalist development in these areas which suggest a rejection or revision of the unilinear and deterministic notion of historical development outlined above. Marx is indeed keen to emphasize that societies develop within their own parameters of circumstance, creating particular challenges and sources of growth. For the late Marx, the stages elaborated above refer to the development of capitalism in Western Europe alone. In an 1877 letter to the editors of *Otechestvenniye Zapiski*, he states that his 'historical sketch of the genesis of capitalism in Western Europe' cannot be transformed

> into a historico-philosophic theory of the general path every people is fated to tread, whatever the historical circumstances in which it finds itself, in order that it may ultimately arrive at the form of economy which ensures, together with the greatest expansion of productive powers of social labour, the most complete development of man. (Avineri 1969: 469–70)

Marx suggests that different historical conditions produce different directions of development, highlighting the disparate courses that 'free peasants, each cultivating his own plot on his own account' took in Ancient Rome and Feudal North Western Europe. While both were 'stripped of everything except their labour-power', only the latter became wage labourers, with the former becoming 'a *mob* of do-nothings more abject than the former "poor whites" in the South of the United States', existing alongside 'a mode of production which was not capitalist but based on slavery' (Avineri 1969: 470).

Leading on from this 'multilinear' account of development is the notion, developed late in Marx's life, that certain societies under particular conditions, might come to skip stages in development. In this account, Marx suggests that the specific social conditions of nineteenth-century Russia might enable a revolutionary society to develop modern modes of production, while preserving elements of the commune compatible with socialism and avoiding the deleterious destructive elements of capitalism (see Lichtheim 1963: 51–2). As he puts it in drafts of his 1881 letter to Vera Zasulich:

> Thanks to the unique combination of circumstances in Russia, the rural commune, which is still established on a national scale, may gradually shake off its primitive characteristics and directly develop as an element of collective production on a national scale. Precisely because it is contemporaneous with capitalist production, the rural commune may appropriate all its positive achievements without undergoing its . . . frightful vicissitudes. (Shanin 1983: 105–6)

For this late Marx, there is the possibility of skipping stages by organizing adopted modern forces of production through the commune:

> Did Russia have to undergo a long Western-style incubation of mechanical industry before it could make use of machinery, steamships, railways, etc.? . . . they [the Russians] managed to introduce, in the twinkling of an eye, that whole machinery of exchange (banks, credit companies, etc.), which was the work of centuries in the West. (Shanin 1983: 106)

Although this might be taken by those, such as Anderson, who wish to advance a 'multilinear' Marx, to suggest that societies can develop socialism in any or a large number of forms, it is apparent that Marx retains belief in the necessity of modern technology and internationalism to progress, such that the value of the commune itself is affected by the extent to which it acquires and harnesses modern forces of production as part of an international movement towards socialism: 'the *contemporaneity* of Western . . . production, which dominates the world market, enables Russia to build into the commune all the positive achievements of the capitalist system, without having to pass under its harsh tribute' (Shanin 1983: 110).

It is not that the commune is an end in itself to be conserved in perpetuity. It is, rather, that it is possible for the commune to be transcended through engagement with modern, international, revolutionary modes of production. Transcendence would enable the commune to 'develop as a regenerating element of Russian society and an element of superiority over the countries enslaved by the capitalist regime (Shanin 1983: 117).

How, then, should we reconcile this apparently multilinear, anti-imperialist Marx with the Marx of *Poverty of Philosophy* – a work he sought to republish in *L'Egalite*, the newspaper of the French Workers' Party, in 1880, around the same time as he was expressing his views on the Russian commune?

> Feudal production also had two antagonistic elements which are likewise designated by the name of the good side and the bad side of feudalism, irrespective of the fact that it is always the bad side that in the end triumphs over the good side. It is the bad side that produces the movement which makes history, by providing a struggle. If, during the epoch of the domination of feudalism, the economists, enthusiastic over the knightly virtues, the beautiful harmony between rights and duties, the patriarchal life of the towns, the prosperous condition of domestic industry in the countryside, the development of industry organized into corporations, guilds, and fraternities, in short, everything that constitutes the good side of feudalism, had set themselves the problem of eliminating everything that cast a shadow on this picture – serfdom, privileges, anarchy – what would have happened? All the elements which called forth the struggle would have been destroyed, and the development of the bourgeoisie nipped in the bud. One would have set oneself the absurd problem of eliminating history. (McLellan 2000: 227)

One explanation for the apparent inconsistency might lie, again, in the particular conditions of nineteenth-century Russia. The late Marx claims that the fate of the commune was seen to be affected by 'neither an historical inevitability nor a theory', but by 'state oppression, and exploitation by capitalist intruders whom the state has made powerful at the peasants' expense' (Shanin 1983: 104–5). Whereas in Western Europe, the internal dynamics of change required the dissolution of elements of the good with the bad, the particular circumstances of Russia, with its access internationally to advanced means of production, presented additional possibilities: stagnation, capitalist development and skipping stages towards socialism. There was the possibility, if appropriate political, economic and social measures were taken, for society to transcend Russia's mode of production effectively in a way that was impossible in feudal society in the West.

Can a 'multilinear' understanding of Marx provide support to the anti-imperialist alliances formed by Marxist groups in opposing US-led forces in Afghanistan? Is it possible to suggest that particular features of Afghan society form the basis for local transcendence towards socialism?

Dysfunctional strategies

Although much is made, by the likes of Anderson, of Marx's apparent Damascene conversion to anti-imperialism, his shift in position may have much less to do with principled objection than tactical assessment. Remaining throughout Marx's work is, first, commitment, often implicit, to the capacity for human flourishing, second, belief in the necessity of technology to progress (as the expansion of the capacity for human flourishing) and, third, instrumental assessment of imperialism according to its effect on progress. Where Marx discusses alliances with political parties or movements which appear to defend 'parochial' or conservative elements of society, he does so while emphasizing clear means by which to challenge that parochialism and conservatism in efforts to promote progress towards socialism. In his address to the Communist League in 1850, for example, Marx evaluates and circumscribes tactical alliances with the petty bourgeoisie in Germany. He states that, in the various German states, there were 'so many relics of the Middle Ages to be abolished' and 'so much local and provincial obstinacy to be broken'. Certain interests and aims of the petty bourgeoisie and revolutionary proletariat overlapped, such as the need to abolish feudalism, enshrine certain *de jure* articulations of equality and 'propose more or less socialistic measures'. However, the petty bourgeois also sought measures which did not meet the interests of workers, such as the desire to replace feudalism with a system of decentralized, free property, in which petty bourgeois peasants would be left in 'the same cycle of impoverishment and indebtedness' seen among French peasants following the 1789 revolution (McLellan 2000: 310). In order to combat counter-revolutionary elements in the petty bourgeois party, Marx proposes that the workers retain their independence, 'Compel the democrats to interfere in as many spheres as possible of the hitherto existing social order' and 'concentrate the utmost possible productive forces, means of transport, factories, railways, etc., in the hands of the state' and transform the reformist democrats into revolutionaries, by taking radical reformist measures in tax and spending (McLellan 2000: 311). The point, then, is that the sort of tactical alliances examined by Marx are governed by the comparatively progressive nature of the ally, the effect of that alliance on progress and the role of the proletarian movement in promoting radical action. In Russia, Marx saw a social structure capable of harnessing modern means of production, while in Germany, Marx saw a potential ally capable of promoting progress denied by existing bourgeois parties. He simply does not entertain 'the enemy of my enemy is my friend' approaches. Indeed, in his aforementioned speech on free trade he states that 'One may declare oneself an enemy of the constitutional regime without declaring one-self a friend of the ancient regime' (McLellan 2000: 296).

Since Marx's death, however, Marxists have rejected or neglected his pragmatic, instrumentalist stance on imperialism and sought, instead, to change the world through forms of 'anti-imperialism', championing Third World 'resistance' movements and regarding the United States as an enemy, rather than an agent, of progress. This trend emerged, most clearly, through Lenin's (1939) *Imperialism: The Highest Stage of Capitalism*, in which the acquisition of capital through imperialism is seen to consolidate capital-ism by diminishing the effects and visibility of exploitation in developed countries. In order to remove this source of amelioration and stimulate revolution in developed countries, revolutionary movements are seen to be required in those underdeveloped countries subject to imperial exploita-tion. This shifted the primary site of revolution from the developed to the developing world, with the October Revolution and the victory of Mao in China firmly entrenching Marxism as an ideology of both development and the developing world. Wallerstein's world-systems theory, in which an international division of labour acts to mirror exploitative relations previ-ously confined to states, developed further this position. This analysis of a conservative, exploitative Western bourgeoisie and progressive, exploited non-Western proletariat, is reflected clearly by Guevara in the following passage:

> The struggle against imperialism, for liberation from colonial or neo-colonial shackles . . . is not separate from the struggle against backward-ness and poverty. Both are stages on the same road leading toward the creation a new society of justice and plenty . . . The practice of proletar-ian internationalism is not only a duty for the peoples struggling for a better future, it is also an inescapable necessity. If the imperialist enemy, the United States or any other, carries out its attack against the underde-veloped peoples and the socialist countries, elementary logic determines the need for an alliance between the underdeveloped peoples and the socialist countries. If there were no other uniting factor, the common enemy should be enough. (Guevara and Castro 2002: 17)

Fundamentally, the association of Marxism with the developing world and belief among Marxists that people in developing countries have a unique interest and role in achieving socialism has served to create a number of difficulties. The instrumentalism which Marx displayed throughout his vari-ous positions on imperialism has been replaced by dogmatic rejection of the value of capitalism as a mode of production and affirmation of the extraor-dinary value of peoples and cultures in developing, non-capitalist societies (see discussions in Warren 1980: 4–6; 47–83; Boron 2005: 16–17). In effect, a crude dichotomy has appeared to emerge in which the capitalist West is regarded as being in some fundamental form inexcusable and irredeemable and the non-West, however imperfect, excusable and redeemable through the overthrow of capitalism and imperialism (with capitalism and imperialism often conflated) (see Bassi 2010: 128).

In this context, anti-imperialist Marxists appear to have been willing to sanction and foster alliances with groups whose ideas and motivations appear intrinsically opposed to those developed by Marx – whether in his pro- or anti-imperialist tracts. The SWP's collaboration with the MAB has been denounced by Nick Cohen, among others, for Islamist support for 'sharia law, with all its difficulties with democracy, women and homosexuals'. In this coalition, the Stop the War Coalition failed to criticize such regressive actions of Iraqi insurgents as kidnappings, beheadings, suicide bombings and sectarianism in emphasizing 'once more the legitimacy of the struggle of Iraqis, by whatever means they find necessary, to secure such ends' (statement cited in Cohen 2004). Indeed, the SWP shunned the Iraqi Communist Party and the Kurds for their collaboration with the United States and attempted to silence trade union opposition to the carnage of the insurgency, while supporting Islamist and, in particular, Ba'athist insurgents. Apologism for Ba'athism should be deeply troubling for Marxists since, under Saddam, 'Iraq had the classic fascist programme of the worship of the great leader, the unprovoked wars of aggression, the genocidal campaigns against impure ethnic minorities, and the suppression of every autonomous element in society, including free trade unions' (Cohen 2004). What defence can there be for such tactical alliances?

For Callinicos, the key contemporary ideological figure in the SWP, the aim of uniting with 'politically diverse', and often conservative, 'forces in action around a limited common objective' is 'to radicalize the anti-capitalist movement by giving it an anti-imperialist edge' in order to develop 'a movement that targets not just the Bush administration and its war drive but the imperialist system itself, with its roots in the capitalist logic of exploitation and accumulation' (Callinicos 2002b). Yet, the politically diverse forces may have absolutely no interest in the realization of communist ends. Halliday (2002: 85) has sought vehemently to oppose such strategic instrumental forms of 'anti-imperialism' on the grounds of their inability to engender, and often hostility towards, progress, with activists 'facilely aligning themselves with a range of regimes whose practice was even more remote from the emancipatory agenda than their opponents'. As Norman Geras claims in his chapter, those involved in these alliances should know better. Callinicos (2001: 398) himself claims to oppose anti-capitalist strategies of 'deglobalization' on the grounds that they risk forfeiting 'the genuine gains that the technologically dynamic and globally integrated capitalism of the present day has brought with it, and . . . tends to idealize petty forms of capitalism that . . . can be more exploitative than the large-scale version'. Callinicos professes to adhere to a universal and egalitarian communism in which national, ethnic, communitarian, cultural and geographical boundaries are dissolved, exploitative hierarchies overturned and modern industry advanced (Callinicos 2003: 106–14).[12] He (2003: 107) emphasizes that

> any alternative to capitalism in its present form should, as far as possible, meet the requirements of (at least) justice, efficiency, democracy, and sustainability … I say that any alternative to capitalism in its present form must meet these requirements in order not to beg the question of whether or not some other version of the prevailing economic system could fit the bill.

This is, though, betrayed by the alliances with regressive forces fighting US-led coalitions in Iraq and Afghanistan. Where, in Marx, tactical alliances are tightly circumscribed in an attempt to ensure that the outcome of action is progressive, in the case of the SWP, there are no such constraints – just references to broader political aims amid intense, reactionary anti-imperialism.

Anti-imperialists may respond that to ignore the possibility of indigenous sources of progress and social organizations capable of realizing socialist progress contradicts Marx's late writings on Russia. The point, however, is that the groups with which anti-imperialist Marxists are aligned are the very same groups which seek to conserve parochial, insular, ethnocentric structures and beliefs and which see in Marxian progress little more than decay, decline and decadence. There is no evidence that the Taliban, Moqtada al-Sadr or Saddam's old allies have any interest in engaging in such processes – that would, surely, herald their own destruction (see Bhatt's 2006 discussion of religious demagoguery). They are the people least willing and capable of harnessing international technological developments to transcend indigenous social structures in advancing local forms of socialism. Moreover, with the fall of the Soviet empire and the transition of China to a form of capitalism, opportunities for international engagement with forms of socialism, however distorted or dysfunctional, are few – though, given widespread Afghan opposition to Soviet occupation, there is little reason to believe that any such engagement would be welcomed anyway by these groups.

Indeed, in terms of the effectiveness of the coalition, if anything it seems that the Islamist allies of the SWP were, and may still be, much more concerned to retain a clear sense of identity and independence and avoid assimilation. Phillips (2008: 103) states that MAB pre-conditions of entering into the coalition were gender-segregation and the provision of *halal* food at meetings and the acknowledgement that, 'while they could overcome misgivings about sharing platforms with some groups (such as socialists and atheists), they could never do so with others (Zionists and Israelis in particular)'. Indeed, past precedents indicate that the SWP's confidence in their ability to inculcate their allies in socialist thought through engagement in single-issue politics may be misplaced. The case of the union of communist and Islamist revolutionary forces in Iran seems particularly relevant, demonstrating that mere opposition to Western capitalism does not necessarily ensure progressive outcomes. Even where pre-capitalist 'Marxist' societies have driven revolutionary change, as in the case of the twentieth-century socialist empires, the outcomes have, in Marxian terms, been disappointing. Despite some 50 years of state socialism, vast swathes of Central Asia, the Caucasus and the Balkans have been left materially underdeveloped, dominated by corrupt political and economic systems and prone to ethnic, religious and cultural conflict.

As Munck's discussion in his chapter suggested, the legitimate response to this, of course, is that the experiences of countries subject to colonial rule by capitalist states or those which have sought to integrate into the global economy through other measures have, at best, been extremely mixed. While Marxists or Marx-influenced Warren (1980), Desai (2004), Harris (2003) and Kitching (2001) have joined neoliberal like Norberg (2003) in extolling the progressive nature of capitalist expansion, many others, such as Munck (2002), Boron (2005) and Lipietz (1982), in addition to Callinicos, have cogently and strongly argued that engagement in the global economy can stunt development and, indeed, undermine local modes of production by flooding domestic markets without adequately advancing locally beneficial alternatives. This has, of course, been a central source of objection to the Washington Consensus and the structural adjustment programmes which have sought to strip developing nations of means by which to protect local economies. Indeed, opponents of capitalist expansion can support their stance by pointing to the way in which mismanagement in the interventions and occupations of Iraq and Afghanistan have failed adequately to produce the new modes of production required to satisfy Marxian criteria of progress.

I do not, in any way, wish to act as an apologist for capitalist activities that undermine the long-term prospects of human beings. As Marxists, it is essential that we continue to challenge capitalist harms. What I do suggest, though, is that we advance objective, consistent means (see Bassi 2010: 121–2) by which to evaluate actions according to their contribution to human interests – the promotion of the capacity for wellbeing. As in Marx's own work, this will mean that the actions of capitalists or capitalist societies are sometimes praised and sometimes criticized. It will also mean that the actions of non-capitalist societies are sometimes praised and sometimes criticized, but not solely on account of the extent to which they oppose the United States or are 'oppressed'. For, whatever the mismanagement, efforts made to change Iraq and Afghanistan in a manner similar to that identified by Marx in nineteenth-century India have been, to varying degrees, undermined, thwarted and repulsed by local insurgents to whom the likes of Callinicos and the SWP have offered at least moral support. Instead of evaluating actions on account of their potential for progress, crude anti-imperialists of the SWP variety have fetishized resistance to such a degree that any and all action taken by 'imperialists' are rejected or denounced and any and all action taken by insurgents applauded or excused (see Bassi 2010 and Bhatt 2006). This is simply antithetical to Marx and should, I suggest, be antithetical to twenty-first century Marxism. Why, though, might this counter-intuitive and apparently self-defeating tendency persist?

Explaining alliances

Despite Callinicos' words of caution on removing capitalism, there is a sense that elements of the Marxist left have moved from having a clear conception of means by which to improve people's lives to fetishized opposition to capitalism in and of itself. That is, Marxism and Marxists have been subsumed within a broader 'anti-' movement against capitalism, capitalist war and capitalist imperialism. If the overwhelming imperative is to oppose, then a strategy of 'the enemy of my enemy is my friend' may appeal (see Bassi 2010: 127). The rationale appears to be that wiping capitalism from the face of the earth will dissolve obstacles to the resolution of the significant problems faced by humanity. Tying into this is the particular motivation of party politics, with the SWP reaching a far greater audience than usual through their participation in StWC (see Phillips 2008: 110). Though there seems little evidence of their 'progressive' ideas permeating their Islamist allies (who have taken steps to avoid losing their identity and goals in the coalition), the attention gleaned from the broader general public may appear seductive to those often dismissed as irrelevant.

Leading from these political explanations is a tendency to conflate the strong with the bad and the weak with the good, such that, in any given confrontation or situation, parties appear to be divided into the powerful, almost intrinsically bad oppressors and the weak, almost intrinsically good oppressed.[13] There are both emotional and analytical reasons for this. Emotionally, common experience of such things as charity appeals tells us that many people, particularly in the modern world, sympathize[14] with the weak – starving Africans, landless Palestinians and neglected animals all being good examples. This is good. We should, as both humans and Marxists, feel concern for other people and beings. However, sympathy appears often to be expressed, destructively, as outrage. The notion that this emotion is, in some way, necessarily constructive is surely misplaced. What sort of society can be created on the basis of uncontrolled aggression? Effective praxis must in some measure be grounded in calm, logical assessment of possibilities, recognition of the parameters of circumstance and consideration of others. Analytically, Marxism generally holds that groups or classes pursue particular interests, with power derived from control over the means of production ensuring that ruling classes can, more effectively than those they exploit, pursue their own ends. The corollary of this is that some Marxists excuse, in lieu of the humane methods which will flourish in communism, the use of destructive measures by the 'weak' or 'oppressed' to attain their goals (see Bassi 2010: 123; 126). This has, perhaps because of post-imperial *zeitgeist* in the West, particular appeal in the case of such international and intercultural conflicts as those in Iraq and Afghanistan, where some Marxists appear to apply different evaluative criteria to the activities of groups according to their level of power. This appears to be apparent in Anderson's (2010: 52) criticism of Marx's 'universalistic secular outlook', which he rejects on the grounds 'that, by condemning all religion, [it] sometimes failed to distinguish between the impact of such attacks on a dominant religion and those on a persecuted minority one'.

The assumption that the weak are innately good and that it is only through oppression that they commit acts contrary to the ends of socialism is, though, dangerous. Power enables groups to do things. There is no reason to assume that, given power and territorial security, the Taliban, for example, will suddenly adopt humanist, socialist forms of praxis. Indeed, previously 'oppressed' Islamist groups, such as the Taliban and post-revolutionary Iranian clerics, among others, have an appalling record of inflicting oppression on others. This cannot simply be attributed to their treatment under previous regimes – even if influenced by circumstance, their actions are, in some measure at least, volitional. Marxism should not entertain obfuscatory forms of romanticism regarding the 'weak' – while employing context analytically as a means of understanding elements of belief, it should evaluate the merits of particular groups and their ideologies independently of their social, economic and political standing.

The final explanation has been discussed by Alan Johnson in his chapter – the desire articulated by Žižek (2008: 119) for enthusiastic, militant, selfless, bloody action. Here, it sometimes seems that anti-imperialist Marxists interpret Marx's eleventh thesis on Feuerbach in the most negative possible form. Any change, so long as it is not capitalist, is to be applauded – all the better if it is violent and filled with emotion.

Unfortunately, the insurgents in Iraq and Afghanistan appeal to crude anti-imperialist Marxists on each of the grounds above: they are opposed to the capitalist West; their cause enables socialist groups to make broader alliances to pursue their party political or cultural ends; they are weak, and they take heroic, selfless action to pursue their ends. For such reasons, apparent proponents of progress are drawn into supporting and promoting forms of conservatism and even regression in the name of Marx.

Conclusion

When Marx wrote *Theses on Feuerbach*, it is hard to believe he intended Marxists to seek action without principle at any cost. In his various positions on imperial actions, there persists an admirable international commitment to advancing human interests. Marx's account of progress persists in both his 'pro-' and 'anti-imperialist' writings. This account of progress transcends national, cultural and political boundaries. It is a view of the way in which all humans can come to develop their uniquely human characteristics and qualities and, ultimately, flourish as social beings. For Marx, such arbitrary, temporal features as Westphalian principles of statehood and cultural identities are evaluated instrumentally – where they promote progress they are affirmed and where they do not they are dismissed. This has led certain modern scholars, imbued with modern post-imperial norms, to denounce and seek to rehabilitate Marx from his 'ethnocentrism' or 'racism'. This, however, misses the point. The 'ethnocentric' works from which Anderson, for example, seeks to extricate Marx, such as *Communist Manifesto*, *German Ideology* and the early articles for the *New York Daily Tribune*, actually highlight an aspect of Marx which is genuinely impressive in the context of his historical epoch: his unstinting commitment to human wellbeing and eagerness to challenge exploitation, oppression and abuse wherever it may occur, by whomever it be perpetuated and against whomever it be inflicted (see Anderson 2010: 98–9). Perhaps the most important tenet that we, in the twenty-first century, can glean from revisiting Marx's work on imperialism and colonialism is that oppression and exploitation is oppression and exploitation whether it be conducted by those we regard as foreigners or those we regard as compatriots. Marx dispels the fetishistic notion that our ethnic, cultural or national allegiances are of any unqualified, innate value.

Yet, it is this very dogma of parochial national, religious and cultural affiliation into which groups such as the SWP play by forging alliances with the likes of the MAB and offering support to insurgents in Iraq and Afghanistan. Only by adopting a clear, tangible vision of progress and associated criteria by which to evaluate practices can such difficulties be avoided. In recent years, movement towards the development of such criteria has actually been driven most clearly by liberals – proponents of the other main strand of Enlightenment thought. The capabilities approach of Martha Nussbaum (as well as, to a lesser degree, Amartya Sen) has advanced a set of concrete criteria by which to evaluate social conditions and, by extension, political, economic and cultural activities. This approach draws on Aristotelian, *eudaemonistic* notions of wellbeing or flourishing and makes explicit reference to the compatibility with, and influence of, Marx's own account of human essence and being. While Nussbaum regards the approach as lying in the Rawlsian tradition of political liberalism, there is scope for development in a range of perfectionist directions. While I do not suggest that he concurs with my arguments above, in the next chapter, Lawrence Wilde revisits Marx's own tactical decision to abstain from moral discourse on justice in order to advance a Marxism committed to influencing the global justice debate. By examining Nussbaum's capabilities approach, he suggests means of transcending Nussbaum's liberalism to promote tangible means of evaluating actions according to objective criteria and promoting, globally, an ethics of self realization.

It is by building constructively upon the gains of liberalism that Marxism can emerge from mere opposition, and the lure of alliances with regressive forces, to make a progressive, positive and distinctive contribution to humankind.

Notes

1 I use square brackets to indicate the year in which the particular piece was written. This helps to trace the development of Marx's thought, particularly with regard to the shift, claimed by the likes of Anderson (2010), towards anti-imperialism in his late writings.

2 See Bhatt's (2006) discussion of the relationship between the left and binary distinctions.

3 Phillips (2008: 110) states that the SWP 'has dominated the leadership of StW nationally and in many local branches'.

4 The MAB eventually left the coalition following the 7/7 bombings in 2005 for fear of entering into conflict with the UK political establishment. They were replaced by the related British Muslim Initiative (Phillips 2008: 107–8).

5 Bassi presents an approach grounded in advancing a 'third camp' revolutionary approach. My discussion, which shares some of Bassi's sentiments, is grounded less clearly in 20th Century revolutionary praxis and more in Marxian scriptural exegesis.

6 It is likely that, were he to express his views on Islam today, Marx would be dismissed as Islamophobic, given his belief in the 'retrograde impact' of faith and religious intolerance in Islamic countries (Avineri 1969: 22). In an article on religious discrimination in the Ottoman Empire in 1854, he claims that 'The Koran and the Mussulman legislation emanating from it reduce the geography and ethnography of the various peoples to the simple and convenient distinction of two nations and two countries; those of the Faithful and those of the Infidels. The Infidel is *"harby"*, i.e., the enemy. Islamism proscribes the nation of the Infidels, constituting a state of permanent hostility between the Mussulman and the unbeliever. In that sense the corsair ships of the Berber States [which raided Western Europe and beyond over several centuries] were the holy fleet of the [sic] Islam'. He adds that, 'As the Koran treats all foreigners as foes, nobody will dare to present himself in a Mussulman country without having taken his precautions' (Avineri 1969: 144; 146).

7 See, further, Shaw (1979: 370–1).

8 See, also, Marx and Engels' references to the Berbers and Chinese in Avineri (1969: 47–8; 67–75; 340–4) and other 'savages' and 'barbarians' in Levin (2004: 28–31).

9 See, also, Marx (1976: 488; 727n2); McLellan (2000: 296); Callinicos (2002a: esp. pp. 249; 260) and Hardt and Negri (2001: esp. pp. xi–xvii).

10 See Hegel (1991: 80; 99). See also Larrain (1991: 181–90) and Levin (2004).

11 The problem of engineering security and professional armies in circumstances with similarities to those encountered in contemporary Afghanistan and Iraq is discussed by Marx and Engels in Avineri (1969: 26–8; 184–90; 442–4).

12 Boron (2005: 32–3) acknowledges that progress has been made towards the realization of these ends in capitalist societies, pointing towards individual liberties, universal suffrage and secularization as bourgeois successes.
13 I recall that, growing up in the 1990s, my own sympathies in the Balkans conflict lay, first, with the Bosniaks due to Serb oppression, then the Serbs, due to Western military support for the Bosniaks, then with the Kosovars when attacked by the Serbs and, finally, with the Serbs when attacked again by the West. This is simply an unhelpful approach to adopt. See the discussion of the postcolonial subaltern in Bhatt 2006 and Bassi's (2010: 122) thoughts.
14 I use the term 'sympathy', rather than the oft-used empathy, for two reasons: first, that the distinction in circumstances, histories and traditions of the 'oppressed' in non-Western societies and Marxists in Western societies means that it is difficult, *precisely*, to understand and comprehend the emotions of others; second, that often the emphasis lies, not in mere comprehension but, rather, in affect, such that Marxists feel and express emotions derived from encountering suffering, but not necessarily the same feelings and emotions experienced by those suffering. It is interesting that the most common example of 'empathy' is actually shared expressions of outrage. It is important that, before validating a claim of empathy, we consider a range of psychological factors in 'empathic' experiences, such as projection and splitting of feelings, as it may be that apparent emotional overlap between two groups conceals the fact that they are affected by events in different ways and for different reasons. Such psychoanalytical understandings of 'empathy' may suggest that the emotions of others are used for personal or political gain, in which case solidarity may shift from having a positive connotation to a rather more negative one.

References

Adamson, W. L. (1981), 'Marx's four histories: an approach to his intellectual development', in B. Jessop and R. Wheatley (eds), (1999), *Karl Marx's Social and Political Thought*, volume 5. New York: Routledge, pp. 537–60.

Anderson, K. B. (2010), *Marx at the Margins: On Nationalism, Ethnicity, and Non-Western Societies*. Chicago, IL: The University of Chicago Press.

Antonio, R. J., (ed.), (2003), *Marx and Modernity: Key Readings and Commentary*. Oxford: Blackwell.

Avineri, S., (ed.), (1969), *Karl Marx: On Colonialism and Modernization*. New York: Anchor.

Bassi, C. (2010) *The Anti-Imperialism of Fools'*, ACME: An International E-Journal for Critical Geographies, 9, 113–37.

Bhatt, C. (2006) *'The Fetish of the Margins: Religious Absolutism, Anti-racism and Postcolonial Silence'*, New Formations, 59, pp. 98–115.

Boron, A. (2005), *Empire and Imperialism: A Critical Reading of Hardt and Negri*. London: Zed Books.

Callinicos, A. (2001), 'Where now?', in E. Bircham and J. Charlton (eds), (2001), *Anti-Capitalism: A Guide to the Movement*. London: Bookmarks, pp. 387–99.

— (2002a), 'Marxism and global governance', in D. Held and A. McGrew (eds), *Governing Globalization: Power, Authority and Global Governance*. Cambridge: Polity, pp. 249–66.

— (2002b), 'The grand strategy of the American Empire', *International Socialism Journal*, [online], 97. Available from: http://pubs.socialistreviewindex.org.uk/isj97/callinicos.htm [Accessed 17 May 2010].

— (2003), *An Anti-Capitalist Manifesto*. Cambridge: Polity.

Chakrabarty, D. (1993), 'Marx after Marxism: history, subalternity, and difference', in B. Jessop and R. Wheatley (eds), (1999), *Karl Marx's Social and Political Thought*, volume 6. New York: Routledge, pp. 223–35.

Cohen, N. (2004), 'The great liberal betrayal', *New Statesman*, 1 November 2004. Available from: http://www.newstatesman.com/200411010022 [Accessed 06 June 2011].

Desai, M. (2004), *Marx's Revenge*. London: Verso.

Guevara, E. and Castro, F. (2002), *Global Justice*. Melbourne: Ocean.

Halliday, F. (2002), 'The pertinence of imperialism', in M. Rupert and H. Smith (eds), *Historical Materialism and Globalization*. London: Routledge.

Hardt, M. and Negri, A. (2001), *Empire*. Cambridge, MA: Harvard University Press.

Harris, N. (2003), *The Return of Cosmopolitan Capital: Globalization, the State and War*. London: I. B. Taurus.

Hegel, G. W. F. (1991), *Lectures on the Philosophy of History*, Amherst, New York: Prometheus.

Katz, C. J. (1990), 'The problems of Europocentrism and evolutionism in Marx's writings on colonialism', in B. Jessop and R. Wheatley (eds), (1999), Karl *Marx's Social and Political Thought*, volume 6. New York: Routledge, pp. 146–63.

Kitching, G. N. (2001), *Seeking Social Justice through Globalization: Escaping a Nationalist Perspective*. University Park, PA: Pennsylvania State University.

Krader, L. (1975), *The Asiatic Mode of Production*. Assen, Holland: Van Gorcum.

Larrain, J. (1991), 'Classical political economists and Marx on colonialism and "backward" nations', in B. Jessop and R. Wheatley (eds), (1999), *Karl Marx's Social and Political Thought*, volume 6. New York: Routledge, pp. 164–95.

Lefort, C. (1978), 'Marx: from one vision of history to another', in B. Jessop and R. Wheatley (eds), (1999), *Karl Marx's Social and Political Thought*, volume 6. New York: Routledge, pp. 83–118.

Lenin, V. I. (1939), *Imperialism: The Highest Stage of Capitalism*. New York: International.

Levin, M. (2004), 'An alternative terminology of development: Engels and Marx on barbarism and civilisation', *Studies in Marxism*, 10, 25–38.

Lichtheim, G. (1963), 'Marx and the "Asiatic mode of production"', in B. Jessop and R. Wheatley (eds), (1999), *Karl Marx's Social and Political Thought*, volume 6. New York: Routledge, pp. 35–58.

Lim, J.-H. (1992), 'Marx's theory of imperialism and the Irish national question', in B. Jessop and R. Wheatley (eds), (1999), *Karl Marx's Social and Political Thought*, volume 6. New York: Routledge, pp. 196–208.

Lipietz, A. (1982), 'Marx or Rostow?', *New Left Review*, 132, 48–58.

Marx, K. (1973), *Grundrisse*. London: Penguin.

— (1976), *Capital*, volume 1. London: Penguin.

— (1981), *Capital*, volume 3. London: Penguin.

— (1992), *Early Writings*. London: Penguin.

Marx, K. and Engels, F. (1967), *The Communist Manifesto*. London: Penguin.

— (1974), *The German Ideology*, 2nd edition. London: Lawrence and Wishart.

McLellan, D. (ed.), (2000), *Karl Marx: Selected Writings*. Oxford: Oxford University Press.

Munck, R. (2002), *Marx@2000*. London: Zed.

Norberg, J. (2003), *In Defence of Global Capitalism*, revised edition. Stockholm: CATO.

Nordahl, R. (1986), 'Marx on evaluating pre-capitalist societies', in B. Jessop and R. Wheatley (eds), (1999), *Karl Marx's Social and Political Thought*, volume 6. New York: Routledge, pp. 1–15.

Phillips, R. (2008), 'Standing together: the Muslim Association of Britain and the anti-war movement', *Race and Class*, 50, 101–13.

Shanin, T., (ed.), (1983), *Late Marx and the Russian Road: Marx and the 'Peripheries of Capitalism'*. New York: Monthly Review Press.

Shaw, W. H. (1979), '"The handmill gives you the feudal lord" Marx's technological determinism', in B. Jessop and R. Wheatley (eds), (1999), *Karl Marx's Social and Political Thought*, volume 5. New York: Routledge, pp. 358–78.

Spier, F. (1996), *The Structure of Big History*. Amsterdam: Amsterdam University Press.

Warren, B. (1980), *Imperialism: Pioneer of Capitalism*. London: Verso.

Žižek, S. (2008), *In Defense of Lost Causes*. London: Verso.

CHAPTER SEVEN

Marx, morality and the global justice debate

Lawrence Wilde

Introduction

Marx is conspicuous by his absence from the burgeoning debate on global justice. Recent summaries of leading contributions, as well as edited collections, barely mention Marx.[1] In the extensive *Global Justice Reader*, edited by Thom Brooks, he fares a little better, but on closer inspection all the references relate to the work of one theorist, Martha Nussbaum (Brooks 2008: 600–18).[2] Nussbaum's use of Marx's philosophy of human potential raises interesting questions about the relationship between liberal approaches to global justice and Marxism, an issue that will be addressed in the final part of the chapter. First, however, I want to deal with the most obvious reason for the neglect of Marx in this field, namely, the hostility he displayed towards moral discourse from 1845 to the end of his life. In this part of the chapter, I argue that this rejection of moral discourse was a tactical choice, contingent on the particular circumstances of the time and no longer appropriate to the circumstances we face today. The second part will argue that there is an ethical viewpoint implicit in Marx's analysis, a eudaemonistic ethics understood as a commitment to self realization through the development of key potentials. The third part will examine how Martha Nussbaum uses

Marx's philosophy to support her capabilities approach to global justice, as set down in *Frontiers of Justice* (2006). I argue that her selective use of Marx could be augmented by a stronger commitment to a project of de-alienation that would require the radical re-regulation of the world economy.

Marx's anti-moralism as a tactical choice

Before 1845, there was a strong moral thrust to Marx's central argument that capitalism is rooted in alienation and has a dehumanizing impact, not only on the working class but also on society as a whole. In *The German Ideology* (1845–6), Marx begins to develop a social science that has no truck with moralizing or indeed with abstract philosophical argument. His impatience with philosophy that does not take into account real social relations in their historical context was evident already in the *Theses on Feuerbach* (1845). Now, on the understanding that it is not consciousness that determines life but life that determines consciousness, morality, along with religion and metaphysics, is treated as epiphenomenal to the development of the social life process (Marx 1976a: 36–7). Having made this general point, Marx goes on to make a number of attacks against individual philosophers for their muddle-headed moralism, and, in an attack on Max Stirner, makes the unequivocal point that 'communists do not preach morality at all' (ibid: 247).

In the *Communist Manifesto* (1848), we find a relativist view of morality whereby all moral, religious and philosophical ideas are seen as reflections of the conditions of material existence, so that 'the ruling ideas of each age have ever been the ideas of its ruling class' (Marx 1976b: 503). Marx anticipates the objection that morality itself has persisted throughout history, despite historical modifications, and therefore if communism rejects 'eternal truths' it runs the risk of acting in contradiction to all past historical experience' (Marx 1976b: 504), but his answer is highly unconvincing. He insists that since all the history of past society has been one of class antagonism, the common forms of consciousness must reflect, in various ways, the exploitative nature of class society. Only with the abolition of class antagonisms can these common forms of consciousness be left behind, so that communism involves the 'most radical rupture with traditional ideas' (Marx 1976b: 504). Marx then abruptly ends the discussion and urges the working class to win the battle for democracy. What we are left with here is an approach that feels free to criticize all moral judgements on the grounds that they reflect particular material interests, but resolutely refuses to be drawn on its own moral position. Nevertheless it should at least be conceded that the communist society of the future will have its own moral principles. At one stage in the third volume of *Capital*, Marx projects one aspect of what a communist moral viewpoint would look like, when he states that the private ownership of land will come to be regarded as just as absurd as the idea of slavery appears to us in liberal society (Marx 1981: 911). However, this is an isolated instance of thinking about what a socialist morality might look like, and Marx in general abjures from discussing how a revolutionary moral consciousness might develop. Instead, all is left to the revolutionary struggle, informed by theoretical analyses of the economic and political conditions.

It is not hard to gauge the reasons for Marx's moral reticence. Put briefly, socialist arguments based on moral objections to unfairness or exclusion run the risk of blocking the emergence of analyses of the conditions confronted by the working class, and such analyses were vital to identifying the most propitious ways of organizing and intervening politically. At this relatively early time in the development of socialist thought, most of the contributions were moralistic or utopian, setting down ideal alternatives without due consideration of how revolutionary social movements could develop under existing conditions and circumstances. Marx wanted to move beyond the twin postures of outrage and yearning, towards developing a better understanding of what was possible under given conditions and circumstances. However, it is important to recognize that Marx was making a tactical choice in shunning moral argument, rather than repudiating the idea that the struggle for socialism has a moral dimension. In other words, his denunciation of specific moral positions should not be taken to mean that all moral utterances are nonsense.

An example of Marx denouncing bad moralizing without rejecting the validity of all moral thinking as such can be found in those parts of the *Critique of the Gotha Programme* in which the German Social Democratic Party claims for all members of society 'an equal right to the undiminished proceeds of labour' and 'a just distribution of the proceeds of labour' (Marx 1974: 341–7). On the 'just distribution' argument, Marx repeats his relativist position by stating that the bourgeoisie would claim that the present system of distribution is just and that they would be right to do so within the present relations of production (Marx 1974: 344). However, Marx makes it clear that by 'just' he refers to a legal concept of right, thereby leaving open the possibility that it may be considered unjust by some socialist standard that anticipates a post-capitalist future. The argument against the 'equal right to undiminished proceeds' is simply that if all people had equal right, that would include those who do not work, and if that was the case then the proceeds of labour would not be 'undiminished'. Marx then goes on to make a number of points about how part of the proceeds of labour must be set aside for public services, including looking after those who are not able to work. Marx terms these demands 'obsolete verbal rubbish' (Marx 1974: 347), but this judgement is quite specific to the cases discussed and should not be construed as a general repudiation of morality *per se*. Not only does Marx concede that ideas of this sort may have 'made sense' at a particular time, but he also endorses a principle of distributive justice for the *future* communist society, already well established in socialist circles – 'from each according to ability to each according to needs' (Marx 1974: 347).

Along with his aversion to moral discourse, then, is an acknowledgement that moral statements can make sense and that moral ideals are an inevitable part of class struggle. When he wrote the Provisional Rules of the First International in 1864, he included a commitment that the members of the International 'will acknowledge truth, justice and morality, as the basis of their conduct towards each other and towards all men, without regard to colour, creed or nationality', followed by a claim for the rights and duties of man and citizen (Marx 1974: 82–3). In a letter to Engels, Marx reveals that he had been 'obliged' to insert these sentences by the sub-committee, adding that 'these are so placed that they can do no harm' (Marx 1987: 18). So, although he would not have adopted this language if left to his own devices, he was quite willing to put his name to these moral commitments. Indeed, in his own Inaugural Address to the International, he urged the working class to oppose the predatory foreign policies of the various governments, in order to 'vindicate the simple laws of morals and justice' which ought to govern both relations between individuals and relations between states (Marx 1974: 81).

Marx never denied that workers were motivated by ideals, despite the passage in *The Civil War in France* in which he argues that the working class did not expect miracles from the Paris Commune and were not trying to introduce a ready-made utopia overnight. He claims that the workers 'have no ideals to realize, but to set free the elements of the new society with which old collapsing bourgeois society itself is pregnant' (Marx 1974: 213). Geras has interpreted this to mean that Marx denied that the workers had ideals at all (Geras 1986: 55), but if we read the 'but' in the sentence as 'except' then it becomes clear that setting free elements of the new society from the status quo is just such an ideal, an ideal of emancipation. This becomes apparent in the relevant passage of the first draft, in which Marx argues that from the moment the workers' struggle became real, the 'fantastic utopias evanesced, not because the working class had given up the end aimed at by these Utopians, but because they had found the real means to realize them' (Marx 1974: 262). It is perfectly clear from this that Marx acknowledges that the workers have ideals, and indeed in the closing paragraph of *The Civil War in France*, Marx declares that the martyrs of the Commune will become part of the collective memory of the working class, fired by outrage against those responsible for their deaths, who will be 'nailed to that eternal pillory from which all the prayers of their priests will not avail to redeem them' (Marx 1974: 233).

Marx chose to downplay moral argument because he considered that it would detract from the imperative tasks of analysing the contradictions of capitalism and formulating an effective political strategy. Yet even if we accept Marx's moral relativism, we are still entitled to ponder what precepts of justice would be appropriate to communist society, and, furthermore, we should be able to identify how those feelings for justice are developing in late capitalism. Marx did not consider it important to dwell on such issues in the nineteenth century, instead relying on a conviction – indeed a faith – that the working class would achieve a consciousness of its own position and create effective revolutionary movements. Despite his frequent observations about competition among the workers, the baleful effects of national and racial prejudice and the moderating effects of parliamentary politics, he had an unwavering conviction that working class political action would replace capitalist society with communist society. Implicitly, there was an assumption that socialist consciousness would grow in step with the growth of the proletariat and its organizations. These hopes have not materialized, and, furthermore, the failure to realize Marx's injunction in the eleventh of the *Theses on Feuerbach* to change the world should prompt a critical reappraisal of his rejection of philosophy and morality. As Adorno (1990: 3) rightly comments at the outset of *Negative Dialectics*, not to do so would constitute 'a defeatism of reason'. Such reappraisal is made all the more urgent by the fact that, in the twentieth century, Marxist movements actually adopted a default moral position of 'the end justifies the means' without any serious consideration of either means or ends, with disastrous consequences, as Steven Lukes argues in *Marxism and Morality* (Lukes 1985: 100–38). Marx's work provides a rich resource for the development of arguments that disclose global exploitation not simply as the manifestation of global class struggle, but also as global injustice. Struggles for economic re-regulation are also struggles for human freedom. It is incumbent on those who accept the truth of Marx's analysis of capitalism and who share the normative goals that are clearly present in his work, to engage in this moral discourse. The moral debate is also a political debate, and, through the process of 'normative framing', radical forces in civil society can mount a serious challenge to neoliberalism. If Marxists have only negative criticisms to offer in relation to the arguments about global justice, they will effectively be adopting the sort of 'political indifferentism' which Marx condemned the anarchists for at the time of the First International (Marx 1974: 327–32).

Marx's implicit eudaemonistic ethics

Having established that Marx's hostility to moral discourse does not involve a rejection of morality *per se*, the question arises as to what sort of ethics can be extracted from Marx's work. What is clear is that there is plenty to work with, for his analysis of capitalism is replete with morally committed references to the extraction of surplus value as robbing, stealing, embezzling or 'pumping booty' out of the workers, and elsewhere as theft and loot (see Peffer 1990: 145). The literature on the implicit ethics of Marx is extensive and has been expertly reviewed by Rodney Peffer in *Marxism, Morality, and Social Justice* (1990), where he identifies two approaches. The first is to attempt to reconstruct Marx's own moral viewpoint, making explicit what is implicit in his work. The second is to re-frame Marx's social theory through the lens of existing moral theories such as Kantianism or utilitarianism; Peffer himself constructs a Marxist moral theory along the lines of Rawls's theory of justice. This second approach has the merits of opening a dialogue with mainstream moral philosophy, but loses the richness of Marx's original perspectives, developed out of his immersion in the ethics of Ancient Greece. So, I opt for the first approach, and, following scholars such as John Somerville, Alan Nasser, Hilliard Aronovitch and Richard Miller (discussed in Peffer 1990: 100–6), argue that Marx's implicit moral position remains as it was in the early writings, firmly in the eudaemonistic tradition (Wilde 1998: 1–50).[3] What is required here is a clarification of what Marx considered human beings in capitalism to be alienated from in order to illuminate his normative conception of human emancipation.

The alienation thesis is the *leitmotif* of the *Economic and Philosophical Writings*. Marx bemoans the fact that work is experienced as deadening compulsion, with the worker feeling free only in functions such as eating, drinking and making love, which, taken abstractly, are animal functions (Marx 1975: 275). The fact that these functions are shared with animals does not mean that they are not also human needs which are being met, but clearly for Marx there must be more to human life than this. In discussing alienation from species-being, Marx elaborates on the difference between humans and animals, much as Aristotle had done when discussing human essence (he had just translated Aristotle's *De Anima* – 'On the Soul' – into German). According to Marx, 'conscious life activity' distinguishes humans from animals, for whereas animals are 'immediately one' with their life activity, humans make their life activity the object of their will and consciousness. This emphasis on rational planning of our 'activity' is followed by a sharper focus on the human capacity for social production, creating products for each other in a consciously planned way. 'It is just because of this that he is a species-being', comments Marx, a conscious being for whom 'his own life is an object for him' and 'his activity free activity'. His argument is that by creating a world of objects, humans prove themselves to be conscious species-beings, or, in other words, they demonstrate their essence. Animals too produce, but only for what they or their young immediately need; they produce only to meet their immediate physical need, while man produces even when he is free from physical need. Indeed truly free production occurs only when immediate needs are taken care of, and humans gain knowledge of how to produce in accordance with the standard of every species and how to produce what we think of as beautiful (Marx 1975: 276–7). In other words, animals can adapt to their environment by changing themselves – autoplasticity – but humans can change the environment – alloplasticity. However, under alienation, the objective demonstration of human essence is contradicted by the subjective experience of the mass of producers, who are condemned to adaptation rather than self realization.

Like Aristotle, Marx holds firm to the idea that we are fundamentally social beings. He expresses this at length in the *Economic and Philosophical Manuscripts* and reiterates it in the *Grundrisse* and the first volume of *Capital* by quoting Aristotle's conception of man as a *zoon politikon*. Marx therefore conceives human essence as conscious and social life activity, but with the development of alienated labour our human essence is deformed into nothing more than a means to our existence. He talks about workers losing their freedom 'in the service of greed', becoming 'depressed spiritually and physically to the condition of a machine' (Marx 1975: 237–8), a metaphor that recurs in the *Manifesto* and also in the first volume of *Capital* (Marx 1976b: 490–1; Marx 1976c: 799). Although the roots of alienation are located in the purchase and sale of labour power, the malaise is not confined to the world of work. Rather the perversion of human potential is achieved through the medium of money, raised to a position of omnipotence, where it confounds and confuses 'all natural human qualities' and turns the world upside down (Marx 1975: 326). It is not only workers who are alienated in the despotism that is the money economy, but it is also the entire society. The task of the communists is to lead society away from this alienation, so that our essential human potentials can be realized. Communism is the 'real appropriation of the human essence by and for man' and 'the return of man to himself as a social being' (Marx 1975: 296).

Paradoxically, while capitalism denies human self realization to those dependent on the sale of their labour power, it simultaneously exhibits the immense capacity of human creativity. The development of industry demonstrates the 'open book of man's essential powers' while at the same time it furthers the 'dehumanization of man' (Marx 1975: 302–3). This conception of dehumanization is present throughout Marx's works, as a loss to be recovered through social struggles. In order to combat it, a communist consciousness must develop in revolutionary activity, through which the working class rids itself 'of all the muck of ages and becomes fitted to found society anew' (Marx 1976a: 52–3). The exploitation of the worker is seen as the deprivation of the worker's social creativity, its perversion into a form of wage slavery, to be redeemed only through revolutionary transformation that will deliver what he envisions in the third volume of *Capital* as the 'true realm of freedom, the development of human powers as an end in itself'. In this projection real freedom can be developed only when producers have full control over the process of production and work-time has been minimized (Marx 1981: 959). The goal is one of self realization, where the self is understood always as a social self (Marx 1973: 611–12; Wilde 1998: 24–9).

Perhaps the clearest indication of Marx's awareness of the centrality of human essence to moral judgement occurs in a footnote in the first volume of *Capital* in which he derides Bentham for applying the principle of utility to human needs without first specifying a theory of 'human nature in general'. Marx, of course, recognized that human nature is also constantly in the process of being 'historically modified', but here he explicitly endorses a eudaemonistic conception of a distinctive human essence. He makes a comparison with the animal world, stating that just as 'to know what is useful for a dog one must investigate the nature of dogs', so too we must consider the nature of humans (Marx 1976c: 758–9n). For all that Marx emphasizes the changing historical dynamics of human needs, he maintains this Aristotelian commitment to human nature 'in general' as both descriptive and normative, looking forward to a future in which alienation is overcome and human potential can be realized to the full by all the peoples of the world. Marx, of course, never developed these insights into an ethical theory, but it is possible to do so, and I have argued elsewhere that the ethical work of Erich Fromm is the closest we have to a developed eudaemonistic ethics in the Marxist tradition (Wilde 2004, 2007; Fromm 2002, 2003). From this 'radical humanist' perspective, moral progress can be assessed – and struggled for – according to the positive development of our potentials for reason, productive work, care and solidarity. Such an approach carries similarities with the capabilities approach to global justice developed by Nussbaum.

The capabilities approach

Nussbaum first sets down her account of the basic human functions in a long polemical article in *Political Theory* in 1992 entitled 'Human Functioning and Aristotelian Justice: In Defence of Aristotelian Essentialism'. At the head of the article is a quotation from Marx's *Economic and Philosophical Manuscripts* in which he extols the virtue of the rich human being in need of the totality of human life, for whom self realization exists as an inner necessity and for whom the greatest wealth is the *other* human being (Nussbaum 1992a: 202, cf. Marx 1975: 304). She introduces her argument by recounting experiences at conferences at which papers by postmodernists defended a variety of traditional cultural practices that would be intuitively deplored by defenders of human rights. The postmodernist view maintained that we should respect the traditions of others, having no right to impose western values or make essentialist judgements about those traditions. At one such event the Marxist historian Eric Hobsbawm responded with a blistering attack on this cultural relativism and was angrily asked to leave the room. Nussbaum objects that these anti-essentialist postmodernists are 'people who think of themselves as progressive and feminist and antiracists', but 'are taking up positions that converge, as Hobsbawm correctly saw, with the positions of reaction, oppression and sexism' (Nussbaum 1992a: 204). She adds that in her own essentialist way she commits to life over death, freedom over slavery, nutrition over starvation and knowledge over ignorance. Here she makes common cause with a Marxist committed to 'a determinate conception of human need and human flourishing' resolutely opposed to what she then termed 'the new subjectivism' (Nussbaum 1992a: 212).

Nussbaum then, exasperated by the sanctification of difference, wants to emphasize what we share in common as human beings. Capabilities are regarded as what people are able to 'do' and to 'be' (Nussbaum 2000: 71; Nussbaum 2006: 70). Her purpose is to identify the most important human functions so that we can make demands on our social and political institutions for their promotion (Nussbaum 1992a: 214). She lists ten 'functional capabilities' in the 1992a article (Nussbaum 1992a: 215) that are substantially retained in later works, in particular *Women and Human Development* (Nussbaum 2000: 78–80) and *Frontiers of Justice* (Nussbaum 2006: 71–6). Table 1 is a summary of her human capabilities, using the headings adopted in the two books:

Table 1 Nussbaum's capabilities

1. *Life.* Being able to lead a full life.

2. *Bodily Health.* Being able to have good health.

3. *Bodily Integrity.* Being able to have physical security, sexual satisfaction and choice about reproduction.

4. *Senses, Imagination and Thought.* Being able to use the senses in a truly human way through education and guarantees of free expression.

5. *Emotions.* Being able to develop our emotions of love, grieving, longing and gratitude.

6. *Practical Reason.* Being able to form a conception of the good and to plan one's own life.

7. *Affiliation.* Being able to live with and for others. Being free from discrimination on the basis of race, sex, sexual orientation, ethnicity, caste, religion or national origin.

8. *Other Species.* Being able to live with concern for animals, plants and the world of nature.

9. *Play.* Being able to laugh and play.

10. *Control Over One's Environment.* Being able to participate politically, being able to hold property on an equal basis with others and being able to work with meaningful relationships of recognition with other workers.

It should be noted that two of the capabilities, practical reason and affiliation, are held to play a special, architectonic, role, holding the project together and making it human.

In proposing her capabilities approach, Nussbaum is determined to stay within the camp of political liberalism, and she sees her contribution as complementary to contractarian and human rights perspectives (Nussbaum 2006: 7). She emphasizes that the approach builds in a respect for pluralism in a number of ways. The list is open-ended and subject to revision, and its abstract and general nature allows for different applications of the same principles. In the most recent version, she is careful to specify that she is talking about capability rather than functioning, so that people may be enabled to do something but may not necessarily choose to do it. For example, a person may have the right to vote but may choose not to participate in the particular polity in which they reside for various reasons. She gives the major liberties of speech, association and conscience 'a central and non-negotiable place', but she also insists that, while her approach provides a good basis for global political principles, it is not intended to justify implementation by force or sanctions (Nussbaum 2006: 78–80).

Why, then, does she consider the capabilities approach superior to that of the contractarian approach? In one sense she is trying to take care of issues which Rawls himself admits are not dealt with adequately by his approach, namely, what is owed to people with disabilities, what is owed to animals, the problem of justice across national boundaries and the problem of saving for future generations (Nussbaum 2006: 23; Rawls 1996: 21). These problems flow from the setting up of the framing of the contract, whereby the framers are considered to be more or less equal abstract individuals within a nation state who are also going to be the recipients of the justice outcome. However, the key moral element that Nussbaum is unhappy with is the presupposition that the pursuit of mutual advantage is the justification for social cooperation. Supporters of contractarianism would view this is a strength because it provides rational grounds to support whatever agreements are reached, where rationality is assumed to equate with narrowly conceived self interest. In other words, it dispenses with altruism, which is intuitively taken to be irrational and simply too demanding. Although versions of the contractarian approach try to build in consideration of others to avoid egoism, the ghost of Hobbes continues to haunt all contractarianism. Nussbaum comments that the pursuit of mutual advantage is not 'less' than a compassionate commitment to the well being of others, 'it is just different', and she considers that adopting the 'parsimonious' starting point of mutual advantage is likely to lead in a different direction than an 'other-committed' starting point (Nussbaum 2006: 35). Nussbaum's intuition here is that this ruling out of sociability and benevolence as a part of what it is to be human leads rather too easily to an acceptance that humans are by nature egoistic utility maximizers. As an Aristotle scholar, she prefers a different starting point, that we are by nature social beings, and she finds support in this view from the young Marx.

On the specific issues of global justice, Nussbaum begins by describing the gross inequalities between the peoples of rich and poor countries (Nussbaum 2006: 224–5). She is sceptical of the efforts of contractarian theorists to deal with this issue. Rawls admits that his original position does not translate to the global sphere, and when Beitz (1999) and Pogge (1989) try to extend it, they ignore the 'circumstances of justice' assumptions that are crucial to the origin of the contract (Nussbaum 2006: 268).[4] The capabilities approach endeavours to identify human needs that have to be met, in a variety of ways depending on cultural difference, if we are to create a more just world. In terms of advancing the development of her capabilities to a minimum threshold, Nussbaum develops another list, this time specifying ten principles to guide our pursuit of global justice:

Table 2 Nussbaum's ten principles for the global structure

1. Overdetermination of responsibility: the domestic never escapes it. All nations, rich and poor, must take responsibility to promote human capabilities up to some reasonable threshold level.

2. National sovereignty should be respected, within the constraints of promoting human capabilities.

3. Prosperous nations have a responsibility to give a substantial portion of their GDP to poorer nations.

4. Multinational corporations have responsibilities for promoting human capabilities in the regions in which they operate.

5. The main structures of the global economic order must be designed to be fair to poor and developing countries.

6. We should cultivate a thin, decentralized and yet forceful global sphere.

7. All institutions and (most) individuals should focus on the problems of the disadvantaged in each nation and region.

8. Care for the ill, the elderly, children and the disabled should be a prominent focus of the world community.

9. The family should be treated as a sphere that is precious but not 'private'.

10. All institutions and individuals have a responsibility to support education, as key to the empowerment of currently disadvantaged people.

(Nussbaum 2006: 315–24)

The contentious issue is the extent to which these principles seek only to ameliorate current distress rather than confront the structural causes of oppression.

Nussbaum's approach reflects her Aristotelian heritage, with the emphasis on good functioning leading to *eudaemonia* or human flourishing, but she also draws also on Marx and assumes an affinity between the two philosophers. In a collection edited by George McCarthy, *Marx and Aristotle*, Nussbaum outlines the Aristotelian basis of the emphasis on function and capability, and at the end of her article, originally presented in 1986, she points out the similarities with the views on fully human functioning expressed by Marx in the *Economic and Philosophical Manuscripts*, citing the passage in which Marx points to the different conceptions of food held by a starving man and one who eats for sensual enjoyment (Nussbaum 1992b: 204–5). The point here is that the capability to function in a truly human way, in this case to express discernment and taste, cannot be fulfilled by those deprived of the requisite material resources. Nussbaum cites Geoffrey de Sainte Croix's *The Class Struggle in the Ancient Greek World* in support of the view that Marx was strongly influenced by Aristotle in the development of his theory of class struggle. She also argues that Marx shifts allegiance from the Hellenistic philosophers (particularly Epicurus) to Aristotle around 1844 (Nussbaum 1992b: 211n47) as part of a move towards a total commitment to political activism. Whereas Epicurus preached withdrawal from public life, Aristotle charged us to make our social institutions consonant with justice (Nussbaum 1994: 11).

Broadly speaking there are two aspects of the young Marx's humanist philosophy that she commends. First there is the commitment to the idea of truly human functioning, involving a wide range of human life activities (Nussbaum 2006: 74). As essentially rational beings we need to exercise our human potentials, and a life reduced to survival is stripped of its humanity. Nussbaum argues that the capabilities approach shares with Aristotle and Marx the view that it is tragic waste when people are not enabled to develop (Nussbaum 2006: 346–7). She also credits Marx's understanding of humans as creatures in need of 'the plurality of life activities', seeing rationality as only one of our functions, and respecting the fact that we share other functions with other animals (Nussbaum 2006: 159–60). In general then, Nussbaum takes from the young Marx the appreciation of 'rich human need', prominently including needs for other people (Nussbaum 2006: 132).

This conception of humans as quintessentially social beings is the second insight she takes from Marx, as well as Aristotle:

the capabilities approach takes its start from the Aristotelian/Marxian conception of the human being as a social and political being, who finds fulfilment in relation with others. Whereas contractarians typically think of the family as 'natural', and the political as in some significant sense artificial, the capabilities approach makes no such distinction (Nussbaum 2006: 85–6).

One of the most important of what Marx termed 'rich human needs' is the need for others (Nussbaum 2006: 132). In *Women and Human Development* Nussbaum refers to a discussion of Marx's view on human nature by Daniel Brudney, which draws attention to the significance of reciprocity in Marx's vision (Brudney 1997: 388–99). The most relevant passages are those from the *Comments on James Mill* when Marx talks about production in communist society 'as human beings', when our production doubly affirms both the producer and the recipient. Marx talks about the satisfaction that the producer would feel in knowing that their products were enjoyed by others, and, in that knowledge, grasping our communality as a completion of our nature (Marx 1975: 227–8). This insight, with its emphasis on the liberating implications of working in a way that arouses awareness of our deep complementarity, is very important for Nussbaum. In her final chapter, she emphasizes the need to cultivate our moral sentiments through education and culture (Nussbaum 2006: 408–15), and this is very much in line with her previous work on the role of art and literature in creating a more human world and about the development of the emotions (Nussbaum 1992c; Nussbaum 2001).

Although she shares Marx's commitment to the fulfilment of human potentials, Nussbaum eschews reliance on any 'deep metaphysics of human nature' which she regards as incompatible with political liberalism (Nussbaum 2006: 86). She insists that she uses the Marxian idea of truly human functioning 'for political purposes only, not as the source of a comprehensive doctrine of human life', adding that Marx made no such distinction (Nussbaum 2006: 74). We may ask why Nussbaum considers the stronger version of human freedom inimical to her substantive goal. It could be argued that this distancing herself from the 'deeper' view of what it is to be human makes it more difficult to ground her own list of capabilities, which might otherwise be considered subjective and arbitrary. After all, she has moved away from moral justification based on mutual advantage and therefore needs to answer the question as to *why* people should be moved to support these capabilities. Nussbaum's reluctance to support a strong view of human nature reflects an anxiety to preserve a commitment to openness to change or flexibility, but it appears to be a retreat from the spirited defence of essentialism contained in the *Political Theory* 1992 article.

A constructive Marxist criticism

In using Marx to justify her entitlement thesis, Nussbaum expresses *only* his positive view of what liberated humanity could be, setting to one side the alienation thesis from which this view is taken. Marx is primarily concerned to show that capitalist relations of production distort human relations and de-humanize the producers. A radical humanist perspective grounded in a Marxian ethical framework would point up the structural obstacles to the fulfilment of human potentials, without using that analytical insight to reject the possibility of any progress towards social justice in the conditions which confront us today. The elucidation and demand for human potentials is a worthy goal, and one that is more consonant with non-Western ethical approaches, but its association with political liberalism is in deep tension with liberalism's attachment to private property. Nussbaum's approach is having a practical impact on UN development strategy in pursuit of the UN Millennium Goals, but the danger is that the demands for fulfilment can become detached from the political imperative of challenging the fundamental direction of global economic governance.[5]

The radical humanist perspective on global justice is concerned that Nussbaum's approach pays inadequate attention to the structural causes of the injustice she wants to redress. This is evident when we look at Nussbaum's principles for the global structure. Although Nussbaum's aims are clearly designed to redress world poverty, some of the principles indicate an unwillingness to confront the structural causes of that poverty. For example, the third principle asserts the need for rich states to give money to the poor, but it does not make the point that 'their' GDPs have grown from the exploitation of the poor. It reads like a moral appeal to charity rather than a 'pay back' demand, and, on this issue of moral responsibility for global poverty; Pogge's negative rights approach and his suggestion for a Global Resources Dividend is more convincing (Pogge 2002). The fourth principle demands that multinationals have responsibilities for promoting human capabilities in the regions where they operate. But what does this mean? All the major global corporations have codes of ethics, and no doubt their spokespersons would claim that they take their responsibilities very seriously, but in practice this is not what they are in business for, and self regulation has been wholly inadequate (Fisher and Lovell 2008). The principle should not be to ask them to accept responsibility, but to insist on it through regulation. Although the fifth principle calls for the main structures of the world economy to be designed to be fair to poor and developing countries, it does not mention how the issue of power in those institutions that control those structures is to be met. And even if some of the glaring inequities were to be removed, such as the huge subsidies employed by the United States and the European Union, what is to prevent global corporations dominating the economies of those poorer states? The 'fairness' demanded would require a level of regulation much more authoritative than that envisaged in the 'thin' global sphere referred to in the sixth principle.

These criticisms of the 'Principles of the Global Structure' are not intended to damn the capabilities approach to global justice. The radical humanism I advocate is not averse to the ethical universalism of Nussbaum, and shares her view of the ethical significance of Marx's conception of the self-realized social being. It also shares her critical observations on the 'mutual advantage' assumptions about human motivation adopted by contractarians since Hobbes. However, although she clearly sees her approach as offering a less 'cynical' view of human nature than that implicit in the contractarian reliance on 'mutual advantage' (Nussbaum 2006: 414), she leaves unanswered the question of the relationship between political liberalism and economic liberalism. Nussbaum, in common with most liberal political theorists, tends to conflate liberalism and democracy, using liberalism in a purely political sense without delving too deeply into its intimate attachment to private property. In doing so she avoids the big questions about how a democratic political culture can emerge to promote human capabilities, if to do so runs against the interests of global corporate capital. Nussbaum has promised to discuss *how* we might develop the resources to advance the normative goals of the capabilities approach in a forthcoming study, *Capabilities and Compassion*, and perhaps then we will be able to form a clearer picture of the distance between her approach and more radical, anti-systemic perspectives.

Notes

1   More precisely, there is one throwaway reference in Simon Caney's *Justice Beyond Borders* (Caney 2005), a single mention in Charles Jones's *Global Justice* (Jones 2001), none at all in Kok-Chor Tan's *Justice Without Borders* (Tan 2004), and two passing remarks in the collections of articles edited by William Sullivan and Will Kymlicka, *The Globalization of Ethics* (Sullivan and Kymlikca 2007) and by Pabo De Greiff and Ciaran Cronin, *Global Justice and Transnational Politics*(De Greiff and Cronin 2002) .

2   Since *The Global Justice Reader* appeared in 2008, Amartya Sen's *The Idea of Justice* has appeared, and he makes use of Marx in a rather different way (Sen 2009: 163–4; 245). Sen, like Nussbaum, operates a capabilities approach.

3   Lukes accepts that there is 'much evidence' to support the view that Marx was implicitly committed 'to an aristotelian realization of distinctively human potentialities and excellences' (Lukes 1985: 87)

4   Nussbaum does not discuss Pogge's negative rights approach adopted in *World Poverty and Human Development* (2002), which demands that we take moral responsibility for the structure of the world economy that systematically deprives people of their rights.

5   Nussbaum's contribution has been criticized from a postcolonialist perspective which invokes Marx structural analysis of the economy, but goes further in rejecting her essentialism, which I do not. See Charusheela (2009).

References

Adorno, T. (1990), *Negative Dialectics*. London: Routledge.
Beitz, C. (1999), *Political Theory and International Relations*, 2nd edition. Princeton, NJ: Princeton University Press.

Brookes, T. (2008), *The Global Justice Reader*. Oxford: Blackwell.

Brudney, D. (1997), 'Community and completion', in A. Reath, B. Herman and C. Korsgaard (eds), *Reclaiming the History of Ethics: Essays for John Rawls*. Cambridge, Cambridge University Press, pp. 388–415.

Caney, S. (2005), *Justice Beyond Borders: A Global Political Theory*. Oxford: Oxford University Press.

Charusheela, S. (2009), 'Social analysis and the capabilities approach: a limit to Martha Nussbaum's universalist ethics', *Cambridge Journal of Economics*, 33, 1135–52.

De Grieff, P. and Cronin, C. (2002), *Global Justice and Transnational Politics*. Cambridge, MA: MIT Press.

Fisher, C. and Lovell, C. (2008), *Business Ethics and Values: Individual, Corporate and International Perspectives*. London: Financial Times/Prentice Hall.

Fromm, E. (2002), *To Have or To Be?*. New York: Continuum.

—(2003), *Man for Himself: An Inquiry Into The Psychology of Ethics*. London: Routledge.

Geras, N. (1986), *Literature of Revolution: Essays on Marxism*. London: Verso.

Jones, C. (2001), *Global Justice: Defending Cosmopolitanism*. Oxford: Oxford University Press.

Lukes, S. (1985), *Marxism and Morality*. Oxford: Clarendon Press.

Marx, K. (1973), *Grundrisse*. Harmondsworth: Penguin.

— (1974), *The First International and After*. Harmondsworth: Penguin.

— (1975), *Collected Works*, volume 3. London: Lawrence and Wishart.

— (1976a), *Collected Works*, volume 5. London: Lawrence and Wishart.

— (1976b), *Collected Works*, volume 6. London: Lawrence and Wishart.

— (1976c), *Capital*, volume 1. Harmondsworth: Penguin.

— (1981), *Capital*, volume 3. Harmondsworth: Penguin.

— (1987), *Collected Works*, volume 42. London: Lawrence and Wishart.

Nussbaum, M. C. (1992a), 'Human functioning and social justice: in defence of Aristotelian essentialism', *Political Theory*, 20, (2), 202–46.

— (1992b), 'Nature, function, and capability: Aristotle on political distribution', in G. E. McCarthy (ed.), *Marx and Aristotle: Nineteenth-Century German Social Theory and Classical Antiquity*. Savage, MD: Rowman and Littlefield.

— (1992c), *Love's Knowledge: Essays on Philosophy and Literature*. New York, Oxford University Press.

— (1994), *The Therapy of Desire: Theory and Practice in Hellenistic Ethics*. Princeton, NJ: Princeton University Press.

— (2000), *Women and Human Development: The Capabilities Approach*. Cambridge: Cambridge University Press.

— (2001), *Upheavals of Thought: The Intelligence of Emotions*. Cambridge: Cambridge University Press.

— (2006), *Frontiers of Justice: Disability, Nationality, Species Membership*. Cambridge, MA: Harvard University Press.

Peffer, R. G. (1990), *Marxism, Morality and Justice*. Princeton: Princeton University Press.

Pogge, T. (1989), *Realizing Rawls*. Ithaca, NY: Cornel University Press.

— (2002), *World Poverty and Human Rights*, 1st edition. Cambridge: Polity.

Rawls, J. (1996), *Political Liberalism*. New York: Columbia University Press.

Sen, A. (2009), *The Idea of Justice*. London: Allen Lane Penguin.

Sullivan, W. and Kymicka, W. (2007), *The Globalization of Ethics*. Cambridge: Cambridge University Press.
Tan, K.-C. (2004), *Justice Without Borders: Cosmopolitanism, Nationalism and Patriotism*. Cambridge: Cambridge University Press.
Wilde, L. (1998), *Ethical Marxism and its Radical Critics*. Basingstoke: Macmillan.
— (2004), *Erich Fromm and the Quest for Solidarity*. New York, Palgrave.
— (2007), 'The ethical Challenge of Touraine's "Living Together"', *Journal of Global Ethics*, 3, (1), 39–53.

CHAPTER EIGHT

Can Marxism make sense of crime?

Mark Cowling

Introduction

The aim of this chapter is to present an overview of the obvious possibilities in using Marxism to make sense of criminological theory. A brief explanation for non-criminologists: criminological theory typically comprises one central part of criminology degrees, the other central part comprises an account of the criminal justice system. Criminological theory looks at theories which purport to explain what is crime and why people commit it. The rest of this introduction discusses issues involved in identifying crime. The main substance of this chapter is a discussion of a series of ways in which Marxism as a social theory might be used in order to make sense of crime. The sections of the chapter correspond to the possibilities I consider: the idea of the lumpenproletariat as the criminal class; possible links between the theory of alienation and crime; crime or the criminal justice system as a reproduction condition of capitalism; the Marxist account of law as the basis for making sense of crime; an analysis based on a Marxist account of distributive justice but linked to an account of criminal justice; and finally the question of whether crime would disappear under communism.

The identification of crime is quite a complicated issue. Typical dictionary definitions refer on the one hand to an act punishable by law and on the other to an act which causes serious harm. It takes only a moment's thought to recognize that these are by no means always fully aligned. At minimum, victimless crimes such as those associated with prostitution and the imbibing of drugs should perhaps be decriminalized, and various activities which are currently not treated as criminal should perhaps be made illegal. A notable example of a crime which is not effectively prosecuted under English law is the war crime of invading other countries without just cause, which is much more harmful than the low-level street crime recorded by the Home Office. The concept of crime is notoriously slippery because crimes come and go: damaging Westminster Bridge and pretending to be a Chelsea pensioner are no longer capital offences. This leads many criminologists, but particularly those on the left, to argue that 'crime has no ontological reality'. They use examples such as that killing people in time of war can be seen as commendable, or that rape within marriage was legal until 1991 in England to claim that pretty much anything can be criminalized or de-criminalized. Marx, Engels and Bonger are then accused of excessive reliance on official statistics. Although I am generally sympathetic to many of the projects and claims of left-wing criminologists, I do not accept this claim. Instead I prefer the idea of a pyramid of crime (see Hagan 1994: 12) in which murder, robbery and rape are deemed basically criminal in pretty much any society. A society in which these were fully decriminalized would be one where life is nasty, brutish and short. As you go down, the pyramid matters become more flexible. The most flexible crimes are those based on paternalism, morality and religion. Even below this come activities that are legal, but generally seen as inappropriate, such as making romantic gestures to your mother-in-law. It is certainly possible to go in the opposite direction from general decriminalization and criminalize virtually anything. Life under the Taliban would be a good illustration of this. Television, alcohol, pork, homosexuality, sex outside marriage, education for women, going out in public unless dressed in a burka and accompanied by a male relative for women, shaving for men were all made illegal, so that all the main forms of entertainment in advanced Western societies were not permitted.

Given the length of time since its main theories were worked out, it is not surprising that some aspects of Marxism no longer work very well. A version of Marxism, which I think works, uses the ideas of informationalism proposed by Manuel Castells as the economic base for historical materialism (see Castells 1996; 2000; 2004; Castells and Himanen 2004). This then fits with many of the main features of globalization. I do not think the idea of revolution on the Leninist model works any more: all that bloodshed in order to produce a society which eventually collapses is simply no longer attractive. Instead I think that some movement towards a socialist world order is possible given the combined efforts of trade unions, social democratic parties and a motley collection of NGOs and globalization protesters.

The lumpenproletariat

In Marx's theories, class is basically defined in terms of relation to the means of production, but Marx also considers class fractions such as industrial, mercantile or financial capitalism, social categories such as state employees, and a rather miscellaneous grouping of displaced members of various classes who have not yet settled down as workers, the lumpenproletariat. Marx offers three definitions of the lumpenproletariat, the most entertaining of which is:

> From the aristocracy there were bankrupted roués of doubtful means and dubious provenance, from the bourgeoisie there were degenerate wastrels on the take, vagabonds, demobbed soldiers, discharged convicts, runaway galley slaves, swindlers and cheats, thugs, pickpockets, conjurers, card-sharps, pimps, brothel-keepers, porters, day-labourers, organ grinders, scrap dealers, knife grinders, tinkers and beggars, in short the whole amorphous, jumbled mass of flotsam and jetsam that the French term bohemian. (Marx 2002: 77–8)

There are a lot of problems with Marx's account. They do not seem to comprise a coherent social grouping. Some of the above, notably the day-labourers, organ grinders, scrap dealers and knife grinders are potentially respectable self-employed people. Stretching a point, the same could be true of card-sharps, given that there is a substantial and generally legal gambling industry in Britain, and brothel keepers could be seen as sex workers. Marx seems to use his account of the lumpenproletariat as a way of vilifying parts of the proletariat that did not behave in a properly revolutionary fashion. However, subsequent accounts from Franz Fanon (1969) and Mao (1967) suggest that the lumpenproletariat can side with the proletariat. I am therefore inclined to agree with Bovenkirk: 'In their [Marx and Engels'] more theoretical works, their definition of the term lumpenproletariat is unclear and inconsistent. Anyone who tries to base further study upon their interpretation of the term will soon be at his or her wits' end' (Bovenkirk 1984: 37).

Worse still, Marx's account of the lumpenproletariat is strikingly similar to Charles Murray's (1996; 1997; 2000; 2001) account of the underclass. Murray argues that, in essence, the over-generous welfare state in the US and Britain has produced a class summarized by one pair of critics as idle thieving bastards (Bagguley and Mann 1992), and that an important objective of social policy should be to get rid of this grouping. Murray's account is a way of vilifying the victims of the neoliberal policies of Mrs Thatcher and President Reagan. His empirical account of their behaviour is thoroughly dubious. In particular, British people have tended not to get married before having children in recent years, so that about half of British children are now born illegitimate. The values of working, and its rewards in the form of a nice partnership, nice home and happy family life do not seem to have been eroded in spite of more than one generation of unemployment in some parts of Britain (see Bagguley and Mann 1992; Macdonald 1994; Johnson et al. 2000: 26; cf Heath 1997).

Finally on this issue, Marx sees the lumpenproletariat as a natural tool of finance capital, which he sees as particularly degenerate. Even in spite of the horrors of the recent banking crisis, there is surely a role under capitalism for a stock exchange as a mechanism for raising and redistributing money capital and trading in commodities and commodity futures. In Marx's terms, some sort of mechanism is needed to translate uneven rates of extraction of surplus value in different capitalist enterprises into a relatively even rate of profit.

Alienation

Marx's theory of alienation states that people are naturally creative, loving, communal and powerful, but that these features get removed from them and attached instead to their economic life, notably the act and product of labour, religion, the state and philosophy. Because this power is turned against them, people experience themselves as dominated by the other features of social life that I have listed (Marx/Engels Collected Works (MECW), 3: 275, 296). There has been a great deal of controversy over the theory. I subscribe to the idea that it was basically dropped around 1846, and that the older Marx makes use of a fairly thin account of human nature (Cowling 1989; 1995; 2006). The fundamental role of the concept of alienation in his youthful writing is replaced by the concept that the other areas of society are determined by the economy (see Cowling 1989; 2006). This sets me at odds with most British commentators on Marx. To the extent that the idea of alienation persists in the older Marx there is certainly an ambiguity: is he arguing that labour can be made creative, or is he arguing that labour under conditions of advanced capitalism is bound to retain some of the features of alienated labour, and that the objective of a socialist society should be to minimize the amount of labour performed by workers so as to allow them a more creative life outside work? (For a good account of this ambiguity, see Wendling 2009.)

Marx himself does not try to use the concept of alienated labour to make sense of crime. One possible use of the concept is found in the early work of Taylor, Walton and Young, which is that a socialist society would allow people full expression of their sexual nature (Pearson 1975: 164). Perhaps this notion could be linked to the ideas of Fourier, whose socialist utopia included arrangements for full sexual expression (see Fourier 1967). However, this could hardly stretch to rape or sex with children under 10, both of which lack consent and are frequently seriously emotionally damaging. Other forms of sexual expression, notably gay and lesbian sex, seemed to be perfectly compatible with capitalism. There is a lively debate between different conceptions of prostitution, with the abolitionist perspective arguing that prostitution is inherently unacceptable and basically a form of rape, in contrast to which the sex worker perspective understands prostitution as a form of work (see Barry 1995; Jeffreys 1997; Sanders 2004). While the concept of alienation could probably be made to fit these issues, it does not add anything useful to existing debates.

A more standard Marxist analysis would say that the workers are so alienated from their human nature that some of them turn to crime; and the objectives of the crime might be to defend the human values of their families. Presumably acquisitive crime directed against capitalists would be seen as relatively acceptable; however, acquisitive crime tends to be directed against other workers. Workers can also try to deaden the effects of alienation by getting drunk and engaging in fights etc. This is fairly similar to the account of the effects of proletarian existence found in Willem Bonger. The theory of alienation adds a moral claim that alienation should be ended. This seems uncomfortably close to the demand that workers should enjoy the full fruits of their labour which Marx gives such short shrift in *The Critique of the Gotha Programme*(MECW, 24: 84–5).

One part of the alienation analysis talks of the alienation of people from nature, and it would be possible to try to construct an ecological version of Marxism on the basis of this. However, Marx also frequently thinks in terms of people dominating nature in one way or another. Actual Communist societies have taken this approach, and tend to have generated worse ecological problems than are generated by advanced capitalism (see Benton 1989).

Marx himself seems to have placed the alienation analysis on the back burner as a result of his encounter with Max Stirner, who took the alienation idea one step further, and thought in terms of claims about human brotherhood etc as a form of alienation from the proper concern of the individual, which is him or herself (Stirner 1907). There is, at any rate, a problem as to why human beings are naturally creative, loving and communal, rather than nurturing, as in feminist, spiritual, as in religious, Aryan, as in Nazi, or individualistic and competitive, as in egoistic, accounts of human nature.

The rather dismal performance of Marxist analysis so far need not be too discouraging: all the remaining four possibilities arguably work better.

The criminal justice system and the reproduction conditions of capitalism

One of Marx's more extended discussions of crime comes in his Economic Manuscripts of 1861–3 (MECW, 30: 307–10). It starts:

A philosopher produces ideas, a poet poems, a clergyman sermons, a professor compendia and so on. A criminal produces crimes. If we take a closer look at the connection between this latter branch of production and society as a whole, we shall rid ourselves of many prejudices. The criminal produces not only crimes but also criminal law, and with this also the professor who gives lectures on criminal law and in addition to this the inevitable compendium in which this same professor throws his lectures onto the general market as "commodities". This brings with it augmentation of national wealth, quite apart from the personal enjoyment which – as a competent witness, Professor Roscher, [tells] us . . . the manuscript of the compendium brings to its originator himself. The criminal moreover produces the whole of the police and of criminal justice, constables, judges, hangmen, juries, etc.; and all these different lines of business, which form just as many categories of the social division of labour, develop different capacities of the human mind, create new needs and new ways of satisfying them. Torture alone has given rise to the most ingenious mechanical inventions, and employed many honourable craftsmen in the production of its instruments. The criminal produces an impression, partly moral and partly tragic, as the case may be, and in this way renders a "service" by arousing the moral and aesthetic feelings of the public.

Marx is actually attacking economists such as Malthus who, he argued, failed to distinguish properly between productive and unproductive labour. He does this by means of a satire in which the criminal is productive because he produces work for the criminal justice system, locksmiths, makers of implements for torture to extract confessions and so on. Because this message is entertaining, it is frequently referred to and reproduced.

In point of fact, Marx's best version of this distinction between productive and unproductive labour, namely that productive labour is productive of profit, still fails to work, particularly in conditions of advanced capitalism. It tells us that state-employed scientists and lecturers in computer science are unproductive and that a capitalist government should sack them and get them flipping hamburgers for a profit making chain. The output of these particular state employees is the main explanation of why Western economies are still in advance of those of India and China. Also, there are productive labourers who have very bad effects on the rest of the workforce, for example gunsmiths, producers of alcohol and tobacco, people employed in making unhealthy food and the like.

Another way to look at Marx's discussion of crime is to conceive of it as one of the reproduction conditions of capitalism. This form of analysis, taking as its starting point one of Althusser's essays, 'Ideology and the state' (Althusser 1970), was very popular in the 1970s, as it provided a way for radical state employees to argue that they were engaged in undermining capitalism (see Hall et al. 1978; Wilson 1977; Corrigan and Leonard 1978; London Edinburgh Weekend Return Group 1980). The reproduction conditions of capitalism are, I would argue, multi-layered. Most basic are the reproduction conditions of human life itself, such as breathable air, food and shelter. Then there are reproduction conditions which are broadly common to capitalist and socialist economies, such as a good general education system and welfare state. Then there are specific conditions of capitalism, such as free workers, an accumulation of money capital, a reasonably extensive market and an ideology which understands profit-making as a reputable activity. A very basic level of the criminal justice system is required by both a capitalist and a socialist economy: both of these are undermined if people are free to murder and steal whenever they see fit. Possibly the criminal justice systems of the Scandinavian countries are quite close to this minimum level of imprisonment needed to run a stable capitalist or socialist economic system. They manage to keep incarceration down to around 70 per hundred thousand of population.[1] Some African countries have lower rates of incarceration, but also suffer from civil war or very poor law and order. The Congo would be an example. In stark contrast with Scandinavia, the British and American criminal justice systems have been afflicted since the 1970s with what Garland calls the culture of control (Garland 2001). He argues that from the early twentieth century to the beginning of the 1970s, there was a culture in Britain and America of penal welfarism, in which prison was much more of a last resort, and the goal of imprisonment was more clearly rehabilitation. What has happened since then, he argues, is that fear of crime has been whipped up by politicians and the media, and imprisonment has come to be much more a matter of deterrence and retribution. Thus in Britain we have roughly doubled the number of prisoners since the time of Douglas Hurd as Home Secretary; and the United States has ended up as the penal capital of the world with 756 prisoners per hundred thousand of population.

Is there anything peculiar about the development of American capitalism since the 1970s which accounts for this massive growth? There has been the relative decline of mass production and manufacturing, which has tended to be shifted to parts of the world such as Mexico and China where labour is cheaper than in the United States. There has also been growing inequality, with stagnating incomes at the bottom of US society and the expansion of extreme wealth of an elite at the top.[2] Given that American culture places considerable stress on material prosperity, this is arguably a criminogenic set of arrangements. This point is, of course, made from the anomie perspective (see Merton 1938; Passas 1990; Messner and Rosenfeld 2012). However, to a somewhat lesser extent, the same developments have been underway in Britain with a much lower rate of imprisonment. A more likely to set of explanations is specific to the criminal justice system. There is the particularly toxic phenomenon of the Republican Southern strategy, which started in a small way with the Nixon presidential campaign in 1968, in which Republicans in the southern states linked fear of crime with fear of black men. This resulted in white Southern voters switching their allegiance from Dixiecrat Democrats to Republicans. It also led to higher rates of imprisonment, which were then used as an argument to show that there was a major danger from crime, particularly black crime. The Democrats fought back by arguing that they were equally tough on crime (see Parenti 1999; Chambliss 2001). This has carried on since the mid-1990s, when levels of crime started to fall quite dramatically. Some other developments have also conspired to inflate the number of prisoners: truth in sentencing, which limits judicial discretion, and means that prisoners get relatively little remission for good conduct; the war on drugs, which has seen the incarceration of large numbers of inoffensive users and low-level dealers; tougher probation, with a more ready tendency to recall men on probation to prison. There is also an argument that crime statistics are manipulated by police authorities and the FBI, either to demonstrate that crime is rampant and that they need to be supplied with extra resources, or to demonstrate that zero tolerance policing works (see Chambliss 2001).

It is worth debating whether there is a more specifically economic explanation. Three major corporations are in the business of providing private prisons; numerous other corporations profit from supplying all sorts of things to the prison sector and to the police and courts. These, together with hangers on such as criminology lecturers, form a significant lobby. However, I see no reason to dispute the view of Christian Parenti that:

> incarceration is a small-scale form of Keynesian, public-works-style stimulus. New penitentiaries can revive economically moribund regions and, acting as anchor industries, can bring in other employers such as medical services and retail chains ... The gulag provides opportunities for localised growth but it does not and will not assume the mantle of *de facto* industrial policy because it cannot and will not replace the role of military and aerospace spending. (Parenti 1999: 217; see also Hooks et al. 2004)

An argument in the opposite direction might in fact be valid. Given that, for example, California is now spending more on its prisoners then it is on education, and that there are more black men in prison than there are in universities, the high rates of imprisonment in the United States are probably a drag on the American economy compared with other possible social arrangements. It would be better for the men who end up in prison to be doing almost anything else: retraining for the informational economy; working as carers for the elderly and disabled; tending civic parks and gardens, putting on operas – all of these would be beneficial and constructive, in contrast with the current arrangements.

The overall conclusion of this section, then, is that capitalist economies have quite a high degree of flexibility and can be run in various different ways. The American pattern of running the economy with such a large criminal justice sector can thus be seen as a contingent rather than a necessary way of reproducing a capitalist economy.

The Marxist analysis of law

Historical materialism conceives of society as comprising an economic base and an ideological and political superstructure, which is determined by the economic base. The role of law in this is problematic. It seems to provide a framework for the economic base and also to be part of the ideological superstructure. It is possible to use law as a framework for accelerating the development of the economic base – consider, for example, legislation to permit enclosure or the setting up of joint stock companies.

Turning specifically to the criminal law, there are broadly two approaches. One, taken by the Soviet jurist Pashukanis (1980), and by the American criminologist Richard Quinney in his Marxist phase (Quinney 1970; 1974; 1977) sees the criminal law as essentially an instrument of the ruling class used against the working class, and thus looks to see the criminal law disappearing with the building of communism. The alternative approach is taken by Paul Q Hirst (1979: 111–14), E. P. Thompson (1990), Douglas Hay (1975) and Hugh Collins (1984). It argues that the law has a relatively autonomous substance of its own. Judges and barristers work within a framework of statute and precedent, using forms of argument which have developed over several hundred years. This activity has, in general, no particular connection to class struggle. This means that the law can, to an extent, be used by subordinate classes against the ruling class. Examples of this could be the refusal of a jury to convict the London Corresponding Committee of workingmen of treason (see Thompson 1991: 19–23); the hanging of Lord Ferrers, a particularly obnoxious aristocrat; the role of health and safety legislation, and legislation to restrict working hours; the refusal of a jury to convict Clive Ponting; the use of the law in the context of the British invasion of Iraq by figures such as Phil Shiner. It is pointed out that the ideological role of the law as something neutral, available to capitalists and workers alike, is enhanced by these relatively limited examples of the law acting to constrain those at the top of society.

Distributive justice and criminal justice

There is a very extensive debate as to whether or not Marx has a theory of distributive justice. It is possible to marshal numerous quotations in both directions from his work.[3] My personal inclination is to go with his official position that historical materialism is not a theory of justice, and that communist revolution is not a revolution motivated by justice. However, I also consider that Marx's arguments to the effect that communist revolution is highly likely have become extremely weak. Contemporary Marxists need to get involved with theories of justice. Moreover, it is by no means clear that the interests of people who work in the interests of justice are identical.

To start with, levels of remuneration enjoyed by different workers are dramatically different: the better-paid employees of Microsoft, for example, leave in a state where they can set up their own businesses; contrast this with workers in Third World sweatshops (see Anderson 2005 on the relative pay rates of third world and US workers who work for Walmart). Worse than this, however, the addition of some labour to a product does not seem to be a particularly good title to the whole of the product. If one considers people's needs, there is a strong argument that carers (usually, though by no means exclusively, women) severely disabled people and some pensioners get a relatively poor deal compared to those lucky enough to be able to do well remunerated work.[4] Justice also demands a reduction in the massive remuneration of those at the very top of businesses and of the bankers who brought about the current crisis. It is thus important to see if it is possible to develop a distinctively Marxist theory of justice. This is obviously a very big task. In terms of Marx's categories we live in a rather peculiar society. We still have capitalism, gross inequality and idle rentiers. On the other hand, we have a welfare state which, to some extent, works on the basis of to each according to his or her needs. This points towards a reformist politics which uses arguments about justice to call for the expansion of the welfare state alongside policies to reduce inequalities in income and wealth.

Where does criminal justice fit with theories about distributive justice? The two tend to be discussed separately. Thus there is about one page on this issue in Rawls' *A Theory of Justice*, if we leave aside a more extended discussion of civil disobedience (Rawls 1973: 575–6). The line Rawls takes is the obvious one that crime tends to upset just patterns of distribution, so that criminal justice restores a just pattern of distribution. One text written by a criminologist tries to make this link by using Marshall's theory of citizenship as her criterion of justice (Cook 2006). If we pursue Rawls' line of thought, I would suggest that we should distinguish between white-collar crime carried out by individuals on their own behalf, corporate crime and street crime. Individual white-collar crime is arguably pursued less vigorously than street crime which nets the same amount of illicit gains, although in recent years some American white-collar criminals have received substantial sentences. Corporate crime is quite often overlooked, or dealt with leniently. An example would be the British Corporate Manslaughter and Corporate Homicide Act (2007), which simply provides for fines on guilty corporations – fines which in the case of Railtrack, hospital trusts or prisons would be paid by the taxpayer. There is also a strong argument that corporate crime does not get enough attention from criminologists, given the massive damage it causes compared to street crime. I was able to review the most significant writing in this area over a few pages of my book (Cowling 2008: 205–8), a task which would be completely impossible for street crime. Just to give a brief illustration of the discrepancy: in the 1990s the Serious Fraud Office had a threshold of £6 million before it would take an interest in cases, and typically had frauds which netted around £5 billion under investigation at any one time. In contrast, the average burglary was estimated to have netted about £370, and the total cost of burglaries was estimated as around £1 billion per annum. Hardly any burglaries were big enough to attract the attention of the Serious Fraud Office if they had been frauds (see Slapper and Tombs 1999: 56–63). Turning to deaths and injuries, in the United Kingdom, there are around 400 deaths and 50,000 serious injuries at work each year (Slapper and Tombs 1999: 68–78). Very many of these are avoidable. The executives who decide whether or not to risk these deaths and injuries obviously hope that nothing harmful will occur, and have nothing against the particular employee who is a victim, but they risk the deaths and injuries in a calculative manner, whereas an individual murderer tends to be enraged and out of control. It is, of course, quite possible to research these matters without a Marxist framework, but this is a pretty clearly territory where Marxist views of the imperatives of capitalism are highly pertinent. It is obviously necessary to develop a Marxist theory of justice in order to properly condemn the crimes discussed in this paragraph as unjust, but this is a major undertaking not appropriate for even a book on Marxism and criminology.

Turning from corporate crime to crime more generally, there are various crimes where a Marxist theory of justice would be relevant. Let us start with the crimes committed by primitive rebels, as Eric Hobsbawm called them. When he was writing in 1959, he had a clear view of the line of march to socialism, and it was relatively easy to see where they would fit (Hobsbawm 1959). Things are less clear if we start engaging in reformist arguments about justice. The line of march towards socialism is messy and unclear. Illegal actions should be largely unnecessary in properly functioning liberal democracies, and are something of a double edged sword in that they legitimate draconian or illicit activities by the criminal justice system or the right against leftists. There may be some role for whistleblowing, leaking, civil disobedience, challenging the way in which demonstrations are policed, symbolic actions against particular targets etc.

What about the victimless crimes advocated by the radical criminologists of the 1970s? People on the left have historically been rather more sympathetic to these than those on the right, but today things are less clear. Existing or recent communist societies have been less sympathetic to homosexuality than today's decadent advanced capitalist societies; in Britain under New Labour the Home Office was dominated by women who accepted the radical feminist view that prostitution is totally unacceptable.

Finally, a brief comment on the relatively petty street crime which dominates criminal statistics. Much of this is relatively harmless – I can recall rejecting the offer of victim support to get me through the trauma of having our lawnmower stolen from our shed and the horror of claiming for a better one on our insurance, or the puzzle of what was the appropriate amount to claim on the insurance for cracked PlayStation games stolen in a minor burglary. Socialist policy would surely be to try to get the young men who are the main perpetrators of this type of crime through their criminal years as untraumatically as possible, rather than labelling and imprisoning them, thus setting them on course for recidivism.

Communism and the end of crime?

Much of the existing Marxist criminology argues that crime would disappear under communism (see Taylor, Walton and Young 1973a: 281–2; 1975: 90; Reiman 1998; Chambliss 2001, the last two arguing that socialist type reforms would greatly reduce crime). It seems reasonable to suppose that the type of situation Bonger describes, where people had the option of starvation, stealing or suicide, would disappear in a communist society, but it has also disappeared in capitalist societies which have a halfway decent welfare state (Bonger 1916: 670–2; Quinney 2002: 167; 187–91).

Marx's slogan for communist society is 'from each according to his abilities and to each according to his needs' (MECW, 24: 87). The older Marx seems to envisage that at least some work would continue to be necessary and disagreeable (MECW, 37: 807).[5] It can therefore be assumed that some people would wish to evade work some of the time. Some things that people legitimately want, such as a car, are ecologically unsustainable for everyone on the planet. Others would have to be rationed in any conceivable situation: the desire to make epic films, the need for emotional care (see Blakeley and Bryson 2005: 138), the demand for space travel should all be available for some people, but do not seem realistic for everyone in the way they might desire and benefit from. We thus have two sorts of situations in which individuals would wish to deviate from the socialist plan; however, it was drawn up. A socialist society will also presumably still have the kind of problem we have today over, for example, the use of the countryside. Farming, house building, quad biking, setting up wind farms and rambling are all legitimate uses to some extent, but are rivals to each other. In capitalist society some people, at least, can get around these problems by spending resources in a way that might not be possible in a socialist society. They might, therefore, engage in various forms of crime or corruption.

Some currently existing crimes are motivated by issues of race or gender. Hopefully these would diminish under socialism, but they would not automatically go away. Although people's sexual desires would hopefully be catered for following Fourier's slogan that 'all perversions are equal under the law' (Fourier 1967), it would surely still be disagreeable to find one's partner in bed with someone else, so to some extent crime based on jealousy would persist. Hopefully a socialist society would take seriously the need of people to live free of fear, and would thus be more effective in prosecuting domestic and sexual violence. Convictions for these might therefore rise rather than fall. Some offences are based on moral and religious beliefs. One might hope that religious beliefs will tend to fade away in a socialist society, but this looks much more realistic in secular Britain than in the United States. Even from a secular point of view, there is a point at which most people would wish to move from polite debate to criminal sanctions – for example, shifting the age of consent to 14 could be dealt with by polite disagreement, but moving it to age 7 would invite criminal sanctions. Similarly, while most enlightened people seem to accept the idea of a spot of sadomasochism such as was at issue in the Spanner trial, there tend to be reservations about consenting cannibalism.

Finally, we should perhaps pause for thought about the consumption of drugs in contemporary capitalist societies. The illegal drugs trade is based on the desire of lots of people for drugs which are prohibited by law. In a socialist society, everything needed for production is supposed to be supplied by the social plan. If this fails and people want to get hold of things needed by enterprises, they are forced onto the black market. This seems to have been one major foundation of the Soviet Mafia: lots of commodities were treated in the same way as illegal drugs in our society.

Overall, then, there seems to be reason to think that in some respects there might actually be more crime in a communist society than in current capitalist society, even if in other respects the communist society was very attractive and provided better opportunities for human fulfilment.

Notes

1　Rates of imprisonment are summarized by Roy Walmsley (2008). Some African countries have lower rates of imprisonment than Scandinavia, but they also do not have very effective capitalist development, and many of them have quite nasty features such as corrupt dictatorships or civil wars. An example would be the Congo, with 22 people in prison per hundred thousand of population, but with a horrible history of corrupt dictatorship and civil war, and a terrible failure to develop the plentiful natural resources of the country for the general benefit of its population.

2　See http://en.wikipedia.org/wiki/List_of_countries_by_income_equality; http://mapscroll.blogspot.com/2009/04/is-us-becoming-third-world-country.html.

3　For an excellent introduction to the quotations, the issues, and the extensive literature, see Geras (1985; 1992).

4　The argument here basically follows that in Geras (1992: 66–9) and Cohen (2000, Chapter 6).

5　For an enlightening and interesting discussion of this change from the youthful alienation theory, see Wendling (2009).

References

Althusser, L. (1970), *Lenin and Philosophy and Other Essays*. London: New Left Books.

Anderson, S. (2005), 'Wal-Mart pay gap', *Institute for Policy Studies* (Washington, DC). Available from: http://www.ips-dc.org/projects/global_econ/Wal-mart_pay_gap.pdf.

Bagguley, P. and Mann, K. (1992), 'Idle thieving bastards? Scholarly representations of the "underclass"', *Work, Employment and Society*, 6, 113–26.

Barry, K. (1995), *The Prostitution of Sexuality*. New York: New York University Press.

Benton, T. (1989), 'Marxism and natural limits: an ecological critique and reconstruction', *New Left Review*, 178, 51–86.

Blakeley, G. and Bryson, V. (2005), *Marx and Other Four-Letter Words*. London: Pluto Press.

Bonger, W. A. (1916), *Criminality and Economic Conditions*. London: W. Heinemann.

Bovenkerk, F. (1984), 'The rehabilitation of the rabble: how and why Marx and Engels wrongly depicted the lumpenproletariat as a reactionary force', *The Netherlands Journal of Sociology*, 20, 13–41.

Castells, M. (1996), *The Rise of the Network Society: The Information Age: Economy, Society and Culture*, volume 1. Oxford: Blackwell.

— (2000), *End of Millennium: The Information Age: Economy, Society and Culture*, volume 3. Oxford: Blackwell Publishers.

— (2004), *The Power of Identity: The Information Age: Economy, Society and Culture*, volume 2 (second edition). Oxford: Blackwell.

Castells, M. and Himanen, P. (2004), *The Information Society and the Welfare State: The Finnish Model*. Oxford: Oxford University Press.

Chambliss, W. J. (2001), *Power, Politics, and Crime*. Boulder, CO: Westview Press.

Cohen, G. A. (2000), If You're an Egalitarian, How Come you're So Rich?, Cambridge MA, Harvard University Press.

Collins, H. (1984), *Marxism and Law*. Oxford: Oxford University Press.

Cook, D. (2006), *Criminal and Social Justice*. London: Sage.

Corrigan, P. and Leonard, P. (1978), *Social Work Practice under Capitalism: A Marxist Approach*. London: Macmillan.

Cowling, M. (1989), 'The case for two Marxes, re-stated', in M. Cowling and L. Wilde (eds), *Approaches to Marx*. Milton Keynes: Open University Press, pp. 1–32.

— (1995), 'Marx's conceptual framework from 1843–5: Hegelian dialectic and historical necessity versus Feuerbachian humanistic materialism?', *Studies in Marxism*, 2, 135–59.

— (2006), 'Alienation in the older Marx', *Contemporary Political Theory*, 5, 319–39.

Cowling, M. (2008), Marxism and Criminological Theory: A Critique and a Toolkit, Houndmills, Palgrave.

Fanon, F. (1969), *The Wretched of the Earth*. Harmondsworth: Penguin.

Fourier, C. (1967), 'Le nouveau monde amoureux', *Oeuvres Complètes de Charles Fourier*, volume VII. Paris: Anthropos.

Garland, D. (2001), *The Culture of Control: Crime and Social Order in Contemporary Society*. Oxford: Oxford University Press.

Geras, N. (1985), 'The controversy about Marx and justice', *New Left Review*, 150, 47–85.

— (1992), 'Bringing Marx to justice: an addendum and rejoinder', *New Left Review*, 195, 37–69.

Hagen, J. (1994), *Crime and Disrepute*. Thousand Oaks, CA: Pine Forge Press.

Hall, S. M. et al. (1978), *Policing the Crisis: Mugging, the State, and Law and Order*. London: Macmillan.

Hay, D. (1975), 'Property, authority and the criminal law', in D. Hay, P. Linebaugh and E. Thompson (eds), *Albion's Fatal Tree*. London: Allen Lane.

Heath, A. (1997), 'The attitudes of the underclass', in D. J. Smith (ed.), *Understanding the Underclass*. London: Policy Studies Institute, pp. 32–47.

Hirst, P. Q. (1979), *On Law and Ideology*. London: Macmillan.

Hobsbawm, E. (1974/1959), *Primitive Rebels*. Manchester: Manchester University Press.

Hooks, G. et al. (2004), 'The prison industry: carceral expansion and employment in U. S. counties, 1969–94', *Social Science Quarterly*, 85, 1, 37–57.

Jeffreys, S. (1997), *The Idea of Prostitution*. North Melbourne, Victoria: Spinifex.

Johnston, L. et al. (2000), *Snakes and Ladders: Young People, Transitions and Social Exclusion*. Bristol: The Policy Press/Joseph Rowntree Foundation.

London Edinburgh Weekend Return Group (1980), *In and Against the State*. London: Pluto Press.

MacDonald, R. (1994), 'Fiddly jobs, undeclared working and the something for nothing society', *Work Employment and Society*, 8, 507–30.

Marx, K. (2002), 'The Eighteenth Brumaire of Louis Napoleon Bonaparte', in M. Cowling and J. Martin (eds), *Marx's Eighteenth Brumaire: (Post)Modern Interpretations*. London: Pluto Press,

Mao T. T. (1967), 'Analysis of the classes in Chinese society', *Selected Works*, volume 1. Peking: Foreign Languages Press.

Merton, R. K. (1938), 'Social structure and anomie', *American Sociological Review*, 3, 672–82.

Messner, S. F. and Rosenfeld, R. (2012), *Crime and the American Dream*. Belmont, CA: Wadsworth Publishing Company.

Murray, C. (1996), *Charles Murray and the Underclass: The Developing Debate*. London: IEA Health and Welfare Unit.

— et al. (1997), *Does Prison Work?*. London: IEA Health and Welfare Unit.

— (2000), *The Underclass Revisited*. American Enterprise Institute Short Publications. Available from: http://www.aei.org/publications/pubID.14891/pub_detail.asp.

— (2001), *Underclass + 10*. London: Civitas.

Parenti, C. (1999), *Lockdown America: Police and Prisons in the Age of Crisis*, London: Verso.

Pashukanis, E. B. (1980), *Pashukanis: Selected Writings on Marxism and Law*. London: Academic Press.

Passas, N. (1990), 'Anomie and corporate deviance', *Contemporary Crises*, 14, 157–78.

Pearson, G. (1975) in I. Taylor, P. Walton and J. Young (eds), *Critical Criminology*. London: Routledge and Kegan Paul.

Quinney, R. (1970), *The Social Reality of Crime*. Boston MA: Little, Brown and Co.

— (1970), *Crime and Justice in Society: The Problem of Crime*. New York: Dodd, Mead and Co.

— (1974), *Criminal Justice in America: A Critical Understanding*. Boston, MA: Little, Brown and Co.

— (1977), *Class, State and Crime*. New York: David McKay.

— (2002), *Critique of Legal Order*. New Brunswick and London: Little, Brown and Company.

Rawls, J. (1973), *A Theory of Justice*. Oxford: Oxford University Press.

Reiman, P. (1998), *The Rich Get Richer and the Poor Get Prison: Ideology, Class, and Criminal Justice*. Boston, MA: Allyn and Bacon.

Sanders, T. (2004), *Sex Work: A Risky Business*. Cullompton: Willan.

Slapper, G. and Tombs, S. (1999), *Corporate Crime*, Harlow: Longman

Stirner, M. (1907), *The Ego and His Own*. New York: Benjamin R. Tucker.

Taylor, I., Walton, P. and Young, J. (1973a), *The New Criminology: For a Social Theory of Deviance*. London: Routledge and Kegan Paul.

— (1973b), 'Rejoinder to the reviewers', *British Journal of Criminology*, 13, 401–3.

Taylor, I., Walton, P. and Young, J. (1975), *Critical Criminology*, London: Routledge and Kegan Paul.

Thompson, E. P. (1990), *Whigs and Hunters*. Harmondsworth: Penguin.

— (1991), *The Making of the English Working Class*. Harmondsworth: Penguin.

Walmsley, R. (2008), *World Prison Population List*. Available from: http://www.kcl.ac.uk/depsta/law/research/icps/downloads/wppl-8th_41.pdf.

Wendling, A. (2009), *Karl Marx on Technology and Alienation*. Houndmills: Palgrave.

Wilson, E. (1977), *Women and the Welfare State*. London: Tavistock.

CHAPTER NINE

Sinicized Marxist constitutionalism: its emergence, contents and implications

Andrew (Chengyi) Peng

Introduction

After three decades of economic reform and opening up to the outside world, China's ideological realm has been significantly transformed and complicated. To borrow Clifford Geertz's (1977: 228) words, 'Things do not merely *seem* jumbled – they *are* jumbled, and it will take more than theory to unjumble them'. This is well manifested in the constitutional discourses concerning the future of China. One notable example is the wide acceptance of the liberal constitutional paradigm among Chinese intellectuals, as shown in the issuing and impacts of the *Charter 08* two years ago by some liberal dissidents, such as Liu Xiaobo who was sentenced to eleven years' imprisonment by the Chinese government but just awarded the Nobel Peace Prize of 2010 for largely the same activities. This perspective historically viewed the constitution of a Marxist–Leninist state as a 'sham' that serves as 'an artifice of propaganda designed to impress and mislead foreigners' (Cohen cited in Wong 2006: 1), or a 'useless' document to rein in the government (Possonycited in Wong 2006: 1). Consequently scholars influenced by this paradigm look contemptuously at the current Chinese constitution, which for them needs to be abolished, significantly revised or judicialized (Jiang 2009: 12). However, in recent years, in light of the significant progress of the constitutional framework of China, including its values and practices regarding the rule of law, this dominant liberal perspective has been challenged. Stephanie Balme and Michael Dowdle (2009), for example, have devoted their latest book *Building Constitutionalism in China* to exploring the empirical impacts of the emerging constitutionalism on many aspects of Chinese society, including its juridical, political and social realms. A US constitutional scholar, Larry C. Backer, has also sought to establish a party-state model to grant legitimacy to China's current constitutional development in the international community. This effort has been echoed by the separate articulations of Jiang Shigong, Lin Feng, Chu Jianguo and Randall Peerenboom as well. The mainstream legal scholars in China have made similar efforts and just convened a conference on 'Socialist Constitutionalism with Chinese Characteristics' in May 2010 in Changsha City of Hunan Province.

In light of these developments, we can see that a new paradigm of sinicized Marxist constitutionalism (SMC)[1] is emerging. Why is SMC emerging? What are its contents and its implications? These are the questions this chapter seeks to explore. The chapter is divided into three sections. The first introduces the emerging context of SMC. The second reviews the main approaches towards SMC as well as their contents. The final section summarizes the chapter and draws some implications concerning the emergence of SMC. As we will see, the emergence of SMC has deep historical roots; the paradigm is quite rich in content and carries some profound implications.

Emerging context of SMC and its historical roots

There are three main sources motivating the emergence of SMC. First, there is the significant progress of the values and practices regarding the rule of law in China over the past three decades. From a virtual legal vacuum at the end of the Cultural Revolution, China has established a comprehensive and well-codified legal system, which has been put into effective practice. The fact of legal progress has been widely noticed and acknowledged by scholars both in and outside China. Because the rule of law is widely taken as the core and defining element of constitutionalism, the achievements in the legal realm provide a foundation for surging interest in constitutional development in China as well as the emergence of SMC. In fact, the constitutional framework of China has also undergone profound changes. During the Reform and Opening Up period, Deng Xiaoping repeatedly emphasized the importance of the institutionalization and legalization of democracy in China. Near the end of the twentieth century, the CPC also called for 'the rule of law and building up a socialist rule of law state' during the Fifteenth Congress of the CPC in 1997 and later entrenched this goal into the Chinese Constitution during the Ninth National Congress in 1999.

Nevertheless, despite the remarkable progress of legal reform in China, mostscholars' attention seems to have been preoccupied with the gap between the Chinese constitutional reality and the ideal liberal constitutionalism developed in the course of Western constitutional experiences. I call the liberal constitutionalism advocated in China an 'ideal' because it is nowhere to be found in practice, nor do those advocates realize the varieties of constitutional tradition in the West. In fact, as most of them are preoccupied with judicial independence, including the 'judicialization of Constitution' (*xianfasifahua*) as practised in the United States, they seem to have only the US 'ideal' in mind without realizing other legitimate alternatives, such as the French or British variants. I will elaborate the problems of this approach more later, but it is worth suggesting that the parochial and ideological nature of this appraoch is perhaps largely due to the dominance of liberal constitutional paradigm in Western academia as well as its deep penetration into the Chinese intellectual realm.

The deep influence of the Western liberal constitutional paradigm is also well manifested in the constitutional scholarship in China. With the steady progress of legal reform in China, especially the official advocacy of 'rule of law' by the CPC leadership in 1997 and the entrenchment of this ideal into the constitution in 1999, the constitutional consciousness in China has increased dramatically; at the same time, scholarship on constitutional law and constitutionalism in China has proliferated. Although constitutionalism is largely a Western idea, it has nevertheless transcended its parochial origin and become a universal norm of the world (Jiang 2009: 11); its influence on Chinese constitutional thinking is also remarkable. As shown in his article 'Western Constitutional Ideas and Constitutional Discourse in China, 1978–2005', the impact of western constitutional ideals and discourses in China is so significant that Yu Xingzhong (2009: 114) acknowledges 'it is no exaggeration to say that Chinese constitutional discourse has been significantly "Westernized"'. It is in this regard that Pan Wei, a well-known coiner and advocate of the notion of 'Chinese Model' (*zhongguo moshi*), regards the realm of legal study as the 'hardest hit area' of Chinese academia by what he regards as Western ideological imperialism (personal communication, June 10, 2010). The impact is also manifested in the sensibilities as well as sense of what problems are most important (*wenti yishi*) of the majority of Chinese constitutional scholars. While not daring to openly call the Chinese constitution a 'sham' or 'useless' as some Western critics did, they nevertheless take the divergence between the constitutional expression and practice as a tacit truism (Jiang 2009: 11). The problems they are most concerned about and preoccupied with are consequently how to revise the current Chinese constitution to meet Western standards, and particularly how to implement the constitution in juridical practice in order to avoid its irrelevance in daily life (Jiang 2009: 12).

Meanwhile, the deep penetration and influence of the Western liberal constitutional paradigm in China has induced two remarkable reactions. The first is the 'constitutionalism abolition thesis' (*xianzheng quxiaolun*) and the second is the advocating of constitutional proposals based on and loyal to China's indigenous traditions by some cultural conservatives in mainland China. The first reaction is mainly shown among scholars of political studies. If the realm of legal studies is indeed the 'hardest hit area' of Chinese academia by Western ideological imperialism, the situation in the realm of political studies is relatively better, perhaps due to greater caution on the part of supervising political authority in China as well as the distinctive natures of the two subjects. The difference is reflected in their distinct stances towards the issue of constitutionalism. Constitutionalism is by no means a hot topic among political scholars in China; in fact, some prominent figures among this group have openly criticized the concept as well as the ideology behind it (Chen 2004; Xie 2004). Their views seem to have been accepted by the political authorities, which is perhaps why some books written on constitutionalism face some implicit barriers for publication (personal communication, anonymous, May 22, 2010). The appeal of the 'constitutionalism abolition thesis' to current political leaders is not hard to understand as soon as one questions where the Four Cardinal Principles (*sixiang jibenyuanze*)[2] that serve as the foundation for China's reform and development are placed in the new constitutional discourse, which usually centres on the three core elements of 'democracy, rule of law and human rights'. This is actually one of the primary motivations for the recent conference on 'Socialist Constitutionalism with Chinese Characteristics' in Changsha in May 2010 by legal scholars in China; most of the participants had the hidden agenda of using the title of this meeting to rectify the name and restore the leading status of constitutionalism in directing China's political reform in future. This may well be shown in the speech of the convener Li Buyun, who confesses his strategic concerns for holding the conference. While the conference was attended by many important figures within the field of legal studies, including several current presidents of the University of Politics and Law (*zhengfa daxue*), and some representatives of major medias in China, such as the People's Daily, as well as an important former state leader, Luo Haocai, the conference received little media coverage and consequently had little impact on the public. The struggle over the issue of constitutionalism has thus not undergone significant changes.

Another reaction to the penetration of the Western liberal constitutional paradigm in China is the emergence of Confucian constitutionalism discourse advocated by some so-called mainland New Confucians, represented by Jiang Qing (*Jiangqing*), Kang Xiaoguang (*Kangxiaoguang*), Sheng Hong (*Shenghong*) and Chen Ming (*Chenming*) (Fang 2006: 6). While having not reached a consensus among themselves for a specific constitutional blueprint, this school is united in bemoaning the fact that the liberal constitutional proposals of the past century, including the amendments of the current Chinese constitution, all lack native features. In other words, contemporary Chinese politics is still diverging from its native tradition and getting more 'Westernized'. As a result, they have been seeking to develop constitutional blueprints that are based on and also loyal to China's cultural tradition. One notable proposal is Jiang Qing's 'Religious Confucian Constitutionalism' (*rujiao xianzheng*), which is supported by his theory of 'political Confucianism', and consists of a series of concrete proposals for realizing the blueprint. An international conference entitled 'Religious Confucian Constitutionalism and China's Future' has just been convened in May 2010 in Hong Kong as well.

If the constitutional achievements of China in the past three decades provide the foundation, while the deep penetration of the WLC paradigm in China serves as a kind of catalyst for the emergence of SMC, interest in exploring and theorizing the so-called Chinese Model (*zhongguo moshi*) within current Chinese academia and the prevailing trend of shaking off the yoke of dominant paradigms in the Western academia may have provided a supporting environment for its emergence. Tacitly endorsed by Chinese government, whose intellectuals have sought to bridge the notion of 'Chinese Model' with the official line of 'The Path and Theoretical System of Socialism with Chinese Characteristics', the exploration and theorization of the 'Chinese Model' based on China's successful modernization path has proliferated in Chinese academia in the past few years, especially in the past two years since the unfolding of the financial crisis in the West. This is well reflected in the change of the number of core social science journal articles published on the theme, as shown in the table below. In the period of 2009–10, there are 91 articles containing the phrase 'Chinese Model' in their titles and 167 articles with 'Chinese Model' as the keyword; this is nearly three times the number published during the period of 2001–8, which has a record of 29 and 57 respectively. There have also been various conferences, research projects, as well as books devoted to the theme in China recently. While it is hard to give a specific definition to the term 'Chinese Model', some key characteristics could be identified, such as its objection to

Table 1 Number of core social science journal articles on 'Chinese Model' (statistics from China Academic Journals Full-text Database)

	1980–2000	2001–2008	2009–2010
'Chinese Model' in Title	6	29	91
'Chinese Model' as Keyword	15	57	167

the prevailing doctrinaire adoption of Western ideas and theories, as well as its emphasis on the theorization of indigenous experiences of the past sixty years.

The current popularity of the 'Chinese Model' does not seem to have spread far from the Chinese border, but nevertheless, in Western academia, there is a trend of rethinking the dominant paradigms as well as reengaging alternative discourses that were previously ignored or suppressed. This trend is particularly well manifested in the area of China studies, since the bare facts of China's rapid economic growth as well as the regime's continuing resilience have betrayed the limitation of the existing frameworks and led some to explore new categories and perspectives to better capture China's realities. This seems to be well shown in Backer, Perenboom, Balme and Dowdle's endeavours. The easier access of information from China as well as increased interactions with Chinese realties due to technological advances and the rising tide of globalization certainly have contributed to this change.

To sum up, we have reviewed three factors in the background that have contributed to the emergence of SMC. As we have seen, the progress of the rule of law and constitutional framework in China plays a foundational role, as without these transformations, the Chinese variant of constitutionalism may not have attracted much attention at all. However, the prevailing acceptance of the liberal constitutional paradigm in China has induced some reactions from various quarters and consequently has served as a catalyst for the emergence of SMC. Finally, interest in exploring the 'Chinese model' within current Chinese academia and dissatisfaction with the dominant paradigms in the West have provided an amiable environment for SMC to emerge. Surely behind all of the three major factors mentioned above is the common denominator of China's continuing rapid economic growth. This may echo Marx's thesis about the dialectical relationship between economic base structure and ideational superstructures. Below, let's have a look at the contents of SMC.

The contents of SMC

As shown in Table 2, we could identify five main approaches towards constitutionalism in China.[3] The first approach is surely the prevailing WLC approach mentioned earlier, which focuses on the gap between China's current constitutional reality and certain Western ideals. Due to the scope and purpose of this chapter, I will not go into details here. The second approach is a little more moderate as it acknowledges and focuses on the legal and constitutional progress seen in China over recent decades, and I call it an 'empirical transitional approach'. This is represented by the chapters in Balme and Dowdle's (2009) edited collection, which are largely

Table 2 A spectrum of approaches towards Chinese constitutionalism

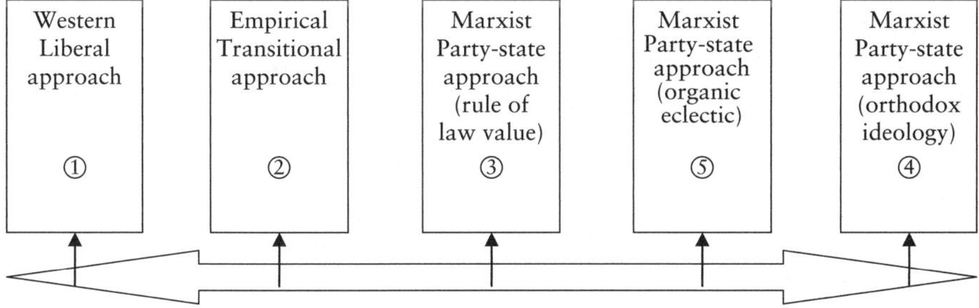

empirical in nature and mainly explore the impacts of this emerging constitutionalism in a variety of areas, including not only the juridical realm such as legal practice, judicial decision making and legal scholarship and education, but also the political and social realms, such as political consciousness, social resistance, mobilization and citizen empowerment. While marking an advance over the first approach, the 'transitional constitutionalism' approach is still operating within the paradigm of WLC, hence suffering the same problems as the first approach. As a result, I will not go over it in detail here. Most relevant to the theme of this chapter are the third to fifth approaches, because they all capture some core elements of Chinese constitutionalism, namely the party-state constitutional order, as well as the importance of ideology in the constitutional framework. Nevertheless, they differ in the gravity centre among the ideological values, with the third approach pivoted on the rule of law value, the fourth approach on the orthodox ideology of regime and the fifth approach on an organic eclectic of previous approaches. Below I will provide a review and analysis of each of the SMC approaches respectively.

Marxist party-state approach pillared on the rule of law

The third approach is well represented by Larry C. Backer's party-state model of Chinese constitutionalism. According to Backer (2009: 110), to understand this model with Chinese characteristics, one needs to first understand that 'the Chinese constitution exists as a combination of polity and governing ideology, on the one hand, and the state apparatus, on the other hand'. A key component in this constitutional arrangement is the Communist Party, not as a political party or private actor in the Western sense, but as the institutionalization of the polity and the source of its substantive values. In other words, the Communist party as an autonomous community serves as the gatekeeper of political citizenship and the provider of the value framework for the state. As a result, Backer (2009: 102) concludes four major features of the party-state model of the Chinese constitutionalism: (1), the division of citizenship between social and economic citizenship held by all and political citizenship exercised through the CPC; (2), the subordination of state power and institutions to political authority; (3), institutionalization of political authority within a collective space (the CPC) beyond the control of any individuals, that serves as the source and conduit of constitutional values to be implemented by the state apparatus; (4), reliance on state and party self discipline for the elaboration of rule of law values.

While this approach is quite distinct from previous approaches in that it brings the CPC as well as its ideologies into the constitutional structure, it is located near the centre of the spectrum because it still emphasizes rule of law as the defining feature of constitutionalism. As a result, Backer (2009: 6) argues that the CPC 'retains its constitutionalist character to the extent that in its internal operations it observes the same rule of law framework as that imposed externally on the state apparatus'. It is Backer's (2009: 2) emphasis on rule of law as the defining feature of constitutionalism that leads him to regard pre-Deng Chinese state governance architecture as anti-constitutionalist, a kind of truism shared with previous approaches. While Backer (2009: 3) is right in claiming that 'the basic premise of constitutionalism is to distinguish it from despotism or tyranny', it seems that further support is needed to argue that the absence of the rule of law necessarily leads to despotism and tyranny.[4]

This approach, represented by Backer's model, is also shared by some famous scholars, like Jiang Shigong and Chu Jianguo in China and Randall Peerenboom at UCLA. Responding to the prevailing sensibilities and problem awareness of the majority of legal scholars in China, especially their exclusive focus on the written constitution, Jiang Shigong (2009) advocates an 'unwritten constitution' perspective to study China's constitutionalism. With some compelling arguments, the author contends that the actual operation of constitutionalism in all countries relies on an unwritten constitution, and he demonstrates that China's constitutional order actually has four sources, namely the party constitution, constitutional conventions, constitutional doctrine and constitutional statutes. The most remarkable characteristics of the Chinese constitutional order, according to Jiang, is the compound interactional structure between the political and the legal, represented by the party and the state respectively.[5] Historically, the PRC is founded politically under the leadership of the CPC with alliances of other political parties. This is well shown in *The Common Program of the Chinese People's Political Consultative Conference* proclaimed in 1949, the first constitutional document of the PRC. According to Jiang, the diverse background of the first political consultative conference attendees as well as their representativeness could well provide the legitimacy needed to politically establish the PRC; however, as a 'political' foundation lacks certain formal elements, it needs a legal foundation to entrench and stabilize the polity, which is the reason for the proclamation of the formal Constitution in 1954. Consequently, Jiang (2009: 22) argues that the sovereignty of China is represented in two ways, the first is through the CPC-led multi-party cooperation system, which consists of representatives based on their political ideas, historical missions and class interests; the second is the People's Congress, which consists in representatives elected through certain legal and formal electoral procedures from the citizenry. This echoes Backer's insights into the two main divisions of citizenship above as well. While emphasizing the unique Chinese constitutional party-state structure, Jiang seems to share the power-constraining dimension of Backer's view. For Jiang (2009: 23), while state sovereignty represented by the People's Congress is indeed a kind of 'rubber stamp' in a neutral sense, since political wills of CPC and NPC are themselves supposed to be identical, legitimization of the party will through the NPC assumes the additional function of 'taming the emperor'. Jiang does not elaborate the reasons but points out the differences through a comparison with that of the Cultural Revolution period where the CPC ruled directly without any resort to legal legitimatization. Conceivably, the need to go through the NPC in order for CPC's will to be elevated to state level may serve to slow the deliberative process, hence making the proposals more cautious as well as representative (remember that the approval rate by the votes in the NPC still indicates something). In fact, this is supported by Robert Benewick's (1998: 447) observation of the dualistic feature of Chinese constitution as 'the Communist Party contending and proposing and the state amending and disposing'. To Jiang (2009: 23), this is similar to the difference between 'absolute monarchy' and 'constitutional monarchy' as manifested and aspired to in recent Chinese history. Another scholar Chu Jianguo (2006: 10) shares this view and further elaborates the advantages as well as necessity of what he calls 'One Party Constitutionalism' (*yidang lixian*) in a web-based article.

Marxist party-state approach pillared on orthodox ideology

If the above approaches are largely preoccupied with constraining governmental power through the rule of law mainly due to the deep influence of the liberal constitutional paradigm, the fourth approach then, as an alternative, concentrates its attention on the constitutional order of Chinese politics as it is, and takes its ideological dimension as the distinctive feature of Chinese constitutionalism. First of all, this approach sees a consistent constitutional developmental trajectory in China and has been well explored in Han Damei (2005), Qing Qianhong and Ye Haibo (2008) and Han Dayuan (2008).[6] Here I will review Ren Xirong's synoptic account as a representative.

In her presentation at the 'Socialist Constitutionalism with Chinese Characteristics' conference, Ren Xirong (2010) from Jilin University reviewed the developmental trajectory of socialist constitutionalism from Mao's time to later leaderships. According to her, Mao Zedong and his contemporary Marxist theorists are the founders of the Chinese Socialist Constitutionalism theory and system. This is so not only because the core of Mao Zedong's constitutional thought, namely 'constitutionalism is the politics of democracy', has deeply influenced the way Chinese people today understand constitutionalism, but also because during Maoist times, the fundamental categorical system of the Chinese socialist constitutionalism, including constituents such as the Constitution, the National Polity (*guoti*), the state/government (*zhengti*), the people, citizenship, democratic centralism, people's congress system, the fundamental rights and obligations, legislative power, judicial power, administrative power, chief of state, autonomous governance and the actual working mechanisms of the constitutional order were formed. The constitutional structure and thought were further developed by Deng and Jiang. During Deng's time, he not only established the 'Four Cardinal Principles' for China's reform and opening up and set up the goal of institutionalizing and legalizing the peoples' democracy, but also developed the ideology of 'Socialist Theory with Chinese Characteristics' (*zhongguotese shehuizhuyililun*).[7] This constitutional trajectory was further developed by later leaderships, as shown in the incorporation of 'the rule of law', 'human rights' and 'Three Represents' clauses into the Constitution.

Second, this fourth approach is distinct for its emphasis on the orthodox ideology. For example, tracing the constitutional development of China from the Common Program of 1949 to the current 1982 Constitution, Kam Wong (2006: 37) points out that the Chinese 'constitutions were not there to limit the government's power but to promote the ideology of the state and advance the cause of the Communist Party, that is, to contribute to building a Communist State under Mao (the 1954 PRC Constitution) or to facilitate the social and economic reforms under Deng (the 1982 PRC Constitution)'. In other words, Wong (2006: 37) further explains, 'Traditional 'constitutionalism' in the West is built upon an individualistic foundation, adversarial processes and a zero-sum gain calculus', but Chinese 'constitutionalism' is 'premised more upon a collective mentality, centred more on a cooperative spirit and on a mutually beneficial understanding [that] Power need not be held in check but must be guided and directed to achieve collective goods'. It is also in this sense that Ren (2010: 2) regards the 'Four Cardinal Principles' as the cornerstone of Chinese constitutionalism and the fundamental feature distinguishing it from its western counterparts. While in his article Wong (2006: 3) points out that the 1982 Constitution of the PRC marks a breakthrough from previous ones by incorporating the ideas of 'rule of law, individual rights, limitation of state powers' for the first time, he does not elaborate much on them, nor regard them as essential for Chinese constitutionalism. In fact, Wong acknowledges that the Chinese authorities drafting the 1982 Constitution did not subscribe to a liberal understanding of these core values, and suggests further research on the impacts of the reform and opening up on the Party's thinking as well as the people's understanding of constitutionalism in the past three decades.

Given this approach's reliance on the orthodox ideology of the CPC as well as its canopy of the Cultural Revolution period, a third feature not hard to conceive is the legacy of Marxist and socialist legal philosophy. Just as the third 'rule of law' approach does not exclude the ideological dimension of SMC, this fourth ideological approach does not exclude the 'rule of law' either, though it presents it in terms of a very different Marxist or socialist understanding. In Western academia, there is very little written on Marxist or socialist legality, let alone their philosophy. This is understandable, since classical Marxism is well known for dismissing law as a class instrument and capitalist institution, which will 'wither away' with the state after the revolution (Wong 2006: 4–5). Nevertheless, Marxist legal theory, advocated and endorsed by state authority, has been hotly explored and discussed in Chinese academia, especially its adaption to the current context. I will leave a review of this aspect till later; what I want to suggest here is a plausible defence of the fourth approach's inclusion of the Cultural Revolution period, which was widely perceived as a lawless era. This reading is taken from Brian Hipkin, who suggests that a key difference between the legal realms of Mao's period and Deng's period is not whether the period has laws or not, but whether the rules of justice are codified or informal. For Hipkin (1984: 126), during the Mao's period, 'rules were created and maintained at the level of interpersonal relationships and it was possible for them to both generate a sense of solidarity and to give the masses a chance to control their situations'; after the transformation, however, 'codification, the intervention of formal state legal organizations, control by higher courts and notions of precedent' emerge and these measures lead to rules that 'stand outside of the interpersonal recognition of solidarity and socialist equality'. Consequently, it has led to the alienation of the ordinary people, particularly the rural peasants and the urban proletariat from legal practices, and partly resulted in future inequality (Hipkin 1984: 126). Hipkin (1984: 125) attributes much of this 'mass-line' style of socialist legality to China's immense cultural heritage, which had contributed to the longevity and efficiency of China's informal justice system as shown in the history of managing such a big country with little more than 5,000 lawyers.

It is beyond the scope of my current project to go into details about the change (*bian*) and continuity (*tong*通) between traditional Chinese jurisprudence and sinicized Marxist jurisprudence, but to help the reader better understand this perspective, I will mention two key theses. The first is the discovery by Yu Ronggen (1998), a widely recognized authoritative scholar on Confucian legal thought, that the distinctive core as well as spirit of Chinese jurisprudence is the trinity of Natural Law or Universal principles (*tianli*), state laws (*guofa*) and commonsensical sentiments or the actual condition of the people (*renqing*). In this framework, the common people are not alienated from the legal realm mainly because they occupy one pole of the trinity, and they can utilize common sense as a weapon against doctrinaire or deviant interpretations of state laws, which is supposed to be consistent with Natural Law which in turn is also based on the sentiments and actual condition of the people (Yu 1998: 14). This is in fact supported by a second thesis advocated by Jin Guantao and Liu Qingfeng, two well-known scholars of Chinese intellectual history. Drawing discoveries from a large quantitative database for the study of modern Chinese intellectual history which they developed, Jin and Liu argue that the Chinese concept of Li as the criteria for judgements of propriety and legitimacy is radically different from the counterpart of rationality in the West (Jin and Liu 2010). For Jin and Liu (2010: 26), one could read the Chinese concept of Li as 'commonsense rationality' (*changshilixing*), which is meticulously entrenched in 'common sense' and 'natural sentiments or facts (*renzhichangqing*)'.

Hipkin's reading of socialist legality clearly renders support for the fourth approach towards SMC. Bearing the two theses mentioned above in mind, we could then also better understand Mao Zedong's statement that 'The peasants are clear sighted. Who is bad and who is not quite vicious, who deserves severe punishment and who deserves to be let off lightly – the peasants keep clear accounts and very seldom has the punishment exceeded the crime' (as cited in Wong 2006: 7), as well as Mao's later shying away from codified laws for governing the people. This perhaps could also help us to understand the current Chinese judiciary's strategic turn towards populism, its re-emphasis on mediation of disputes (Peerenboom 2010: 21), as well as the hot debate in China over the advantages of substantive justice (*shitizhengyi*) over procedural justice (*chengxuzhengyi*), and established legal scholars' surging interest in 'soft law' (*ruanfa*).[8]

Marxist party-state approach supported by a new organic eclectic ideology

The fifth approach towards SMC marks the latest turn in constitutional thought among the leadership as well as some leading established intellectuals in China. First of all, it is worth pointing out that given the dense liberal flavour of the notion of 'constitutionalism' in the Chinese context, which has induced the 'constitutionalism abolition thesis' mentioned earlier, the terminology is rarely used by party leaders and established intellectuals, with the exception of some legal scholars mainly in the legal community. Party leaders have used the notion of the 'rule of Constitution' (*yixianzhiguo*), but the most common counterparts of 'constitutionalism' in the Chinese discourse have been 'socialist democratic politics', 'Chinese style democracy' and 'socialist political civilization'. Since the political authority's public pronouncement and advocacy of these notions with Chinese characteristics, the literature devoted to these themes has proliferated. Though these different notions emerged in different contexts and differ to some extent in terms of their respective intensions and extensions, they all share an essential core in the Chinese case, which is the organic unity of 'the leadership of the Party, the position of the people as masters of the country and the rule of law'. This constitutional trinity was included in the reports of both the 16th and the 17th CPC National Congresses. Since then, an enormous literature has been devoted to this constitutional trinity as well. Below I will just take Wang Jinyuan's explication of the organic relationships among the trinity as representative.[9]

The three parts are held to be organically united since the leadership of the party is the guarantee of the latter two, while the people as masters is the essential requirement of socialist democratic politics and rule of law is the fundamental strategy of the CPC to lead the people to govern state affairs (Wang 2003: 30). According to these authors, the leadership of the CPC has been proven by both history and reality to be indispensable for the setting up of the socialist system and the continuing march towards socialist democracy in China. In fact, from the very moment of the birth of the CPC, it has embraced the realization and development of people's democracy as its main task, so there is no divergence between the leadership of the CPC and the people as masters. Accordingly, all Chinese leaders have repeatedly emphasized the crucial leading role of the CPC for the socialist causes and endeavours China is aiming at (Wang 2003: 30–1). As for the people as masters, that is surely a necessary requirement of socialist democracy, which itself is the inherent nature and requirement of socialism (Wang 2003: 32). The people as masters means that all endeavours should serve the interests of the people, who have the inherent rights to participate in governing state affairs and supervise the operation of state apparatuses. At the same time, rule of law as an important mark of modern civilization has been accepted as the necessary requirement of socialist democratic politics and also the guarantor of the realization of the latter, and consequently the goal of people as the master. Rule of law is also the bridge as well as nexus between the CPC and the people as masters.

From this brief introduction, we can see that the fifth approach combines certain core ideas from both liberal constitutionalism and Marxist constitutionalism as reviewed earlier. In this regard, it is similar to the effort of the third approach, but it transcends the third approach by developing an organic outlook on the three core elements rather than tilting towards the rule of law value. As we can see from the spectrum of Table 2, this latest development of constitutional thought also could be regarded as the result of the interactions and dialogues between liberal constitutionalism and Marxist constitutionalism. Marxist constitutionalism, as shown in the fourth approach, takes the orthodox ideology as the defining element of constitutionalism and to some extent adopts a kind of consequentialist philosophy which enables the government to use ends to justify means as practised during the pre-Deng eras. However, due to increasing western influences as well as China's own development, the importance of the rule of law and individual rights has been widely accepted by both the authority and the public and consequently integrated into this latest constitutionalism discourse. This eclectic reading is also supported by He Baogang (2010), who argues for a constitutionalism that is able to transcend both the left and the right ideologies and maintain a dynamic coordinating balance among them with a comprehensive outlook.

The eclectic nature of the fifth approach is also well illustrated in the new discursive terminologies of the current ideology. Shying away from the slogans of the Maoist period yet without embracing Western values in a wholesale manner, party leaders and established intellectuals have sought to develop a 'theoretical system of Socialism with Chinese Characteristics' that incorporates those newly coined ideas such as the 'Three Represents', 'Scientific Outlook on Development', 'People-centeredness', 'Harmonious Society', 'Socialist Political Civilization' and 'Socialist Legal Ideas'. This discursive turn of Chinese ideology has been well captured by China scholars in Western academia as well. For example, through the application of discourse theory to an analysis of the newly emerging ideology of 'Socialism with Chinese Characteristics' and 'Scientific Outlook on Development', Guoxin Xing (2009: 213) argues that the Chinese party leaders and established intellectuals have 'boiled socialism down to abstract values, independent of and autonomous from the economic base, marking a retreat from class and class struggle'. Nicholas Dynon's (2008) article 'Four Civilizations' and the Evolution of Post-Mao Chinese Socialist Ideology' also offers an in-depth analysis of the emergence of 'civilization discourse' in China's current ideology. What is remarkable about this collection of terminology is that both the left and the right could interpret and utilize them in ways consistent with their respective core tenets, while the 'Party rhetoric defines the opportunity structures for debate' (Gilley and Holbig 2009: 342). For example, employing a similar attempt to take 'people centeredness' as the foundational norm of Chinese constitutionalism, liberals try to associate it with the protection of human rights and dignity (Liu and Yang 2004; Li and Zhu 2005; Yuan 2010), while Marxists tend to emphasize the superiority of the Marxist understanding on the issue over that of Western liberal alternatives (Xu and Xie 2005; Chen and Jin 2009).

A related issue worth pointing out is the emergence of corresponding legal theory in the name of 'Socialist Legal Ideas' for SMC. It is a summation and theorization of China's legal reforms both in its practical and theoretical dimensions over the past three decades; it is also an inherent part of the theory of 'Socialism with Chinese Characteristics' and deals with juridical aspects of the grand theoretical system. It is a direct result of the adaptation and innovation of Marxist jurisprudence in the contemporary Chinese context. As mentioned earlier, while Marxist jurisprudence is not so popular in mainstream Western academia, it is nevertheless a hot topic in Chinese legal studies. This is well shown in the number of articles written on this theme, especially its sinicization. For example, the core social science journal articles that have 'Marxist jurisprudence'in their title have increased from 5 in 2000 to 31 today.[10] The focus of this literature has also shifted from mainly an introduction to the original legal theory of Marxism to an exploration of its sinicization for application in contemporary China; the recent high-level conference devoted to this theme in the summer of 2010 at Renmin University is a good illustration of the ascendance of this topic.[11] A more telling statistics perhaps is the number of articles written on 'Socialist Legal Ideas', explicitly claiming to be a result of the process of the Sinicization of Marxist jurisprudence in China. Since the term was first coined in 2006, there have been a total of 43 articles in the core journals containing this idea in their title.[12] State authorities have tried to advocate it in society with promotional campaigns, such as knowledge and speech contests. The Politics and Law Committee of the CPC has also published a *Socialist Legal IdeasReader* in 2009 and have included 'Socialist Legal Ideas' in China's Judicial Test (*sifakaoshi*) as a separate, weighty section, starting in 2009. There is no need to go into further details about the contents as well as justifications for these ideas; it is enough to point out that the core essence of 'Socialist Legal Ideas', as the official expression puts it, is the constitutional trinity explicated earlier. Consequently, 'Socialist Legal Ideas' has eclectically combined values such as 'respect and protection of human rights', 'maintenance of the authority of law' and 'leadership of the CPC' (*dangdelingdao*).

Conclusion and implications

To sum up, in this chapter we first described the emerging context of the newly developed SMC. The progress of the rule of law in both its theoretical and practical dimensions over the past thirty years in China surely plays the foundational role for the surging interests among scholars on the issue of constitutionalism in China. Meanwhile, the deep penetration and domination of Western liberal constitutionalism have induced two reactions from scholars outside of the legal realm, namely the articulation of the 'constitutionalism abolition thesis' as well as some cultural conservatives' proposal of developing constitutionalism that is based on and also loyal to China's indigenous tradition. Within the legal realm, it has pushed some to rethink the preconceptions of the WLC paradigm both in and outside China, and catalysed their articulation of the SMC paradigm. The fad of advocating the 'Chinese Model' within Chinese academia and popular trend of shaking off the yoke of current dominant paradigms in the West, especially since the Western financial crisis, may have offered an amiable and supporting environment for the emergence of SMC as well.

We then reviewed the three main approaches towards Chinese constitutionalism that are under the canopy of SMC. The first one is represented by Larry Backer's model, which takes into consideration the CPC as well as its ideologies, but still emphasizes rule of law – the defining feature of constitutionalism. This approach does not elaborate much on their understanding of the rule of law, but it seems that they share that of the liberal paradigm. The second also takes the party-state structure into the constitutionalism, but emphasizes more the orthodox ideology. Its understanding of rule of law is also significantly different from that of the liberal paradigm, and is more akin to jurisprudence such as Critical Legal Theory, that are largely marginalized in the contemporary western legal realm. The third is the one currently developed and promoted by the political authority as well as the established scholars in China. It combines certain core ideas from the previous two approaches and emphasizes the organic trinity of party leadership, democracy and rule of law. This approach has also developed corresponding legal theories such as the 'Socialist Legal Ideas' to match it.

The implications of SMC could be profound. First of all, the emergence of a lively heterogeneous constitutionalism certainly poses a challenge to dominant WLC and consequently contributes to the pluralistic orientation of current constitutional discourses both in China and around the world. It will perhaps force some liberal scholars to rethink their preconceptions of constitutionalism and generate more dialogues between different constitutional communities. Second, it may remind us of the relevance of Marxism in contemporary China as well as within the global society. After thirty years' embrace of a market economy and the penetration of external forces, is Marxism–Leninism still relevant in China as the official line proclaims? Are the top CPC leaders who call for cadres at all levels to 'truly study, truly understand, truly believe and truly apply' 'the stand, viewpoint and methodologies of Marxism', or what they call the 'living soul of Marxism' merely hypocrites or are they doing something imprudent or deluded? We did not tackle this problem directly in this chapter, but the answer may be quite obvious. The constitutional structure of China has remained largely the same throughout the past six decades and the current ideology of the regime is eclectic and vague enough to retain flexibility for both left and right turns. To a clairvoyant observer, the current Chinese ideology is very much taking Marxist values as the Ti and liberal values as the Yong, though with both adapted and contextualized to the current reality and time. In fact, there is sufficient evidence to support such a reading, such as the current leadership's heavy investment in the Marxism Theory Research and Construction Project, which aspires to lead the whole humanities and social science world in China, and its firm stance towards reforms in the area of civil and political rights that lie at the core of the liberal paradigm. The third implication is then the impacts of such a 'communist' China on the world order. While the ideology has successfully shied away from traditional class politics and incorporated a market economy as well as private property, it still subscribes to the 'stand, viewpoint and methodology' of Marxism; hence, it is perhaps unacceptable to hardcore liberals. This certainly necessitates more careful research and reflection for anyone who is concerned about the future of the world order and peace.

Notes

1　The reason I prefer the title of 'Sinicized Marxist Constitutionalism' over other titles such as 'Party-State Constitutionalism' or 'Socialist Constitutionalism with Chinese Characteristics' has to do with its semantic range as well as preciseness, which will be clearer later.

2　The 'Four Cardinal Principles' includes the 'leadership of the Communist Party, guidance of Marxism–Leninism and Mao Zedong thought, people's democratic dictatorship and adherence to socialism'. It was advocated by Deng Xiaoping in 1979 as the foundational or baseline principles for China's reform and opening up. It was explicitly written into the Charter of the CPC, and implicitly included in the Preamble of the Constitution. For the latter, see 'Chapter 2, The Fundamental Principles of Chinese Constitutional Law' of Lin Feng (2000).

3　The boundaries among the five approaches may not be clearly delineated, nor are the categorization of the scholars to the approaches absolute; the preliminary categorizations are for general organizational as well as illustrative purposes.

4　The assumed dichotomy of either the rule of law or despotism seems to have been taken for granted by the liberal paradigm; nevertheless, we should be aware that this preconception has excluded some plausible alternatives. For example, as I have shown and elaborated in another paper, the core of Confucian constitutionalism is to design a subtle cultural mechanism to contain the potential abuses of government power without excessive reliance on legal means; for some, the socialist legal system as practised in China during Mao's period is founded on a 'radicalized version of Confucianism', and also representing a socialist alternative to the liberal paradigm (Hipkin 1984: 125).

5　For a more detailed discussion of the compound feature of China's political reform as well as the overall Reform and Open Up movements of the late 1970s, see Tong Dezhi (2010: 8–23).

6　This is a major reason for my preference for using the title 'Sinicized Marxist Constitutionalism', because only it precisely and comprehensively covers the whole period; other titles, such as 'Party-state Constitutionalism' and 'Socialist Constitionalism with Chinese Characteristics' tend to be either not indicative of its philosophical foundation as the former, or not comprehensive enough as the latter which tends to be associated with Deng's reform period in the Chinese context. For a more detailed elaboration on the evolution and continuity of Marxism in China, see Ni Degang (2009).

7 According to Chinese scholars, this theory system was developed during Deng's time, but theorized afterwards.
8 This is well shown in the growing number of articles containing 'soft law' in the title: before 2005, there is only five articles, and now the number has increased to 29 in total (statistics from China Academic Journals Full-text Database).
9 I only provide a brief account of the organic relationship here. For a discussion of what each pole entails, see Zhang and Jiang (2002: 646–7).
10 Statistics is from China Academic Journals Full-text Database.
11 The conference is attended by over 120 leading legal scholars and practitioners in China, with some important political figures present in the opening ceremony, such as the Vice-president of the Central Party School, the former Director of the Central Military Committee Office, etc.
12 Statistics is from China Academic Journals Full-text Database.

References

Backer, L. C. (2009), 'The party as polity, the Communist Party, and the Chinese constitutional state: a theory of state-party constitutionalism', *Journal of Chinese and Comparative Law*, 16, (1), 161–5.

Balme, S. and Dowdle, M. W. (eds), (2009), *Building Constitutionalism in China*. New York: Palgrave Macmillan.

Benewick, R. (1998), 'Towards a developmental theory of constitutionalism: the Chinese case', *Government and Opposition*, 33, (4), 442–61.

Chen, H. (2004), 'Some reflections on the problem of constitutionalism', *Political Studies*, 3, 1–11.

Chen, X. and Jin, Y. (2009), 'People-centered: centered on what kinds of people and what of a person', *Marxist Philosophy*, 8, 15–21.

Chu, J. (2006-last update), 'One Party Constitutionalism: The New Path of Chinese Constitutionalism'. Available from: http://chinaelections.net/newsinfo.asp?newsid=99982[Accessed 10/11/2010].

Dynon, N. (2008), '"Four civilizations" and the evolution of post-Mao Chinese socialist ideology', *The China Journal*, 60, 83–109.

Fang, K. (2006), 'The three letters about the current problem of neo-confucianism on the Mainland', *Academic Exploration*, 2, 4–10.

Geertz, C. (1977), *The Interpretation of Cultures*. New York: Basic Books.

Gilley, B. and Holbig, H. (2009), 'The debate on party legitimacy in China: a mixed quantitative/qualitative analysis', *Journal of Contemporary China*, 18, (59), 339–58.

Han, D. (2005), *A Study of the Constitutionalism of New Democracy*. Beijing: People's Press.

Han, D. (2008), *The 1954 Constitution and Chinese Constitutionalism*. Wuhan: Wuhan University Press.

He, B. (2010), 'Constitutionalism and trascending the competition of the left and the right', *Jinyang Journal*, 4, 21–4.

Hipkin, B. (1984), 'Book review of justice and politics in People's China: Legal order or continuing revolution by James P. Brandy', *Journal of Law and Society*, 11, 124–7.

Jiang, S. (2009), 'The unwritten constitution of chinese constitution: a new perspective to understand Chinese constitution', 12, 10–39.

Jin, G. and Liu, Q. (2010), *A Study of Conceptual History: The Formation of the Important Political Concepts of Modern China*. Beijing: Law Press.

Li, L. and Zhu, K. (2005), 'The transcendental dimension of constitutionalism and the constitutional meaning of "people-centredness"', *The Journal of Henan Politics and Law Cadre Management School*, 1, 64–9.

Lin, F. (2000), *Constitutional Law in China*. Hong Kong: Sweet & Maxwell Asia.

Liu, J. and Yang, Z. (2004), '"People-centredness" and constitutional civilization', *Jiangxi Social Science*, 5, 163–6.

Ni, D. (2009), *A Study of Sinicization of Marxism*. Beijing: Central Documents Publishing House.

Peerenboom, R. (2010), 'Social foundation of China's living constitution.' Available from http://ssrn.com/abstract=1542463 [accessed 01/03/2011]

Qing, Q. and Ye, H. (2008), *A Study of Socialist Constitutionalism*. Jinan: Shandong People's Press.

Ren, X. (2010), 'The developmental prospects of socialist constitutionalism with Chinese characteristics: from Mao, Deng to Jiang', *The Theory and Practice of Socialist Constitutionalism with Chinese Characteristics*, Changsha, Hunan, May 21–3, 2010.

The Politics and Law Committee of CPC Central (2009), *Socialist Legal Ideas Reader*. Beijing: China Chang'an Press.

Tong, D. (2010), 'Introduction', in J. Gao and D. Tong (eds), *Chinese Democracy*. Tianjin: Tianjin People's Press, 3–31.

Wang, J. (2003), 'The relationship between political civilization and constitutionalism', *Chinese Legal Studies*, 6, 33–40.

Wong, K. C. (2006), 'Human rights and limitation of state power: the discovery of constitutionalism in the People's Republic of China', *Asia-Pacific Journal on Human Rights & the Law*, 7, (1), 1–37.

Xie, Y. (2004), 'Could constitutionalism be used as a fundamental political concept of China', *Political Studies*, 3, 12–14.

Xing, G. (2009). 'Hu jintao's political thinking and legitimacy building: A post-marxist perspective.' *Asian Affairs: An American Review*, 36, (4), 213–26.

Xu, X. and Xie, L. (2005), 'The institutional condition for realizing the constitutional ideal of "people-centred" socialism: a reading of Marx's whole-person development theory from the constitutional perspective', *Philosophy Study*, 7, 34–8.

Yu, R. (1998), 'The conflicts and integration of natural law, state laws, and commonsensical sentiments of the people: the inner core of confucian law and traditional resources ofmodern legality', *Chinese Cultural Forum*, 4, 12–19.

Yu, X. (2009), 'Western constitutional ideas and constitutional discourse in China, 1978–2005', in S. Balme and M. W. Dowdle (eds), *Building Constitutionalism in China*. New York: Palgrave Macmillan, pp. 111–24.

Yuan, J. (2010), '"People-centredness" and Constitutionalism', *Theoretical Investigation*, 6, 163–6.

Zhang, X. and Jiang, Z. (2002), 'The three-represents thought: the foundation of China's constitutional thoughts', *Wuhan University Journal*, 55, (6), 641–7.

CHAPTER TEN

Varieties of constitutionalism: a response to 'Sinicized Marxist Constitutionalism' by Andrew (Chengyi) Peng

Terrell Carver

Andrew (Chengyi) Peng's article 'Sinicized Marxist Constitutionalism' provides a very welcome window on recent and continuing political developments in China. As Peng explains, the whole idea of such an area of interest has been almost unthinkable within Western scholarship, and is only recently opening up in the last couple of years. This was because – from most Western perspectives – Marxism and constitutionalism did not go together in the first place, so one never really needed to look for it at all. There was no 'it' to look 'at' in any serious way.

By way of comparison, it took quite a long time for serious study of the Soviet state bureaucracy to emerge, as opposed to minutely detailed interest in the Communist Party and its hierarchies, purges, intrigues, secret speeches and the like, all of which was taken to sum up the political realm. Only with *perestroika* and its various devolutions did Soviet studies begin to embrace a genuinely pluralist (as opposed to merely factional) model for Soviet politics, but the applicable time period was all too brief. Since then, the situation has grown even more complex, and pluralist assumptions seem to hold rather poorly in grasping post-Communist realities.

China is of course a double puzzle in this regard. Western access to the documents, elites and publics involved was even more limited by linguistic and cultural considerations than was the case with the Soviet Union, not to mention distance, lack of informants and state restrictions and constraints (which persist). And it was also limited by the persistence of the pervasive Western view about constitutions that 'if it's Marxist, then it's a sham'. Since the 1990s, Westerners have had a further double puzzle. Given radical changes in economic policies and successive waves of ideological vacuity, in what sense is China still credibly Marxist, as it claims? And if it is no longer Marxist, how then are we (in the Anglophone West) to understand its politics?

Perhaps we are unhappier than are the Chinese with our rather out-of-date selection of models – one-party state? devolved and competing bureaucracies? Authoritarian capitalism? developing country? emerging economy? and so on. The Western press focuses overwhelmingly on human rights protesters and government responses, because we understand that at once. It fits into our civil rights and civil disobedience discourse, and particularly after the Tiananmen Square protests and massacre of 1989 – now an iconic world-historical sequence of events – we are on the case for those issues 24/7. We were there ourselves in our own Western histories beforehand in terms of demonstrations, protests and martyrdoms, as we built and developed constitutional regimes, and we are still there, having more or less regularized the balance – so we might think – between citizens' rights (as derived from popular sovereignty) and legal obligations (as required for social order).

Or so we might have thought till the 9/11 securitization and Global War on Terror brought home to the United States such un-Western practices as incarceration without trial (or credible trial of the usual sort), secret rendition and torture, remission of American citizens into military prisons, pervasive surveillance and 'profiling' for lists, murder-by-drone and 'collateral' casualties, etc. While some of these practices had occurred historically, and indeed reflected legally entrenched racisms and paranoia, they were hardly celebrated in the acronymic ('USA PATRIOT' Act) and Orwellian ('Homeland Security') terms proudly promoted by the G. W. Bush administration and overwhelmingly approved and funded by Congress. Whether and to what extent this represents some 're-balancing' of the rule of law and constitutional rights, on the one hand, with public order considerations of security, on the other, is still a hotly debated question. And of course some of these issues unfold directly and indirectly in other constitutional states, such as Canada, Western Europe and elsewhere. This is to say that even where the Western press likes to draw a line between 'us' and 'them', to some readers, anyway, the idea that the West exemplifies rule of law derived from stable constitutional structures, whereas China does not, seems more than somewhat debateable at present. The Chinese leadership, understandably, has not been slow to play this card, but I am not convinced that their comments are always reported to us in full, or indeed at all, in major media sources.

Peng's article informs us about 'Sinicized Marxist Constitutionalism' as a Western-derived and therefore possibly common – or at least translatable – paradigm applicable to the developing political situation in China. It is thus offered as a way of summarizing and understanding the history and trajectory of political practice in terms that supplant the Party-only model, or even the Party-State model, through which communist states were formerly and exclusively viewed. Crucially this paradigm focuses on rule of – or by – law within a constitutional framework that is said to have credibility, or is at least gaining credibility. In other words, a legislative and judicial system that had some genuine independence from a party-executive governmental system would have to be in place, and indeed the latter would have to be visibly accountable to the former, rather than the reverse.

How much credibility and for whom are of course the operative questions. Peng argues that credibility seems to be growing in terms of the way that citizens and lawyers in China use legal processes which have a regularity and consistency that we recognize. Ultimately, within the paradigm, this must come from the judiciary interpreting the law and the state then respecting the judiciary's interpretations, rather than power and influence flowing the other way. Thus we are looking at a practice of constitutionalism, not just the letter of any current constitution, and we might indeed be looking towards revisions as these processes develop, which is, of course, a normal part of constitutionalism. The paradigm itself does not have to fit current realities exactly; rather it characterizes those realities one way, rather than another, and thus guides us into a predictive mode where we think it likely that we will see more of the same constitutional regularities – barring unpredictable and countervailing events, of course. Then – as in the United States most recently – public discussions must ensue.

My response here is not to argue that constitutionalism is or is not a good way to interpret Chinese politics at the moment, but rather to suggest that one aspect of opening this kind of window on China is that it should make us usefully question our own understandings of constitutionalism more closely, and in that way expose ourselves to things that we may already know as matters of detailed variation, but which in this geopolitical context, are really matters of definitional significance. Put bluntly, I am saying that we have a considerable variety of significant constitutional variation already in the West, and that this derives both from formal differences in terms of texts and legal systems and from circumstantial differences in terms of local or cultural practices and presumptions.

My starting point is to note, as Peng explains, that over the last 30 years a significant number of Chinese intellectuals have accepted the 'liberal constitutional paradigm', and are thus committing themselves to understanding and developing political practices in China in those terms (and on occasion to suffering notable consequences for this). The article lucidly details the ways that this ideal is interpreted and pursued in contemporary China. My task here is to reflect further on this ideal so that we guard against idealizing ourselves and losing our critical sense of just where and why our own practices should come up for scrutiny. Taking a critical position about policies and practices elsewhere is fine, but we should use that opportunity to watch our backs even more closely and thus to resist the temptation to glory in the way that others idealize what we say we stand for. Is our ideal really as consistent as that? Are our practices really exemplars of the varied and often conflicting ideals that we espouse?

Taking the constitutional route, critics of China – even from within China, as Peng explains – focus on the lack of judicial independence, compared to the West and particularly to the United States. But this discussion in China, as explained by Peng, seems to me to reflect an over-emphasis on the role of the US Supreme Court in reviewing and striking down both Federal and state legislation. These are not powers granted to the Court by the US Constitution at all, but were rather arrogated to the Court itself by early justices and their decisions – a process not uncontroversial at the time. Moreover both the stability and the steady progress of democracy in America are highly questionable presumptions. The US Civil War was specifically constitutional in character (approximately half a million casualties and untold internecine suffering), and for almost 100 years the Supreme Court consistently upheld racial segregation and institutionalized prejudice (whereas the slave system had been controversial from its introduction in the seventeenth century).

A quick review of French, German, Italian and Eastern European history reveals that Western democracy is highly fragile, and that its course of development has been far from smooth, given the number of constitutional states that have 'gone under' to fascism, authoritarian militarism and the like over the years. Indeed if we go to the pre-War period, most were not all that democratic in their constitutionalism anyway, particularly with respect to women and working class people generally. And many were self-justifying and self-promoting empires, with scant interest in credible constitutionalism for their 'possessions'. Commonplace judgements of stability require not just the long view, but an active process of erasure and forgetting.

While it is true that the United Kingdom is only just now establishing a supreme court independent of the legislative branch (which of course is famously not separated from the executive), it is rather a mistake to see judicial independence as peculiarly American. It is in fact the foundational argument of John Locke's (1988) *Two Treatises of Government*, first circulated and published in 1688/89, and widely reproduced and translated since then. The 'Second Treatise' on 'Civil Government' is probably the most successful political tract in history to date, and is unquestionably the largest stone in the foundations of liberalism. It argues that people form a 'politick' society and then derogate their individual executive powers to a government, precisely so that this common executive can protect their persons and property by enforcing the decisions of 'known and indifferent' judges or magistrates (II§§124–5).

Most commentators on democracy focus on the representative institutions through which laws are made and on the party political processes through which governments come to hold the power to execute the law. Judicial processes and judicial independence thus tend to disappear, especially if formal review of legislation against constitutional provisions and rights is not part of the process, or is – as is usual – exercised with great restraint. Even worse, courts are sometimes dismissed as undemocratic (though many state judges in the United States are directly elected), whereas they are in fact crucial to liberalism, conceived as a constitutional system that guarantees the rights of citizens against unwarranted government actions. As Locke says, governments have but a 'fiduciary power' from the people to act only for the 'publick good' (II§§131, 149). 'Rule of law' is thus often taken for granted in Western constitutionalism, poorly understood in theoretical terms, and – tragically – rather easily suspended. Under the G. W. Bush administration, it was perverted at times into a simulacrum, notably in the novel 'trials' and 'procedures' operating in (or at least planned for) the detention centres at Guantánamo Bay.

Arguing that courts are inherently undemocratic is thus a mistake. Locke was rightly worried that governments would be tempted into the 'absolute and arbitrary' power (II§23 and *passim.*) that is the 'evil other' in his theory, and it is the independence of the judiciary – and the popularly enforced requirement that governments respect this – that generates the whole enterprise of liberal democracy (though Locke used neither word to describe his theoretical edifice). This of course may be off the point as to what either Chinese intellectuals or Western commentators think is going on. But then my point is that Peng's article should be provoking us into thinking again, and thinking carefully.

Somewhat the same process is evidently going on in China. Political studies are more popular there than constitutional studies, because the authorities are not keen on documents and practices that 'interfere' with what they want to do. Constitutional and legal studies are indeed flourishing in the United States, but then to what extent are they already informed with local and cultural content that has become normalized as 'just part of the ideal'? In fact the British parliamentary system has been copied more often as a model of democratic practice throughout the world – even in post-war zones of sole or hegemonic American occupation such as Japan and Germany – than the US model, which has full separation of powers, a directly elected chief executive, judicial review at the highest level and a highly devolved federal system. Peng rightly points this out. I would not enter into any debate about what local content is or is not helpful or appropriate (or even what counts as generically 'Chinese') as argued through in current debates in China. But it is certainly the case that liberal democracy has recognizable and distinct French characteristics, as well as British and American ones, not to mention the intriguing constitutional issues raised in recent years by Aboriginal and Maori politics in Australia, Canada and New Zealand (obviously the cases of local variation can be multiplied considerably from here). From China, it may all look Western, and the West in that view may well be exemplified in the US Constitution as amended. But trust me, US constitutionalism plays well in Peoria, but not in Paris or Pisa or Poznań.

But what about the one-party state? I would not dream of defending this, but any discussion on this point should note that some Western democracies have had very long periods of quite uncompetitive one-party rule (e.g. Sweden, Japan), and that the supposedly crucial constituent of democracy – classically formulated by Joseph Schumpeter (2010: chs 21–2) as a party-competitive system of elections – is rarely if ever embodied in constitutions themselves. How much difference there may in fact be between competing parties, how broad a choice voters actually have, how honest and accountable party leaderships are (not to mention how open their candidate selection procedures are) and numerous other debates about political parties are characteristic areas where the 'Western liberal paradigm' has simply not settled, or if it has, a lot of us are unhappy about it, wherever we are. Gestures in China towards party pluralism and non-party representation in consultative bodies may look feeble, but then in what sense are political parties credible just because they are (usually) competing?

The founding theorists of liberalism were – to a man – hostile to faction and party. In a notable essay, Carole Pateman (1983: 204) crisply remarked that, 'For feminists, democracy has never existed; women have never been and still are not admitted as full and equal members and citizens in any country known as a "democracy"'. Her target was largely the party political presumptions and procedures that formed the sexist (and racist) basis from which governments were constructed and through which courts – however independent or not – construed legality. Given our own confusions and erasures regarding the party political process, we lack a sound basis for dismissing out of hand any of the current Chinese discussions on the party-state configuration, or indeed the 'Han Chinese' settlement projects in the Far West, given exclusionary and replacement practices in place in some Western locales until quite recently. While anti-racism and other multi-cultural activisms against unwarranted forms of discrimination have a lengthy history in Western politics, the reconciliation of these ideals with constitutionalism has been and still is a slow and painful process. Saying sorry on a national basis in some of these cases might mean something, but many of these processes continue, and it is not always obvious that constitutionalism as such generates sufficient consistency in practice to warrant belief that it is a solid bulwark against structural inequality and sectarian bigotry.

Indeed the liberalism/Marxism boundary is itself more porous than many (inside China or within Western countries) might think; not all democracy on the Marxist side of things is utterly sham. Marx was an economically oriented left-democrat, committing himself to middle-class groups working for constitutional reform (and indeed for constitutions in the first place, over and against non-constitutional, highly authoritarian monarchies).[1] While Marx then – and Marxists along the line – looked over and beyond liberal politics and its presumed free-market deficiencies and ideological smokescreens, it is not the case that the overall vision within Marxism is illiberal as such. Rather there is overwhelming evidence that its socialist character was specifically intended as an advance on democracy, recouping its basic assumptions and improving on its practice – in theory anyway, whereas practice often works out otherwise, of course. The problem for Marxists was that liberal democracies preserved economic inequalities (which are now more extreme in many places than was the case in post-war times) at the expense of class-rooted exclusion and misery, not just 'fair competition' and 'equal opportunity'. Arguably the economic construction of democracy today as pro-'private enterprise' and anti-'state interference' has not simply taken a toll on the kind of democratic *and* economic advances that Marx himself predicted and promoted – such as minimum wages and hours, health and safety at work, realistic pensions and unemployment benefits and the like. These have been rolled back not just by neoliberal legislation and executive action (or inaction, in the case of regulatory agencies), but also by interpretations of constitutional principles that support this 'free market' ideology. Judicial independence is quite a strictly constructed practice; constitutional decisions are necessarily political – rather than sublimely Olympian – in all cases.

Discussions along these lines may or may not be taking place in China, and may or may not be very genuine in all cases, but given a convergence of systems between Western capitalisms and current Chinese economic management (or at least comparable levels of economic growth and social stratification), there is more common ground here – as Peng argues – than many might assume. I put this kind of question personally to a Chinese interlocutor at a conference on contemporary capitalism in China in 2006. My way of conceptualizing this was to ask about concepts of social democracy that 'the left' (outside the United States, usually) rather takes for granted, even if the onward march of neoliberalism (not to mention neo-conservatism) has made many 'leftists' feel beleaguered. 'Ah', my Chinese friend replied, 'we've got over Lenin, but we're not yet allowed Bernstein' (see Bernstein 2009).

This is just where Marxist constitutionalism gets interesting and well before it gets 'Sinicized'. At its simplest (which is historically located in the 1840s) Marx's and Engels's common political project was piggy-backed on radical constitutionalism, which was itself not just revolutionary in political terms but also in economic presumptions. The economic presumption involved was not merely that humans were by nature entrepreneurial as producers and utility-maximizing as consumers, but that politics and specifically the state must be organized so as to allow this to flourish, rather than to inhibit it on grounds of tradition, morals, religion or anything else. In practice this was a self-conscious attack on hierarchies of 'birth' and 'time-honoured' institutions which prevented or discouraged this realization, and thus on the non-representative and unaccountable monarchies which stood in the way. Constitutionalism was a means to an end, and as Marx correctly saw – and many openly acknowledged – the 'end' was to be a state structure and political practice amenable to financial and industrial entrepreneurs at the expense of feudal and rentier classes. Marx, and many others, discounted the ideological claims commonly made that this outcome would liberate 'all' – including everyone without substantial property and wealth – but he supported *pro tem* the political alliances that would – as was done in a day during the French Revolution – abolish feudalism, and open the way to trade, industry and financial gain without limit.

This state structure – termed 'bourgeois' by Marx and understood as commercial or middle class more generally – evolved in fits and starts in ways that mirror the Lockean perspective from the late seventeenth century. This was unsurprising, as Locke's relentlessly anti-feudal and pro-commercial narrative – 'God gave the world to the use of the industrious and rational' – says not a word about monarchy, constitutional or otherwise, precisely to obtain clarity about popular sovereignty, albeit refracted through a lens of commercial privilege (II§34). This was said to be a politics of majority rule, but in institutions that specifically or by implication failed to include all adults. 'Majority of whom' is always an interesting question. Western democracy thus evolved in tandem with Western economics, against which Chinese authoritarianism and hostility to trade (after the late fifteenth century) make an important historical contrast and controversial subject of contemporary debate. Given the economic changes in China since the 1990s and the liberalization of commercial practices, it is easy to identify a parallelism in Western experience. '*Enrichissez vous*' was François Guizot's famous slogan, and the West has hardly looked back since he proclaimed this in the 1840s. In China this has been translated into what is said to be a Marxist imperative to 'Build the productive forces' at this stage in history, with consumer capitalism and high finance put in place (and let rip) to do the trick.

Marx himself was not quite on board for this strategy, though it is less than completely clear what political and intellectual strategy he in fact espoused from the later 1850s onwards, once the revolutionary wave of constitutionalism had receded. It left behind in its wake a string of modernizing, post-feudal constitutional regimes, mostly monarchies that balanced land-owning and industrializing interests through various forms of representative and responsible government. Representative of what and responsible to whom were good questions with – throughout the nineteenth century – quite a clear answer: propertied males. Suffrage and electoral restrictions were a notable feature of 'liberal' constitutionalism, notably the US Constitution (see the passages on 'free persons' and 'Indians not taxed', with women tacitly excluded), and the German Imperial Constitution (with a strong monarchy and institutionalization of 'Junker' class privilege), not to mention the successive struggles for electoral reform and enfranchisement in the United Kingdom (of Great Britain and the whole of Ireland), at Westminster and elsewhere.

Marx's position on these regimes was excoriatingly critical for the exclusion of working-class (male) voters, to the detriment of their economic interests. His comments on peasant farmers and other excluded classes of society were sketchy and not exactly flattering, though his views on colonial subjects were generally anti-imperialist, if not always upbeat about economies and cultures. Personally he excluded himself from active partisan and electoral participation in Prussia and the successive formations of the non-Austrian German state up to 1871. Though his citizenship had been revoked, he could possibly have got it back, but in correspondence he demurred from returning to Germany from English exile. His politics there was very largely expatriate in character and mindful of his position as a resident alien. This is not to say that a political thinker's immediate politics has to be 'on-side' with his ideas, or even activist or participatory in any dramatic way. Marx was a prolific correspondent and committee-man in his time, though whether this really qualifies him for the posthumous and commonplace Marxist claims that he was a great revolutionary as such seem open to question. However, it does cut off a route of argument. Had he returned to Germany, become openly active (prior to the Anti-Socialist law of 1878) and/or clandestinely active (up to his death in 1883), then we would know more about precisely where he stood on questions of social democracy (as opposed to proletarian revolution, at least in the longer term). The immediate goals of the *Communist Manifesto* of 1848 (Part II) are notably social democratic and indeed broadly overlapping with many current and at least semi-constitutional institutions, for example, central banks, income tax, industrialization of agriculture, free education etc. (Marx and Engels 1976: 505).

We don't know if Marx was on the road to becoming Bernstein; it is somewhat clearer that Engels wasn't. The 'revisionism' debate of the early years of the twentieth century is precisely relevant here, when considering Marxist constitutionalism today (in China or elsewhere, Cuba or Vietnam for example). The crux is the extent to which a constitutional, party-political system is open to possibilities other than capture by commercial and financial interests, and a monopolization of the terms of policy debate that suit their own interests (not to mention media ownership, also an issue dating from these early days). On the whole Marx and Engels got used to the idea – or even celebrated it – that enfranchised voters would elect governments that would reform or restrain capitalism (which Marx had exhaustively analysed, at least in its basic conceptual terms). Having put these mandated agencies in place, they thought it would follow that capitalist terms of *unequal* competition (say, between largely property-less workers and well-off shareholders and rentiers) would succumb to legislation, regulation and popular, comprehensive socialization.

These are exactly the terms of debate (whether overt or covert) in China today. Except that the world has moved on, and those involved now have more complexities to deal with, precisely because there is more evidence to consider, one way or another, and precisely because the stakes are so high in China (and arguably much higher in planetary terms). If commercialism and capitalism are indeed the way to build up the forces of production, then does this process go better with Western multi-party constitutionalism, or indeed require it? Are Chinese state and Communist Party structures for consultation in decision making and liberalization in enterprise and communication an adequate substitute for this, or a pragmatic and moral perversion of it? On the other hand, if commercialism and capitalism are inherently wasteful and counter-productive to majority interests in the Chinese population, then exactly what alternative interests do they have and what structures would help to realize them? 'Social democracy in one country' has been a goal in many Western nations, especially Scandinavia. Possibly this was the case 'with Japanese characteristics', and perhaps it persists in Japan. But on the whole the 'pro-market' and 'pro-privatization' forces backing neoliberalism have won considerable victories in various kinds of electoral systems, and as I have suggested, these regimes have indeed altered some of the values through which Western constitutions are interpreted. Social democracy in one country would be an interesting project in China, and one with Marxist credentials, even if 'revisionist'.

The fault-line between what is clearly Marxist and what isn't dates back to the 1880s, and it has been drawn in different ways on varying grounds. Initially and consistently it has been about proletarian revolution, most excitingly conceived as a *coup d'état* and popular takeover, not achieved even as a purely theoretical claim until Lenin's arrival at the Finland Station in 1917. China's engagement with Marxism has been far more Leninist than anything else in the Marxist tradition. From that perspective even Karl Kautsky's revolutionary rhetoric (but reformist participation) was 'renegade'. Lenin was wounded by a bullet from a would-be assassin in 1918 and was dead by early 1924, so there is little record to go on (notwithstanding an industry of justification and demonization ever since as to his 'real' intentions, beliefs and doctrinal legacy). Has China today cranked up an NEP (an early Soviet 'New Economic Policy' allowing limited markets and individual accumulation and investment) of gargantuan proportions? Or is the current mode of production in China something completely different? Either way, are proletarian revolution and communist society meaningful or vacuous as political goals?

The other notable fault-line between what is Marxist and what isn't takes us via Bernstein back to Western constitutionalism itself. Are the institutions of representative and responsible government inherently capitalist, as ideologues on both sides have notably claimed? Marx was quite clear that capitalism was inherently anti-egalitarian in substantive results, ideological claims of trickling down and levelling up notwithstanding. However, in terms of a socialist or social-democratic politics, at least of transition, he was somewhat more informative, sketching out a bottom-up system of mandated representatives and responsible assemblies intended to protect the economic interests of the vast majority of any given population, or so he saw it at the time (Marx 1986: 332–3). In these days of capitalist near-collapse and squeezed middle classes, this 'vast majority' looks rather more plausible than in more prosperous times of middle-class hegemony. However, Marx's thoughts are just a sketch, and they say nothing about competitive partisan politics, which has come to be the *sine qua non* of credible democracy and – by extension – credible constitutionalism.

On the one hand Marx's perspective – and that of Marxists generally – is substantive, rather than procedural. The right institutions are those that deliver the good (and the goods) that the people want (on some aggregation of interests), or that serve the public interest (as somehow determined in a singular way). Western constitutionalism is procedural, in that the good institutions are those that protect the natural rights of each individual to security of the person and possession of property. Who has exactly what by way of access to goods and services is thus a procedural outcome rather than substantive goal. Moreover good structures are those that resist the incursion of substantive goals into areas of procedural purity, imposing a so-called patterned distribution of income and wealth. The questions here are not always economic ones in the first instance; witness the resistance to civil rights and anti-discrimination decisions taken by the 'Warren Court' and its successors in the United States, where purity of principle in relation to individuals and their rights, and in relation to the terms of the Federal system of governments, have played a very large role. This is a very large fault-line indeed and one that is currently debated – though not very explicitly – in Western constitutional regimes. In Chinese terms, given the heritage of Marxist emphasis on substance over procedure and the limited and unsuccessful experience in the Republican period with Western norms that value procedure over substance, it seems clear that debate in China will be on this ground and will concern outcomes and the means to get them. There may of course be a realm of disingenuousness, as there always is in politics; politicians may reward themselves and their cronies with the opportunities of proceduralism while declaring that these outcomes – or that future outcomes – will be to the substantive benefit of 'all'. Our own concern with bankers and industrialists and their bonuses, incentive-schemes and pension-pots comes to mind here, given their claims that we will all be worse off if we 'interfere'.

My conclusions from this brief and rather sketchy chapter are: that liberal democracy is necessarily a broad church, with considerable local content; that it rests on judicial independence at all levels as a bulwark against governmental usurpations; that Marxist jurisprudence is not necessarily a wilder shore than the more familiar systems of common law and Roman law; that the fault-line between procedure and substance is not exclusive to Marxism; and that Peng's article opens a window on varieties of constitutionalism *tout court* as a matter of common global interest.

Note

1   For an exposition of this view, see Carver (1998: ch. 6).

References

Bernstein, E. (2009) [1911], *Evolutionary Socialism: A Criticism and Affirmation*. Whitefish, MT: Kessinger Publishing.

Carver, T. (1998), *The Postmodern Marx*. Manchester: Manchester University Press.

Locke, J. (1988), *Two Treatises of Government*. Cambridge: Cambridge University Press.

Marx, K. (1986) [1871], *The Civil War in France*, in Marx, K., and Engels, F., *Collected Works*, volume 22 (London: Lawrence & Wishart), pp. 307–59.

Marx, K., and Engels, F. (1976) [first pub. 1848], *The Communist Manifesto*, in *Collected Works*, volume 6 (London: Lawrence & Wishart), pp. 477–519.

Pateman, C. (1983), 'Feminism and democracy', in G. Duncan (ed.), *Democratic Theory and Practice*. Cambridge: Cambridge University Press, pp. 204–17.

Schumpeter, J. A. (2010) [1942], *Capitalism, Socialism and Democracy*. Milton Park: Routledge.

CHAPTER ELEVEN

Revolutionary subjectivity in post-Marxist thought: the case of Laclau and Badiou

Oliver Harrison

Introduction

Since Ernesto Laclau and Chantal Mouffe's publication of *Hegemony and Socialist Strategy* in 1985, the term 'post-Marxism' has been understood in at least two senses. First, using Laclau's and Mouffe's terminology, in a *post*-Marxist sense it refers to the view that the development of Marx's work was built on principles that were *always* wrong; either in terms of his notion of 'subjectivity and classes', his historical predictions regarding capitalist development, or his notion of a communist society (Laclau and Mouffe 2001: 4). In a second – post-*Marxist* – sense, however, it accepts that the process of going beyond Marx cannot be one of straight forward abandonment but, rather, must involve working through him – and the

Marxist tradition. This distinction between different forms of post-Marxism was reiterated by Tormey and Townshend (2006). For them, it is possible to identify 'strong' and 'weak' forms of post-Marxism. The former denotes those who 'wished to be seen or perceived as working within the Marxian problematic', whereas the latter refers to those more self-consciously antagonistic to the Marxist project (Tormey and Townshend 2006: 4). More recently, Göran Therborn (2009: 165) referred to post-Marxism 'in an open sense, referring to writers with an explicitly Marxist background', whose 'work has gone beyond Marxist problematics and who do not publicly claim a continuing Marxist commitment'. Neo-Marxism, interestingly, is distinguished from post-Marxism only on the basis that 'an explicit commitment' to Marxism remains.

What seems clear is that the term post-Marxism is not as straightforward as it might appear. Furthermore, as Tormey and Townshend (2006: 1) point out, far from being a 'badge of self-identification', the term is frequently used in a derogatory way to describe the work of others. At the heart of the problem, perhaps, is the extent to which post-Marxism conclusively leaves Marx behind. After all, one could argue that any attempt at going beyond Marx is always in the same instance a process that involves going back to him (Tormey and Townshend 2006: 11). The purpose of this article is to demonstrate this ambiguity with particular reference to the theories of revolutionary subjectivity articulated by Ernesto Laclau and Alain Badiou. Drawing on Marx's own theory of revolutionary subjectivity as an analytical framework, I consider the extent to which Laclau's and Badiou's theory can be considered post-Marxist. I argue that, although both Laclau's and Badiou's theories of revolutionary subjectivity break decisively with Marx, they do so by drawing on the insights of two thinkers who were both indebted to Marx and who sought explicitly to remain Marxist: Antonio Gramsci and Mao Tse-Tung respectively. This continuing fidelity to Gramsci and Mao confounds the decisiveness of Laclau's and Badiou's break from Marx. After outlining the conditions I associate with Marx's own theory, as well as then mapping Laclau's and Badiou's against these conditions, and conclude by suggesting – in line with the post-Marxism of Michael Hardt and Antonio Negri – that one condition of Marx's theory remains an important tool for considering the question of revolutionary subjectivity today.

The centrality of productive labour

Marx and Engels regarded the emergence of the capitalist mode of production as a progressive development in the evolution of productive activity (Marx 1993: 70). With the transition from the 'formal subsumption' to the 'real subsumption' of labour to capital, the labour process was radically transformed (Marx 1990: 1021, 1035). While the formal subsumption of labour to capital involved the extraction of absolute surplus value, the period inaugurated by real subsumption involved an increase in the working day's intensity – one that was achieved through a radical restructuring of the division of labour. This process found its classical form in the application of large-scale industry.

Through machines, capital found a means to overcome the physical limitations of human labour and dissolve the unity of its collective struggle. However, far from diminishing class antagonism, this process merely displaced it to a different level, with the struggle over the length of the working day being supplanted by the struggle over its relative intensity. Crucially, according to Marx, this process had significant effects on the composition and subjectivity of the working class. Although the strategic employment of machinery was instrumental in disciplining the 'refractory hand of labour', in the long run this only increased the socialization of labour and, in so doing, brought with it new forms of highly productive and co-operative subjectivity (see Marx and Engels 1976: 455–91). While Marx certainly criticized this process in its capitalist guise (Marx 1990: 486), ultimately he believed that capital brought with it both the objective and the subjective conditions for its eventual supersession.

The objective tendency of capitalist production

Marx believed that capitalist development would be plagued by persistent crises. With a rise in the 'organic composition of capital', he predicted an increased concentration and centralization of social wealth, a swelling in the ranks of the industrial reserve army of labour and, ultimately, a long-term tendency of the rate of profit to fall (Marx 1990: 777–89). For Marx, it was in and through capitalist crises that a template could be established to identify means by which to overcome the instability of capital. The increased socialization, centralization and concentration of capital brought glimpses of an alternative form of society which Marx believed would convince the working class of the necessity of social revolution. What capital's objective tendencies revealed overall, then, was the fact that, far from being the most 'rational' form of society, capitalism was in fact a highly contradictory system that, when fully matured, only blocked the further development and realization of social needs and consciousness (Callinicos 1995: 159).

As an objective tendency, then, capitalist development would work 'towards its own dissolution as the form dominating production' (Marx 1993: 700). However, social revolution required more than objective conditions alone. As Peter Hallward (2009) explains, 'what is most fundamental in Marx is not the "inevitable" or involuntary process whereby capitalism might dig its own grave, but rather the way in which it prepares the ground upon which the determined diggers might appear' (Hallward 2009: 18). Communist revolution, in other words, required the development of 'the greatest productive power' of all: 'the revolutionary class itself' (Marx and Engels 1976: 211).

The subjective tendency of capitalist development

Although the objective contradictions of capitalist development revealed the 'revolutionary, subversive side' to the working class' increasing misery (c.f. Marx and Engels 1976: 178), revolutionary subjectivity was unlikely to develop out of pauperism or social destitution alone (Clarke 1993: 171; Draper 1979: 55). The real effects of the 'general law' of capitalist development lay in the shared experience that this situation induced. With the progressive development of the division of labour, capital creates a subjectivity that is collectivized, highly concentrated and whose interests and conditions of life become more and more 'equalized' (Marx 1993: 75). In this sense, by virtue of its very existence, the working class was already a 'class against capital' (Marx and Engels 1976: 211). Yet, through its increased strength in numbers, improved means of communication to co-ordinate its struggle and the 'political and general education' provided by the bourgeoisie themselves, Marx believed that the working class could transform itself from being a 'class against capital' to a revolutionary 'class-for-itself'.

While the most immediate form of working class struggle was conducted through the trades unions, Marx believed that this organizational form had to extend the scope of its influence, enlisting 'the non-society men into their ranks', and thus convincing society at large that their interests were not narrow and secular, but broad and inclusive to all the 'downtrodden millions' (Marx 1992b: 92). The problem, however, was how to theorize this revolutionary transformation for, as Lebowitz (2003: 179) explains, in the ordinary run of things, one has to accept that capitalism produces the sort of workers that it needs, and the working class subjectivity that it encourages is anything but revolutionary.

Marx's answer was that the working class had to develop its own revolutionary political party, one that 'unites and concentrates its forces', which is not 'separate' from, but works alongside, the various workers' organizations already established. Although Marx believed this party would be guided by an advanced theory, this theory had to link dialectically to the actual movements of the class struggle (Marx 1993: 80; Marx 1992b: 99; Marx and Engels 1975: 182). Crucially, Marx believed that the working class must ultimately educate *itself* gradually and independently with the assistance of the communist party (Marx 1993: 330; Blackburn 1976: 23). In sum, for Marx, it was through the educative process of class struggle that the working class could become revolutionary. In line with capital's objective development, then, the subjective development of the working class emerges (Lebowitz 2003: 180).

The necessity of political power and the establishment of a classless society

For Marx and Engels, the only lasting way the working class could sustain its revolutionary subjectivization was through raising itself 'to the position of ruling class, to win the battle of democracy' (Marx 1993: 86). As a vital element in this process the conquest and retention of political power was, in itself, an educative experience (Lebowitz 2003: 193). What Marx famously called the 'revolutionary dictatorship of the proletariat', was to be a very particular form of state power – one that governed the transition from capitalist society to communist society (Marx 1992b: 355). Using the Paris Commune as his model, Marx stipulated that, although it would principally be a working class government, it would also be the 'true representative of all the healthy elements of French society' (Marx 1992b: 209, 212, 216). This latter aspect was crucial, highlighting the fact that Marx was well aware of the necessity of tactical alliances in the quest for political power, particularly among elements of the peasantry and petty bourgeoisie (Draper 1979: 358; Callinicos 1995: 165).

The 'true secret' of the commune was, not only that it provided the space for the working class to continue its revolutionary transformation, but also that it served as a means of consolidating its power for the tasks that lay ahead in the future (Marx 1992b: 212). The dictatorship of the proletariat, then, although instrumental to the goals of revolutionary subjectivity, does not in any way effect its dissolution. This point, Marx (1993: 87) argued, could only occur with the establishment of a communist society capable of liberating the socially cooperative powers of labour so as to provide for the needs of all. Only then, they argued, would class antagonism dissipate (Marx 1992a: 426).

Alongside the three conditions outlined above, Marx's theory of revolutionary subjectivity reveals two recurrent themes. First, revolutionary subjectivity emerges through the educative process of class struggle. Capitalist development might bring the conditions necessary for the emergence of this subjectivity, but these conditions require an additional subjective supplement. Second, Marx and Engels were well aware that, although the industrial proletariat was expected to be the vanguard of workers' struggles, these workers – and the party that guided them – would have to be tactically astute, particularly with regard to revolutionary alliances. These two themes would be taken up most significantly in the work of Antonio Gramsci and Mao Tse-Tung. In expounding the notion of 'hegemony', Gramsci considers strongly the issue of tactical alliances, arguing that, central to a Marxist theory of revolutionary subjectivity, is the construction of a 'national-popular collective will' which moves beyond the 'economic corporate' interests of the working class to integrate the interests of other social groups into a united 'social bloc' (Gramsci 1999: 152, 329, 353, 406). Mao, on the other hand, continually emphasizes the importance of political practice, especially in relation to the development of intellectuals, the role of the communist party and the more generic search for 'knowledge' and 'truth' (Tse-Tung 1965). By now comparing Laclau's and Badiou's theories of revolutionary subjectivity to that of Marx, I will trace the legacies of Gramsci and Mao in post-Marxist thought.

Hegemony, populism and 'the people'

The starting point to Laclau's (2005) theory of revolutionary subjectivity is the emergence of what he calls a basic 'social demand'. This demand, Laclau argues, is an attempt to articulate something that is deemed absent from a particular social order. If this demand is dealt with – and thus remains merely at the level of a 'request' – then 'that is the end of the matter'. In a situation where this demand is not met, however, then the possibility arises that other – equally unmet – demands might start to link themselves together (Laclau 2005: 73) creating an 'internal frontier': a division of the social space into two antagonistic camps, one consisting of the emergent 'chain' of unmet demands, and the other, a social order that is unwilling or unable to settle them (Laclau 2005: 74). Hence, what were once isolated and quite particular 'democratic' demands can now develop into 'popular' collective ones.

This movement from democratic to popular demands depends entirely on how they become articulated. Building on a distinction established in his earlier work with Laclau and Chantal Mouffe (2001), what Laclau calls a 'logic of difference' describes a strategy whereby each demand asserts only their own particularity and, in consequence, remain isolated from one another. In this case, the formation of an internal frontier does not occur, and in consequence, neither can the emergence of a collective revolutionary subjectivity (Laclau 2005: 78). Laclau is adamant that the pure particularism often associated with 'identity politics' is a 'self-defeating exercise' that 'can only lead to a political blind alley' (Laclau 1996: 26, 48). What is needed, Laclau claims, is a strategy that employs the alternative 'logic of equivalence', in which each demand becomes equivalent to one another, with at least one demand dissolving its own particularity and becoming the universal inscription for all the others (Laclau 1996: 81).

Crucially, for Laclau, there is no underlying demand that is *a priori* more significant or universal than any other. The extent to which one demand might become universal is entirely contingent, dependent on its own hegemonic construction.[1] It is at this point that the influence of Gramsci's notion of hegemony emerges. For Laclau, revolutionary subjectivity must be constructed out of various – at times disparate – elements. This is a process that rejects an emphasis on one particular social demand, unless, as stated above, this emphasis is hegemonically constructed. Of resonance, here, is Gramsci's reiteration of the need to create a tactical 'social bloc' that transcends particularism and seeks the possibility of universality. Yet, there is clearly a significant difference between Gramsci's and Laclau's starting point, and this difference allows us to understand Laclau's rejection of the first condition of Marx's own theory. For Laclau, revolutionary subjectivity is not defined in any *a priori* manner, let alone through the prism of productive activity. Although he accepts that class may have been a dominant presence in emancipatory political movements in the past, the contrasting conditions of the present mean that it is no longer (Laclau 2000a: 206; Laclau 2000b: 299, 300).

Putting contemporary trends aside, for Laclau, the problem with Marx's theory is twofold. First, his philosophy of history forced him to privilege *a priori* one particular (class) identity as the embodiment of revolutionary subjectivity. Although the question of class alliance was indeed present in Marx's work, the historical significance he ascribed to productive activity meant that Marx's revolutionary subject was always-already the working class. Perhaps more importantly, however, the problems with Marx's theory in fact ran deeper than this, due to his acceptance of the very notion of 'the subject' as a self-contained, fully transparent entity. In *Hegemony and Socialist Strategy*, Laclau and Mouffe had accepted that the privileged *political* status of the working class should not be rejected outright, but that concern should lie in rejecting the ontological category of 'the subject' itself (Laclau and Mouffe 2001: 181).

When considering the conditions necessary for the emergence of revolutionary subjectivity, Laclau shares with Marx the idea that a crisis in an established social structure is a basic prerequisite (Laclau 2005: 85). In an earlier work, however, Laclau (1990) explicitly distanced his own understanding of structural crisis from Marx's. Drawing on Lacanian theory, Laclau employed the notion of 'dislocation' to refer to the idea that, at base, every social structure is deficient, in some respect. Due to this 'gap' within the structure, Laclau argues that the emergence of revolutionary subjectivity must always be conceived as an attempt by rival hegemonic political forces to contend its closure (Laclau 1990: 41, 44). Thus, whereas, for Marx, structural crises can be explained logically through reference to the internal contradictions of the structure, for Laclau, dislocations follow no such dialectical logic. According to Laclau, it would do so only *if* that structure was fully 'sutured' in the first place. Dislocation, in other words 'is not a necessary moment in the self-transformation of the structure' (Laclau 1990: 46, 47). The consequence of Laclau's notion of 'dislocation' is that he breaks with the second condition of Marx's theory of revolutionary subjectivity.

Revolutionary subjectivity, for Laclau, does not emerge entirely immanently from the structure which it aims to revolutionize.

The final aspect of Laclau's theory of revolutionary subjectivity concerns the mechanism required in order to link successfully an equivalential 'chain' together. As stated above, the construction of revolutionary subjectivity is dependent on one particular demand 'splitting' itself into becoming a 'signifier of a wider universality' (Laclau 2005: 95). In the same instance, however, the particularity of the other demands must also split, and this is because they too must put aside their own particularity and rally around the universal demand that comes to constitute the unity of the chain. For Laclau, the unity of this equivalential chain – and hence the possibility of revolutionary subjectivity – depends on the production of what he calls 'empty signifiers'.

Empty signifiers unify an equivalential chain by signifying what is commonly held to be deficient in a particular social order. A useful example of what Laclau has in mind here is the common populist reference to 'the people'. Since Roman times, the question has always pertained to whether 'the people' refers to the whole of the political community or rather the disenfranchised 'part' (Canovan 2005: 12, 15). Laclau takes this 'stubborn ambiguity' between the 'populace' and the 'plebs' a little further and argues that the distinctiveness of populist discourse is the claim by the latter to be the only 'legitimate' form of the former: 'a partiality which wants to function as the totality of the community' (Laclau 2005: 81). In this sense, 'the people' does not refer to the totality of an *existing* community, but is rather the signifier (or name) that attempts to articulate the deficiency within the community itself. What is equally significant with regard to Laclau's claim that revolutionary subjectivity is never inscribed *a priori*, however, is the fact that revolutionary subjectivity is only ever constituted through the very process of naming itself. Revolutionary subjectivity, in other words, does not exist prior to the name it is given, whether this be 'the people' or any other particular signifier (Laclau 2005: 103, 108).

For Laclau, revolutionary subjectivity is thus always the outcome of the hegemonic construction of a 'people' (Laclau 2005: 239). Interestingly, however, Laclau accepts that a signifier such as 'the people' can be articulated in a number of different ways, none of which are constricted by any necessary or underlying ground. There is, in other words, nothing intrinsically progressive about appeals to 'the people'; history has repeatedly proven this signifier's political elasticity. Due to its Gramscian heritage, then, Laclau's theory of revolutionary subjectivity is highly attuned to means by which particular signifiers can become attached to – or dislodged from – a particular discursive framework. This reminds us, again, that Laclau's revolutionary subject is only ever the outcome of a protracted hegemonic struggle.

One particularly useful example of how Laclau's theory of empty signifiers links to contemporary events is the signifier of 'change' in the Presidential election of Barak Obama in 2008. Initially, Obama's appeals to change referred to something relatively specific, such as foreign policy in

Iraq and Afghanistan or reform in the health care system or the banking sector. In a more generic sense, however, the signifier of 'change' was clearly used to articulate a deficit in the Bush Administration. During the election campaign, however, this signifier progressively became empty and, in consequence, managed to unite a mass of diverse social demands. The (initial) hope and euphoria that reached its peak at Obama's inauguration was an impressive spectacle and can be explained well through the ambiguity that such appeals to 'change' managed to create. The Obama administration's problem, however – as continually witnessed today – was that once elected, this promise of 'change' had to become something much more specific. It was at this point, arguably, that the enormity of Obama's promises became clear, as did the structural barriers to change in the US political and economic system. Change at one level, in other words, can sometimes have unappealing ramifications for change at another and, hence, whereas an element of strategic ambiguity might prove essential for creating collective/ revolutionary subjectivity, in the same instance, attempting to keep this subjectivity alive establishes very real tensions.[2]

Returning to the issue at hand, we have seen that Laclau's theory breaks with Marx's first two conditions of revolutionary subjectivity. To understand how it breaks from the third, we must return to his notion of empty signifiers, the primary function of which, it would appear, is to unify an equivalential chain. At base, however, their significance lies much deeper. Put simply, the ultimate significance of empty signifiers is that they deny the very possibility of achieving a resolutive form of the social. Although there is nothing in Laclau's theory that rejects the strategic necessity of seizing political power, the idea that 'society' could ever be a fully constituted totality – now or in the future – renders the third condition of Marx's theory nothing less than a totalitarian fantasy. What Laclau does accept, however, is the *aspiration* for totality, or, as he puts it, totality understood as a 'horizon and not a ground' (Laclau 2005: 71). It is this aspiration that lies behind repeated acts of identification on the part of the subject, and hence, ensures the vitality of both the continued emergence of different forms of 'the people', and in consequence, democracy itself (Laclau 2005: 170).

Event, truth and the faithful subject

Badiou's theory of revolutionary subjectivity hinges on his notion of 'the event'. According to him, every event is a reactivation – within a particular 'situation' – of something that was 'counted' either not properly or perhaps not at all. The event itself is highly mysterious in the sense that it cannot be explained merely on that basis of its 'localization' within a particular situation. What the event brings is something completely unforeseen and exceptionally novel. In this sense, it is the event – understood as a highly indiscernible structural crisis – that can be said to revolutionize a situation. Understood as a 'kind of flashing supplement that happens to a situation', the event leaves behind a 'trace'. In order properly to understand the event's significance, 'someone' has to engage in a series of 'inquiries' (Badiou 2002: 72).

It is at this point that Mao's emphasis on political practice becomes clear. Unless 'someone' wagers on the possibility that an event has indeed occurred, from within the situation 'it will always remain doubtful whether there has been an event or not' (Badiou 2005: 207). Significantly, then, before an event, every situation is composed merely of 'individuals', not subjects. The transformation of the former into the latter only occurs through a sustained engagement with the consequences – or 'truth' – of an event itself (Badiou 2002: 40; Badiou 1999: 108). Badiou's subject, then, 'is absolutely non-existent in the situation before the event' (Badiou 2002: 43).[3] In consequence, and in contradistinction to the first condition of Marx's theory, the 'faithful' – revolutionary – subject is not defined by anything other than the truth that it decides to investigate. While it might be true that the working class does not 'exist' as the revolutionary subject until it becomes conscious of itself as the subject–object of history (c.f. Lukács 1971), the working class was always-already the historical candidate to take up this task due to the fact that Marx defined revolutionary subjectivity through the prism of productive activity. In a similar way to Laclau's 'people', faithful subjectivity is not the work of a predisposed 'hero', but rather a complex and highly contingent set of procedures. Any philosophical narrative (i.e. historical materialism) that suggests otherwise was precisely that which the events of May 1968 and the Chinese Cultural Revolution (CCR) ended up extinguishing (Badiou 2010: 55).

Like Marx and Laclau, then, Badiou's theory of revolutionary subjectivity hinges on the occurrence of some form of structural or objective crisis. In the same instance, this crisis is not enough, in itself, to guarantee the emergence of revolutionary subjectivity. Yet, just as there were discrepancies between Laclau's theory and the second condition of Marx's, there is a major difference in the way Badiou conceives of this crisis. We have seen that, for Marx, revolutionary subjectivity emerges subjectively alongside objective *tendencies*. For Laclau and Badiou, however, revolutionary subjectivity emerges alongside objective *anomalies*: 'dislocations' or 'events' that fundamentally disrupt any historical narrative that purports to understand why, and indeed predict when, they might occur. The consequences of this reveal the distance between Badiou's theory of revolutionary subjectivity and Marx's second condition. In a similar way to Laclau, then, due to the fact that revolutionary subjectivity is only ever the possible consequence of a highly unpredictable crisis, in Badiou's schema this subjectivity only ever emerges *partially* immanently to the system which it aims to revolutionize. Hence, while Badiou's theory accepts that there is some kind of immanence at work, it does so only to the extent to which it *enables* revolutionary subjectivity to become a possibility (Badiou 2002: 16).

The final step in Badiou's theory of revolutionary subjectivity – the work of a faithful subject – is for the 'truth' of an event to be 'forced', and ultimately, 'normalized' (Badiou 2005: 342). What Badiou calls 'the law of the subject' involves the establishment of its own 'subject language'; one that traverses the encyclopaedic knowledge of a situation, supplanting it with that which was revealed to be excluded. Due to the undecidable nature of the event, the subject sustains itself through a radical commitment – a 'confidence' or 'belief' that inquiries will not be conducted in vain. What Badiou (2002: 48) calls the 'subjective principle', then, is, as Bosteels (2005: 581, 584) has argued, the principle aspect of Badiou's aforementioned fidelity to Mao and, in particular, his 'materialist theory of knowledge' (see Tse-Tung 1965: 303). Alongside Mao's emphasis on the primacy of political practice being the sole criterion of truth, what Badiou quite clearly retains in this respect is the Maoist emphasis on 'faith' – not necessarily in 'serving the masses', but in the more generic sense of 'serving the truth'.

If revolutionary subjectivity is the process by which one is faithful to the consequences of an event, what might this entail today? Does Badiou's account of politics offer anything as useful as Laclau's notion of empty signifiers, for example? This raises interesting issues, particularly considering Badiou's vehement rejection of conventional political processes, being as they are, intrinsically tied to what he calls 'capitalo-parliamentarianism'. Badiou's own politics is largely experimental and, yet because of this, highlights some interesting suggestions as to how we should conceive radical politics today. Following what he sees as the exhaustion of the second sequence of the communist hypothesis (1917–75), Badiou argues that revolutionary subjectivity today finds itself in an 'interval period'; one which, following the event–subject–truth schema outlined above, must continually relate back to the lessons learnt from the events of May 1968 and the failures of the CCR.

What is at stake today, then, is the opening of a new sequence that has the courage to move beyond the models and referents of the past (Badiou 2010: 37). In more concrete terms, what Badiou has in mind here is what Peter Hallward (2003) has called a 'politics of prescription'. Judging by the activities of Badiou's own political organization – *L'Organisation Politique* – this politics is highly localized, and involves interventions in particular 'sites' where the state's repressive counting procedures are most evident. Using the axiomatic principle of equality as its starting point – not as something that is to be 'researched or verified' but as a fundamental principle of political action – *L'Organisation Politique* has intervened directly on a number of issues, particularly over the plight of undocumented migrants in France (see Badiou 2008: 44). In recent times, revolts from those at the margins of society have been a recurrent issue in the recent riots throughout Europe (Paris

2005, Britain 2011, etc.) and, even more recently, the protests against the Dale Farm eviction in October 2011.

Like Laclau, then, aspects of Badiou's theory of revolutionary subjectivity can offer a useful viewpoint on what radical politics entails today, particularly from the perspective of so-called post-party politics. Yet, we are still left with the question as to how Badiou's theory relates to the final condition of Marx's. What seems clear is that, as in the case of Laclau, the core of Badiou's post-Marxism is premised on his rejection of Marx's philosophy of history. Yet, due the fact that he insists on the continued possibility of universal truths, might one claim a lingering form of dogmatism such as that which some have associated with the former? After all, as Peter Hallward (2003: 36) has noted, Badiou's politics has always been one in which a 'disciplined purification prevails over a politics of alliance and negotiation'.

Badiou deals with this problem through establishing what he calls a 'typology of fidelities'. In contrast to the 'deviations' associated with 'spontaneous' and 'dogmatic' fidelities, Badiou's 'generic fidelity' is one that basically does this job properly – seeking to separate those aspects of the situation which are positively connected to the event from those which are not. For Badiou, in other words, there is no one form of truth procedure, just as there is no one particular form of post-eventual subjectivity. By recognizing this, Badiou avoids the excesses of a totalizing notion of truth, one that might potentially involve a 'total destruction or reorganization of absolutely every multiple in the situation' (Badiou 2005: 237).

All of this reveals the extent to which Badiou breaks with the third condition of Marx's theory. This condition stipulated that, with the conquest of political power, the eventual abolition of private property would destroy the heart of capitalist society and, in so doing, would involve a complete reorganization of the social space. What we see from the above, however, is the extent to which Badiou believes this should in fact be avoided. Badiou (2002) reiterates this point by establishing what he calls a second 'ethic of truths'. One of Badiou's claims regarding a truth procedure is that it must necessarily traverse the existing knowledge and language of a situation. Only this way can the true novelty of an event be established. The danger here, however, is that the emergent 'subject language' might attempt to re-arrange *all* the elements of an existing situated knowledge (Badiou 2002: 83). If this occurred, he claims, the truth procedure would not just reorganize the distortions associated with the language/knowledge of an existing situation, but in fact revolutionize *everything* on the 'absolute authority of truthful nomination'. In a remarkably similar way to Laclau, then, Badiou believes that every situation will always be built on some form of exclusion and hence, in his terms, there will always be something to every truth that will, and must, remain 'unnameable'. By consequence, any revolutionary change such as that stipulated by the third condition to Marx's theory would only ever end in 'disaster'. Hence, Badiou's second ethic of truth appears to involve an explicit denial that there can ever be an imposition of one totalized truth and, in as much, he moves decisively beyond the third condition of Marx's theory of revolutionary subjectivity.

Conclusion

Laclau's and Badiou's theory of revolutionary subjectivity clearly breaks with all three conditions of Marx and, in this sense, their work has to be characterized as operating in some form of CCR post-Marxist terrain. Interestingly, although Laclau has been perfectly willing to characterize his work as such, Badiou has argued that post-Marxism leads to a politics resigned to the continued dominance of capitalist society (Badiou 2002: 114). This aside, Badiou's theory of revolutionary subjectivity clearly exceeds the confines associated with the account of Marx. The claim of this chapter, however, has been that both Laclau's and Badiou's post-Marxism hinges, paradoxically, on the continued inspiration drawn from a particular Marxist thinker. For Laclau, it is Gramsci's theory of hegemony – pushed to what he sees as its logical conclusions – that necessitated his break from Marx. Freed from its underlying class bias, Laclau (2005) today regards the 'hegemonic construction of a people' as *the* fundamental task in radical politics. For Badiou, in a similar way, it is the lessons learnt from the two major sequences of the 'communist hypothesis' that have necessitated the move beyond Marx (Badiou 2010). Citing the failures of the CCR in particular, Badiou continues to display 'fidelity' to Mao through his insistence that revolutionary subjectivity today involves a sustained commitment to a truth procedure generated by an 'event', and belief that this commitment must be one that continually unfolds the revolutionary consequences of that truth *in practice* within a particular situation. Hence, although Laclau and Badiou break all three conditions to Marx's theory of revolutionary subjectivity and can, therefore, rightly be called 'post-Marxists', their continued reliance on Gramsci and Mao is enough to retain a link – however distinct – to the theory from which their mature work has tried so hard to distance itself.

The unifying principle of Laclau's and Badiou's post-Marxism is their shared hostility to Marx's philosophy of history. Because of this, perhaps the main strength of their work lies in their shared emphasis on contingency of revolutionary subjectivity itself. In consequence, each theory is highly attentive to theorizing not only the emergence of revolutionary subjectivity, but also its potential for deviation or inconsistency. Strengths aside, however, both theories have their weaknesses. Laclau's insistence that 'class' is just another species of identity politics restricts the true importance of the category and, as Slavoj Žižek has claimed, raises questions as to whether some demands are intrinsically more able than others to become hegemonic in the first place (Žižek 2000: 320). Additionally, changes in class stratification do not necessarily signal the 'demise of class itself' (Thoburn 2007: 87). When considering Badiou's theory, his weaknesses are reflected in the strengths of Laclau's. Although the former's theory seeks to explain how 'miracles can happen', it lacks an understanding of how different forms of 'faithful' fidelity might in fact converge. In other words, Badiou has no theory of hegemony. Also, due to his insistence that revolutionary politics must abstain from conventional political processes, many have questioned the effectiveness of his own particular brand of political action (Hallward 2003: 283; Hewlett 2007: 56).

The reason that Marx defined revolutionary subjectivity through the prism of productive labour was because he believed that this development held the key for understanding how – through an analysis of tendencies in the present – a post-capitalist society could become a possibility. Laclau's and Badiou's rejection of this condition limits their ability to do this. Yet, not all post-Marxists go this far. Although explicitly stating the need to go 'beyond' Marx, because of their retention of the first condition to Marx's theory, Michael Hardt and Antonio Negri continue to offer a materialist analysis of the viability of a post-capitalist society and, from that, an attempt to understand how that society might function.[4] While there might be some danger associated with their more speculative dispositions, Hardt and Negri continually seek new and innovative means of conceiving social production. This, it seems to me, remains the strongest and most valuable legacy of Marx. It is one that we certainly should not be quick to abandon.

Notes

1   This is not to say, however, that in principle all demands are equally able to do this. Due to the 'unevenness of the social' and the fact that every structure is composed of 'sedimented' relations and social identities, every conjuncture must be analysed on its own very particular basis. See Laclau (1990: 34, 35).

2   The very same tension confronts those who form part of the recent 'We are the 99%' occupation movement. Indeed, as McVeigh (2011) has reported in relation to the 'Occupy Wall Street' movement in New York, one of the major issues that threatens the unity of this particular 'equivalential chain' is the extent to which *specific* demands should now be put forward.

3   At this point, it is important to note that in his *Logic of Worlds* (2009), Badiou would supplement the 'faithful' subject with two other 'subjective figures'. As a consequence, whereas one could claim that the actions of the faithful subject certainly corresponds to what we understand to be revolutionary subjectivity – that is, because it connects itself to the consequences of a radical and unforeseen break in a situation – the actions of the other two subjective figures deviate substantially from this model. I do not have space here to discuss these figures, but this move by Badiou is significant because, as in Laclau, it proves his continual interest in theorizing, not just the emergence of revolutionary subjectivity, but also its propensity for deviation and inconsistency.

References

Badiou, A. (1999), *Manifesto for Philosophy*. New York: SUNY.
— (2002), *Ethics*. London: Verso.
— (2005), *Being and Event*. London and New York: Continuum.
— (2008), *The Meaning of Sarkozy*. London: Continuum.
— (2009), *Logic of Worlds*. London and New York: Continuum.
— (2010), *The Communist Hypothesis*. London: Verso.
Blackburn, R. (1976), 'Marxism: theory of proletarian revolution', *New Left Review*, 97, 3–35.
Bosteels, B. (2005), 'Post Maoism: Badiou and politics', *Positions*. 13, 575–634.
Callinicos, A. (1995), *The Revolutionary Ideas of Karl Marx*. London: Bookmarks.
Canovan, M. (2005), *The People*. London: Polity Press.
Clarke, S. (1993), *Marx's Theory of Crisis*. Basingstoke: Palgrave.
Draper, H. (1979), *Karl Marx's theory of Revolution; Volume 2*. New York and London: Monthly Review Press.
Gramsci, A. (1999), *Selections on the Prison Notebooks*. London: ElecBooks.
Hallward, P. (2003), *Badiou: A Subject to Truth*. Minneapolis and London: University of Minnesota Press.
— (2009), 'The will of the people: notes towards a dialectical voluntarism', *Radical Philosophy*, 155, 17–29.
Hewlett, N. (2007), *Badiou, Balibar, Rancière: Rethinking Emancipation*. London and New York: Continuum.
Laclau, E. (1990), *New Reflections on the Revolution of Our Time*. London: Verso.
— (1996), *Emancipations*. London: Verso, pp. 20–35.
— (2000a), 'Structure, history and the political', in J. Butler, E. Laclau and S. Žižek (eds), *Contingency, Hegemony, Universality*. London: Verso, pp. 182–213.
— (2000b), 'Constructing universality', in J. Butler, E. Laclau and S. Žižek (eds), *Contingency, Hegemony, Universality*. London: Verso, pp. 281–308.
— (2005), *On Populist Reason*. London: Verso.
Laclau, E., and Mouffe, C. (2001), *Hegemony and Socialist Strategy: Towards a Radical Democratic Politics*, 2nd Edition. London: Verso.
Lebowitz, M. (2003), *Beyond Capital: Marx's Political Economy of the Working Class*. Basingstoke: Macmillan.
Lukács, G. (1971), *History and Class Consciousness*. London: Merlin Press.
Marx, K. (1990), *Capital*, volume 1. London: Penguin Books.
— (1992a), *Early Writings*. London: Penguin Books.
— (1992b), *The First International and After*. London: Penguin Classics.
— (1993), *Grundrisse*. London: Penguin Books.
Marx, K., and Engels, F. (1975), *Collected Works*, volume 3. London: Laurence and Wishart.
— (1976), *Collected Works*, volume 16. London: Laurence and Wishart.
— (1993), The Revolutions of 1848: Political Writings: Volume London: Penguin Classics.
McVeigh, K. (2011), 'Wall Street protesters divided over Occupy movement's demands' in *The Guardian*, Wednesday 19th October. Available from: http://www.guardian.co.uk/world/2011/oct/19/occupy-wall-street-protesters-divided?intcmp=239 [Accessed 19 October 2011].

Therborn, G. (2009), *From Marxism to post-Marxism?*. London and New York: Verso Books.

Thoburn, N. (2007), 'Patterns of production; cultural studies after hegemony', *Theory, Culture and Society*, 24, (3), 79–94.

Tormey, S., and Townshend, J. (2006), *Key Thinkers from Critical Theory to Post-Marxism*. London and California: Sage Publications.

Tse-Tung, M. (1965), *Selected Works*, volume 3. Peking: Foreign Languages Press.

Žižek , S. (2000), 'Holding the place', in J. Butler, E. Laclau and S. Žižek (eds), *Contingency, Hegemony, Universality*. London: Verso, pp. 308–29.

CHAPTER TWELVE

'Post' or 'Past'?: does post-Marxism have any future?

Stuart Sim

Introduction

A quarter-century has elapsed since the publication of the work which, more than any other, established post-Marxism as a brand in its own right on the theoretical spectrum: Ernesto Laclau and Chantal Mouffe's *Hegemony and Socialist Strategy* (Laclau and Mouffe 1985). As I discussed at some length in my book *Post-Marxism: An Intellectual History* (Sim 2000), we can identify post-Marxist tendencies well before that event, but there is no denying that Laclau and Mouffe's book served to bring together these somewhat disparate strands into a coherent theoretical position, which many others then proceeded to rally around. The result was a period of bitter infighting on the left, with insults being freely thrown around by those on both sides of the Marxist divide: what was post-Marxist to some was anti-Marxist to others, what was a necessary recognition of a changed global reality to the former was more like a betrayal of the revolutionary cause to the latter (Geras 1987). Nevertheless, post-Marxism was now firmly on the theoretical map, along with a series of other 'posts' from the later twentieth century: poststructuralism, postmodernism, post-industrialism, post-feminism, post-humanism, even post-philosophy. 'Post' seemed to be very much the flavour of the age, which was developing a very sceptical streak when it came to cultural totems.

Much has happened culturally and politically in the interim (not least the disappearance of the Soviet empire), so it is worth taking stock of what post-Marxism now means and asking whether it has anything of note to contribute to socio-political debate – especially now that communism is no longer a force of any note in the West, and at best a very distorted image of itself in China, where capitalist economics is being openly promoted by the state. (One of the issues I will be considering at a later point in the chapter is whether we can consider China to be a post-Marxist phenomenon – and whether that would be a good or a bad thing.) So I am posing the question as to whether there is any future for post-Marxism as a theoretical movement in the twenty-first century: is it still relevant to political debate on the left, or have we moved inexorably from 'post' to 'past'?

Post-Marxism and postmodernism

Speculating on what the prospects might be for post-Marxism is made all the more problematical given that it is so tied up with the history of postmodernism, the status of which is currently very much under review now that many of its major figures have passed away: Michel Foucault, Gilles Deleuze, Jean-François Lyotard, Jacques Derrida, Jean Baudrillard, for example – all of whom were in dialogue with Marxism to some degree or other over the course of their careers. Post-Marxism from Laclau and Mouffe onwards is very much influenced by postmodern thought (and I include poststructuralism within that general category), and it is motivated by very similar ideals: such as, breaking free from an intellectual tradition felt to be restrictive and authoritarian, and pushing the case for a more pluralist politics where difference and diversity are given their full due instead of being systematically marginalized. But we have to wonder whether postmodernism itself still means all that much, particularly now that its main target, modernity, seems to be in such trouble on the economic front (the term 'post-postmodernism' has even been bandied about of late). Neoliberals would certainly agree with Habermas's contention that 'modernity is an incomplete project' (Habermas 1985), and have done their level best to keep it going on the economic front through the insistent spread of market fundamentalist principles and globalization in recent decades. Yet we are all uncomfortably aware of just how much of a mess that project is presently in as national economies collapse around us (with Ireland and Greece merely the latest of a growing list of casualties), and it is an interesting question as to whether it can ever reconstruct itself as it was before. Without its economic successes to proclaim, modernity loses much of its cultural authority, since economic growth was always its strongest suit. Indeed, it is entirely possible to argue, and I did so myself in a recent book, that we might actually be witnessing the 'end' of modernity (Sim 2010): that it is just no longer sustainable as a system, that its contradictions and limitations have been brutally exposed by the unprecedented severity of the banking crisis we have undergone. We could ask where that leaves postmodernism: does it mean it loses its force as a concept as well? Is it locked into a binary relationship with modernism/modernity such that if that can't survive then it can't either? I will be returning to this topic in a later section.

Several commentators have already written postmodernism off as a late twentieth-century phenomenon that has now passed its sell-by date and need concern us no longer: Alan Kirby going so far in an article as to proclaim that it's 'dead' (Kirby 2006: 34). I think that judgement is more than a little premature (although I would concede that having just edited the 3rd edition of *The Routledge Companion to Postmodernism* (Sim 2011) means that I am not exactly an unbiased witness in this respect). However, it does mean that a case has to be argued for its continuing relevance, as it does too for its post-Marxist strand.

Post-Marxism and post-*Marxism*

So what can we claim for post-Marxism? What has it actually achieved as a theory? On the negative side, that is easy enough to say, in that it has significantly damaged Marxism's reputation as a philosophy and cultural theory by its confrontational style of critique and refusal to abide by any party line; but on the positive side it is much more difficult. The distinction that Laclau and Mouffe themselves made between *post*-Marxism and post-*Marxism* can be usefully drawn on in this context. They tended to emphasize the importance of Marxism as a starting point for their theories, which proceeded to advocate 'radical democracy' as the way forward for the left, whereas others, like Lyotard and Baudrillard took a more virulently anti-Marxist stance. Both approaches have attracted their share of followers: you either consider yourself to be engaged in revitalizing a tradition of thought, or unapologetically consigning it to historical oblivion. The distinction is a fairly loose one and I would not want to push it too far, but it can be helpful in trying to assess the impact of post-Marxism as a theory.

Laclau and Mouffe forcefully brought to our attention the revolutionary potential of the diverse social and political protest movements that had sprung up around the globe by the later twentieth century – ethnic, sexual, environmental and so on. It was a revolutionary potential that Marxism was turning a blind eye to because it did not fit into its prescriptive scheme of how revolution was supposed to emerge and then be conducted. Their argument was that Marxism was doing what it always did when faced by discrepancies with its socio-historical vision and taking refuge in its theory of hegemony in order to discount the importance of such phenomena: from the classical Marxist point of view, the new protest movements were mere diversions from the real business of class struggle, which would eventually re-assert itself as the overriding concern. Laclau and Mouffe's critique of hegemony is long and exhaustive, but the gist of it was that Marxism could not really think outside its preconceptions; that it could not shake off its commitment to its basic principles; that it had become doctrinally rigid and dogmatic. (Feminist theorists, of course, had been saying similar things for some time – if with a more specific agenda, which at one point, memorably enough, called for a 'divorce' to be drawn up between Marxism and feminism (Hartman 1981).) Nevertheless, Laclau and Mouffe's work still suggested that it was motivated by the spirit of Marxism: it wasn't quite going to the lengths of recommending a divorce, although maybe it did sound a bit like a trial separation. They just felt that it was time to strike out in new directions in order to keep that spirit alive, to lose the doctrinaire attitude that they felt was inhibiting its development and leading to its decline as an influential theory. If post-*Marxism* was to mean anything it would have to seek out new methods and approaches rather than just go on repeating the mantras of the classical Marxist past, a past that provided little guidance about how to adapt, and turn to account, rapidly changing cultural circumstances.

When we turn to such thinkers as Lyotard and Baudrillard, however, that spirit seems to have disappeared and we do seem to have entered divorce territory. Baudrillard inveighed against Marxism's fetish for production in *The Mirror of Production*, and was completely dismissive of its pretensions as a socio-political programme:

> The concept of production is never questioned; it will never radically overcome the influence of political economy. Even Marxism's transcending perspective will always be burdened by counter-dependence on political economy. Against Necessity it will oppose the mastery of Nature .... The political order is at stake here. Can the quantitative development of productive forces lead to a revolution of social relations? Revolutionary hope is based 'objectively' and hopelessly on this claim. (Baudrillard 1975: 59)

Baudrillard is such a determinedly maverick figure in theoretical terms, however, that it is hard to identify much in the way of development in his post-Marxist stance from that point in the 1970s onwards; whereas Lyotard can be turned into a veritable case study of *post*-Marxism. On the face of it, the evidence would seem to suggest that Lyotard is anti-Marxist, the criticism made by Norman Geras of Laclau and Mouffe. *Libidinal Economy* alone constitutes compelling forensic evidence on that score, where instead of detailed breakdowns of the history of the theory of hegemony and how it had been deployed to uphold the 'truth' of Marxist doctrines, we are treated to withering asides such as: 'Why, political intellectuals, do you *incline towards* the proletariat? In commiseration for what?' (Lyotard 1993: 115). Or could we say that, in a sense, Lyotard is always 'post-Marxist' (in the more general sense, without emphasizing either side of the term), and that he demonstrates just how difficult it can be to try to occupy such a position on the theoretical spectrum? That is, temperamentally far left, but intellectually increasingly sceptical, and even despairing, about the belief system this entails.

Libidinal Economy certainly appears to be a vicious attack on Marxism, which is taken to be everything that is wrong about the art and practice of theory by the time of the later twentieth century. As Lyotard boldly declares, before launching into a diatribe against Marx on both a personal and a theoretical level: 'We no longer want to correct Marx[.] . . . We have no plan to be true, to give the truth of Marx' (Lyotard 1993: 96). It is a cardinal sin of theory, as Lyotard sees it, to believe that it can explain everything within its domain, that it can provide a comprehensive picture and thus a basis for authoritative predictions and assessments (exactly what Derrida was objecting to in structuralism of course, its universalizing tendencies). Lyotard argues that the impact of libidinal energy alone would dispute that claim, since it is neither predictable nor, ultimately, controllable: it is instead an 'excess' (a favourite concept of the postmodern movement) that always evades the schemes of the political theorist – Marxists no less than anyone else:

> Now, therefore, we must completely abandon critique, in the sense that we must put a stop to the critique of capital, stop accusing it of libidinal coldness or pulsional monovalence, stop accusing it of not being an organic body, of not being a natural immediate relation of the terms that it brings into play, we must take note of, examine, exalt the incredible, unspeakable pulsional possibilities that it sets rolling, and so understand that *there has never been* an organic body, an immediate relation, nor a nature in the sense of an *established site of affects*. (Lyotard 1993: 140)

Libidinal Economy is full of such outbursts in its quest to resituate Marx's *Capital* as 'a work of art' rather than a text bearing any kind of 'truth' (Lyotard 1993: 96), and that of course changes the ground rules of debate on the left quite radically. Marx's basic premises are effectively being rubbished as totally misguided, in what is a quintessentially *post*-Marxist gesture, iconoclastic to a fault: what could be more wounding than comparing it to fiction? Coming in the aftermath of 1968, this is a devastating indictment of the entire Marxist enterprise as being founded on false and unsustainable premises, which have become an end in themselves for the party machine rather than a means to bring about a fairer, less exploitative, society. Marxism has ceased to have any positive connotations at all for Lyotard, who can only regard it henceforth as a target for abuse.

The rest of Lyotard's career is largely spent in making us aware that difference will keep intruding to disturb any grand plans that we may have in either the social or the political arena – and even the aesthetic. Hence, his later obsession with the 'sublime', that ultimate signifier for the unknown and the unknowable, all the 'excess' that we can never account for. As far as Lyotard is concerned there is no escaping the fact of the sublime: knowledge can only ever be partial in its scope; aesthetic endeavour has no alternative but to bear witness to the existence of the unpresentable and make that known to its audience; there is always something that our theories must fail to encompass, something that can disrupt and distort even the most painstakingly worked-out plans. It is all very persuasive, if more than a bit depressing for anyone trying to think how we could construct a political plan to achieve radical change of the kind that leftists traditionally have been geared towards. As so often in post-Marxism, positive proposals to bring about that state of affairs prove to be a bit thin on the ground; but let's have a brief look at what these actually are in Lyotard to see if they offer any guide at all as to how post-Marxism might develop as a political philosophy in future.

Lyotard lays great store by 'little narrative' as a means of challenging the supremacy of grand narratives, whether in the political domain or elsewhere (Lyotard 1984). There is no set model being put forward here: a little narrative is effectively a protest movement which does all it can to undermine the operations of whatever grand narrative it chooses to take on – the greens versus the multinationals, the anti-capitalist and anti-globalization movements versus the World Trade Organization (and everything that it represents), for example. The whole point of the exercise is to exist *only* as a protest movement, and crucially, for only as long as the particular circumstances of the protest demand: once a specific objective has been completed then the little narrative is expected to dissolve, rather than to allow itself to mutate into a power base and so replicate the system it has set out in the first instance to challenge. This has proved to be a difficult concept for the traditional left to get its head around, since the episodic nature of operations it involves opens up the prospect of recurrent power vacuums being created as each subsequent little narrative winds itself up, mission apparently completed. The assumption is that grand narratives would simply move into such vacuums and re-establish control. Marxism in particular cannot countenance such a way of proceeding, which appears to have no overall trajectory, no teleological dialectic as it were, and to leave far too much to chance: hence its opposition to the student-trade union alliance against the de Gaulle government in 1968. By the standards of the traditional left, this approach to political action is just too *ad hoc* ever to work truly effectively; that, however, is precisely its attraction to a thinker like Lyotard, for whom long-term planning is an illusion – in the political domain above all, human behaviour being just too erratic to forecast with any accuracy. And he does have a point: who could have forecast the exact character of the *événements*? One does have to wonder, however, just how effective the little narrative method could ever be as a way of destabilizing a grand narrative in the longer term, a process which usually requires far greater continuity of action than is being promised here. While one can understand the distrust of power bases being displayed by this kind of disenchanted leftist, this nevertheless has to be seen as a drawback in the process of fighting entrenched systems, which can regroup after each little narrative confrontation: the aftermath of 1968 in France was not particularly pretty in this regard.

Then there is the concept of 'paganism' to consider, Lyotard's attempt to construct a workable system by which to make value judgements, as in legal cases, without the use of pre-established criteria in which authority is deemed to reside. He argues for this to be done on a 'case by case' basis, without reference to previous practice or experience, and cites Aristotle as a model of how we ought to proceed (Lyotard 1985: 28). The success or otherwise of any particular judgement can only really be assessed in retrospect by its consequences (there is more than a suggestion of utilitarianism to this method, it should be said), and it probably does reflect how most of us operate in everyday, small-scale, decision-making situations. It is far more problematical when it comes to larger-scale moral issues, however (a point consistently made against utilitarianism), and that is precisely where relativism always comes unstuck – and postmodernism is never less than defiantly relativist in outlook. Value judgement is undeniably postmodernism's weakest point as a system of thought, and where post-Marxism most differs from its Marxist source with its absolutist stance. Judgement without criteria is not something that Marxists can ever really accept – they know exactly what their ultimate objective is and how they are supposed to expedite it: difference merely clouds the issue and is to be marginalized wherever possible. Neither relativism nor pragmatism square with the classical Marxist world-view, which can only equate these with making things up as one goes along – empiricism rather than scientific socialism.

Returning to a point I raised earlier, we might well ask if China qualifies as post-Marxist in character. It certainly has its roots in Marxist theory, and at least in principle still claims to be a Marxist state, although pragmatism seems to be very much in evidence there in its present phase of development. It has openly embraced the market economy, quite aggressively so in recent years, and has done its best to integrate itself into the world trading community: ironically enough for such an apparent tyro in this game, it seemed to suffer less from the credit crisis than the majority of the developed nations did. There are political commentators who consider it to be on the verge of eclipsing the United States and the West to become the next global superpower of the twenty-first century, the world's future economic centre (Jacques 2009). So it is not unreasonable to classify it as some kind of post-Marxist political entity, officially Marxist in ideology but in practice capitalist in exhorting its citizens to 'become rich' as their patriotic duty. What it is not so good on is encouraging difference and diversity, which are completely at variance with its authoritarian ethos. This is hardly what Laclau and Mouffe envisaged in *Hegemony and Socialist Strategy,* but nevertheless it does need to be seen as representing one direction that post-Marxism *could* take: tight political control from a centralized party apparatus, plus carefully monitored economic freedom. Whether the Western left would regard this as still being in the spirit of Marxism is a moot point. Another way of looking at it would be to see it as combining the worst of the two systems in question: a somewhat schizophrenic mix of repression plus economic free-for-all. All the same, it does maintain many of the ideological trappings of a Marxist state and does indicate that classical Marxism, or Maoist Marxism at any rate, has some capacity for adaptation.

Radical democracy

China therefore constitutes one possible solution as to how to construct a post-Marxist politics. Another way that post-Marxism can distance itself from its Marxist shadow, however, is to evolve into something else entirely: as in the case of radical democracy, which gives us something more concrete, and manifestly less authoritarian, to enter onto the positive side of the Western post-Marxist ledger. Radical democracy enshrines difference and diversity, and wants to restructure political life in such a manner that these are always respected and given a platform, rather than being diluted in the compromise politics of the West or suppressed altogether in the one-party vision of traditional Marxism. Pluralist debate is at the forefront of the system that is envisaged, with Mouffe arguing for what she calls an 'agonistic' style of politics that precludes the possibility of compromise (Mouffe 2000) – to her, that being the great curse of Western political systems, by which a deadening consensus is achieved, stifling debate in the process. The pluralist commitment takes us, Laclau and Mouffe both feel, past Marxism, which is to be regarded as an ideological dead end from this viewpoint.

Radical democracy is an interesting development; although it would have to be said it does have limitations and so far has promised more than it has delivered. As several critics have pointed out, there are some rather glaring 'deficits' in it as a political theory. It is unclear, for example, how we could form political institutions under its aegis: agonistic politics does not lend itself to that very easily, since it usually requires some measure of compromise and consensus between competing groups to establish anything viable in this line. As David Howarth has remarked of the problem of implementing radical democracy in the current political system, 'less attention is paid to the economic, material, and institutional obstacles that block its realization, as well as the precise composition and configuration of such impediments' (Howarth 2008: 189), than should be by its leading theorists. Howarth and Jason Glynos go on to assert that radical democracy suffers from being essentially 'theory-driven' as a concept (Glynos and Howarth 2007: 167), thus substantially limiting its practical application: a criticism that might well be made of postmodernism in general when it comes to its political ambitions.

The classical Marxist alternative to consensus is one-party rule, which is the antithesis of what this kind of a post-Marxist wants to see. We face the same dilemma here that we do with paganism, the central problem for anyone on the left who espouses a post-Marxist position, and that is how to justify value judgements. This returns again and again to haunt relativists, and it has to be admitted that it is a major obstacle to anything like post-Marxism making a major breakthrough into the arena of mass politics. Could you really have mass politics without *some* kind of consensus between competing factions? Even Mouffe seems to concede that the answer is probably no, although the way she puts this in her book *On the Political* raises some awkward questions: 'A democratic society cannot treat those who put its basic institutions into question as legitimate adversaries' (Mouffe 2005: 120). It depends on how you interpret 'into question' and 'legitimate', of course: one suspects that those words could only too easily be abused, by radical democrats as much as anyone, as Mouffe herself goes on more or less to admit when she cautions that: 'The agonistic approach does not pretend to encompass all differences and to overcome all forms of exclusion' (Mouffe 2005: 120). How this state of affairs differs from the kind of consensus we already see in play in parliamentary systems is by no means clear, and it sounds as if it would in its turn merely create yet another class of alienated individuals, thus storing up future trouble for the proposed 'radical democratic' society.

It is worth reflecting at this point on Žižek's theories of how ideological systems, especially authoritarian ideological systems, work in psychological terms at the level of the individual. Žižek identifies a bias towards 'saving the phenomena', upholding the system, even if one can recognize that it is signally failing to achieve its goals, and indeed, looks highly unlikely ever to do so. We then enter into a condition of what he calls 'enlightened false consciousness', preserving the illusion, the 'fetish' in Žižek's terminology (Žižek 1989: 29), of loyalty to the system in spite of its recognizable shortcomings. It is Žižek's contention that the Soviet system only managed to survive as long as it did because it eventually generated this rather desperate form of 'consensus' among many of the populace as a coping mechanism. We can see exactly that happening again of late in terms of neoliberalism and the free market, which still continue to inform policy among the political class of most countries despite the all-too-evident structural flaws in the global economic system. We would have to lose our disposition towards saving theories in this manner, towards attaining the condition of consensus no matter how desperate it turned out to be, if we were to have any hope of a transition to an agonistic political set-up where there is no central core of belief to hang onto, illusory though that may always prove to be in real terms.

Marxism and the crisis of modernity

Perhaps we need to situate the debate between Marxism and post-Marxism within the wider debate about the future direction of modernity as a project, because that is probably the key cultural debate of our time. Unlike artistic and architectural modernity, economic modernity never went away, although it is now in deep trouble; nevertheless, like it or not, those in political power are committed to resurrecting it, and at least in theory 'business as usual' is what is being aimed at by policy-makers (no doubt they will be pleased to hear that in places like Ireland and Greece). The notion of full-scale structural renewal, which had so much public support a couple of years ago when the credit crisis really started to bite and the full extent of the system's internal contradictions were remorselessly coming to light, has been quietly sidelined: 'enlightened false consciousness' seems to have set in again, the brief public flare-ups in Greece and the student protest movement in the United Kingdom notwithstanding.

There is the not inconsiderable problem that Marxism itself is part of modernity as a project, equally as entranced by the prospect of progress as any capitalist institution, it would seem; a point made very firmly by Zygmunt Bauman in his *Intimations of Postmodernity*:

> Throughout its history, communism was modernity's most devout, vigorous and gallant champion – pious to the point of simplicity. It also claimed to be its only true champion. Indeed, it was under communist, not capitalist, auspices that the audacious dream of modernity, freed from obstacles by the merciless and seemingly omnipotent state, was pushed to its radical limits: grand designs, unlimited social engineering, huge and bulky technology, total transformation of nature. (Bauman 1992: 179)

True, as Bauman goes on to point out, such schemes almost invariably went horribly wrong somewhere along the line, but Marxism certainly wanted the economic and technological progress, just not the capitalist method of bringing it about: it is that fetish for production that Baudrillard railed against declaring itself yet again. China gives every indication of still being addicted to such grandiose transforming projects however, whether social or environmental. This is all the more reason to be wary of its brand of post-Marxism, and yet further proof that it might be taking in the worst of both systems it is drawing upon for its current working ideology.

If Marxism is to continue to mean anything it would have to reconsider its attitude towards modernity therefore, and be much more critical of its goals and not just its methods. In fact, Marxism can never really return to its old form; too much has happened in the interim, and in a sense Marxism itself will always henceforth be post-Marxist.

Conclusion

So *is* there a future for post-Marxism? It could be said that post-Marxism is as much a symptom of a problem as a solution to the left's ills; the problem being that radical politics has become very dispersed in the last few decades. The anti-capitalist movement, the anti-globalization movement, the various versions of the greens to be found around the world, none of these are very homogeneous entities, and neither do they necessarily agree even on the most basic points of what needs to be done to rectify the situation, or how. Yet capitalism, particularly in its neoliberal form, still needs to be opposed. There is manifestly a desperate need for *some* kind of radical leftist movement to articulate the opposition to neoliberalism as we move into a very uncertain post-credit crunch world, and it will have to take account of Marxism – whether as what Derrida referred to as a 'hauntology' or otherwise (Derrida 1994: 10). However, it will also have to take account of post-Marxism (in whatever form), with its dissenting cast of mind, rejection of dogmatism and generally anti-authoritarian outlook. As long as Marxism continues to have any kind of intellectual presence in our culture, and by that I mean as more than just a historical phenomenon to be studied by academics, then there will be a need for an internal critique of its workings, and at the very least we now have a history of how this can be formalized.

Where does this leave post-Marxism in yet another rapidly changing cultural environment however? Do we really want post-Marxism on the Chinese model? My own preference would be to follow the 'radical democracy' route and see where that might take us, what we might be able to do with it, whether its limitations can be overcome so that it can start to exert some mass appeal. That, of course, is the crucial difference between Marxism and post-Marxism: for all its abstract theoretical basis, the former *could* exert such appeal – there was no institutional deficit to report. Yet if Marxism ever *did* resurrect itself as a significant opponent to neoliberalism, it would of necessity have to include a post-Marxist element within it. It has undoubtedly been one of Marxism's greatest failings as a socio-political theory not to recognize the value, indeed the sheer necessity, of internal dissent; as Jean-Paul Sartre remarked of the conflicts over the imposition of the party line in the French Communist Party in the late 1940s, 'the opponent is never answered; he is discredited' (Sartre 1967: 190). That reputation for intolerance is something Marxism will always remain 'haunted' by, and deservedly so. From this perspective, post-Marxism might be seen as the guardian of that 'hauntology', and I would argue it would justify itself on that basis alone.

But 'radical democracy' plainly demands to be taken much further, to be developed in such a way that it overcomes its institutional deficit. At the moment, the post-Marxist tradition has no fully coherent option to offer to the neoliberal system, and that has to change. Bauman warned us back in the early 90s of the likely adverse consequences of 'living without an alternative' (Bauman 1992: 175), as he put it, to Western capitalism, and that has been borne out by the excesses committed in the name of a neo-liberal economics with no real check on its activities: 'casino capitalism', as one commentator dubbed it, at its very worst (Strange 1986). Whether we call it post-Marxism or radical democracy, something will have to step into the breach that the collapse of communism has created, otherwise we face a future of 'casino capitalism', run for the benefit of fanatical market fundamentalists only – and as we now realize only too well, you can lose really big-time in this particular casino. So there is definitely an opening for a radical political alternative, which at the very least would have to be informed by the experience of post-Marxism.

The point that I am making overall is that *post*-Marxism probably is now 'past', that it has served its purpose of knocking Marxism off its intellectual pedestal and making it all but impossible to have an idealized view of it any longer, either as theory or politics. A certain degree of cynicism with regard to Marxism's chequered history in the twentieth century is no bad thing, I would venture to suggest. Post-*Marxism*, however, remains relevant in that it has the potential for development and adaptation, the desire to take on the same socio-political evils that motivated Marxism to enter into cultural combat in the first place. It was harder to make a case for post-*Marxism* when market fundamentalism and neoliberal globalization were sweeping all before them: but not now that the system has revealed its weaknesses quite so graphically. I suggested before that the key cultural debate of our time was over the direction that economic modernity would take, and that requires attention to be drawn to the insidious role of enlightened false consciousness in allowing neoliberalism to go unchallenged in any really serious way. Post-*Marxism* was designed above all to offer precisely that kind of serious challenge and we can build on the lesson it taught us in this respect.

Referring to the 'evident truths' of left-wing thought, Laclau and Mouffe spoke of 'an avalanche of historical mutations which have riven the ground on which those truths were constituted' (Laclau and Mouffe 1985: 1): this is surely even more the case than it was in 1985 when they were writing. Classical Marxism has no answer to the impasse we find ourselves in a post-credit crunch environment, exactly the sort of situation which it believes should be breeding revolution, but to cite the appearance of yet another 'hegemonic' moment. That alone would be enough to generate the cynicism and nihilism that so often accompanies *post*-Marxism; but on the other hand it also ought to spur us on to re-investigate what can be done in the name of post-*Marxism*. If we are going to problematize the fetishization indulged in by both neoliberalism and classical Marxism, then that is where we have to start: ideological fetishization in general is the 'past' we should really be doing our utmost to turn into a 'post'.

References

Baudrillard, J. (1975 [1971]), *The Mirror of Production*, trans. M. Poster. St. Louis, MO: Telos Press.

Bauman, Z. (1992), *Intimations of Postmodernity*. London: Routledge.

Derrida, J. (1994 [1993]), *Specters of Marx: The State of the Debt, the Work of Mourning, and the New International*, trans. P. Kamuf. New York and London: Routledge.

Geras, N. (1987), 'Post-Marxism?', *New Left Review*, 163, 40–82.

Glynos, J. and Howarth, D. (2007), *Logics of Critical Explanation in Social and Political Theory*. London: Routledge.

Habermas, J. (1985), 'Modernity: an unfinished project', in H. Foster (ed.), *Postmodern Culture*. London and Concord, MA: Pluto Press, pp. 3–15.

Hartmann, H. (1981), 'The unhappy marriage of Marxism and Feminism: towards a more progressive union', in L. Sargent (ed.), *The Unhappy Marriage of Marxism and Feminism: A Debate on Class and Patriarchy*. London: Pluto Press, pp. 1–41.

Howarth, D. (2008), 'Ethos, agonism and populism: William Connolly and the case for radical democracy', *British Journal of Politics and International Relations*, 10, (2), 171–93.

Jacques, M. (2009), *When China Rules the World: The Rise of the Middle Kingdom and the End of the Western World*. London: Allen Lane.

Kirby, A. (2006), 'The death of postmodernism and beyond', *Philosophy Now*, 58, 34–7.

Laclau, E. and Mouffe C. (1985), *Hegemony and Socialist Strategy: Towards a Radical Democratic Politics*. London: Verso.

Lyotard, J.-F. (1984 [1979]), *The Postmodern Condition: A Report on Knowledge*, trans. G. Bennington and B. Massumi. Manchester: Manchester University Press.

Lyotard, J.-F. and Jean-Loup Thébaud (1985 [1979]), *Just Gaming*, trans. W. Godzich. Manchester: Manchester University Press.

Lyotard, J.-F. (1993 [1974]), *Libidinal Economy*, trans. I. H. Grant. London: Athlone Press.

Mouffe, C. (2000), *The Democratic Paradox*. London: Verso.

— (2005), *On the Political*. London: Routledge.

Sartre, J.-P. (1967 [1948]), *What is Literature?*, trans. B. Frechtman. London: Methuen.

Sim, S. (2000), *Post-Marxism: An Intellectual History*. London and New York: Routledge.

— (2010), *The End of Modernity: What the Financial and Environmental Crisis Is Really Telling Us*. Edinburgh: Edinburgh University Press.

— (2011), *The Routledge Companion to Postmodernism* (3rd edition). London and New York: Routledge.

Strange, S. (1986), *Casino Capitalism*. Oxford: Blackwell.

Žižek, S. (1989), *The Sublime Object of Ideology*. London and New York: Verso.